Poland's Kin-State Policies

The increased engagement of states with their co-ethnics abroad has recently become one of the most contentious features of European politics. Until recently, the issue has been discussed predominantly within the paradigm of international security; yet a review of the broader European picture shows that kin-state engagement can in fact have a positive societal impact when it actually responds effectively to the claims formulated by co-ethnic communities themselves.

Poland's Kin-State Policies: Opportunities and Challenges offers new insights into this issue by examining Poland's fast-evolving relationship with Polish communities living beyond its borders. Its central focus is the Act on the Polish Card (generally known as *Karta Polaka*). Tracing policymaking processes and the underlying political agendas that have shaped them, the volume situates Poland's engagement within broader conceptual and normative debates around kin-state and diaspora politics and explores its reception and impact in neighbouring states (Ukraine, Germany, Lithuania). The volume highlights how the issue of co-ethnics abroad is increasingly being instrumentalised, most especially for the purposes of attracting labour migration to resolve the demographic crisis in Poland.

The chapters in this book were originally published as a special issue of the journal *Ethnopolitics.*

Andreea Udrea co-convenes KINPOL Observatory on Kin-state Policies at the University of Glasgow. With Professor David Smith, she led a two-year project entitled 'Poland's Kin-state Policies: Opportunities and Challenges' funded by the Noble Foundation Programme on Modern Poland.

David Smith is Professor and Alec Nove Chair in Russian and East European Studies at the University of Glasgow, where he co-convenes the KINPOL Observatory on Kin-state Policies and the Glasgow Baltic Research Unit.

Karl Cordell is Emeritus Professor of Politics at the University of Plymouth.

Poland's Kin-State Policies
Opportunities and Challenges

Edited by
Andreea Udrea, David Smith and
Karl Cordell

LONDON AND NEW YORK

First published 2022
by Routledge
2 Park Square, Milton Park, Abingdon, Oxon, OX14 4RN

and by Routledge
605 Third Avenue, New York, NY 10158

Routledge is an imprint of the Taylor & Francis Group, an informa business

© 2022 The Editor of Ethnopolitics

All rights reserved. No part of this book may be reprinted or reproduced or utilised in any form or by any electronic, mechanical, or other means, now known or hereafter invented, including photocopying and recording, or in any information storage or retrieval system, without permission in writing from the publishers.

Trademark notice: Product or corporate names may be trademarks or registered trademarks, and are used only for identification and explanation without intent to infringe.

British Library Cataloguing-in-Publication Data
A catalogue record for this book is available from the British Library

ISBN13: 978-1-032-04028-8 (hbk)
ISBN13: 978-1-032-04029-5 (pbk)
ISBN13: 978-1-003-19028-8 (ebk)

DOI: 10.4324/9781003190288

Typeset in Times New Roman
by codeMantra

Publisher's Note
The publisher accepts responsibility for any inconsistencies that may have arisen during the conversion of this book from journal articles to book chapters, namely the inclusion of journal terminology.

Disclaimer
Every effort has been made to contact copyright holders for their permission to reprint material in this book. The publishers would be grateful to hear from any copyright holder who is not here acknowledged and will undertake to rectify any errors or omissions in future editions of this book.

Contents

Citation Information	vii
Notes on Contributors	ix

1 *Karta Polaka*, Poland and its Co-ethnics Abroad   1
   Andreea Udrea, David Smith and Karl Cordell

2 *Karta Polaka*—New Wine in Old Bottles   12
   Dorota Pudzianowska

3 The Paradoxical Nature of Diaspora Engagement Policies: A World Polity
   Perspective on the *Karta Polaka*   25
   Bastian Sendhardt

4 Divided Nationhood and Multiple Membership: A Framework for Assessing
   Kin-State Policies and Their Impact   39
   Myra A. Waterbury

5 Pragmatic Trans-Border Nationalism: A Comparative Analysis of Poland's
   and Hungary's Policies Towards Kin-Minorities in the Twenty-First Century   53
   Magdalena Lesińska and Dominik Héjj

6 Minority Protection and Kin-State Engagement: *Karta Polaka* in
   Comparative Perspective   67
   Andreea Udrea and David Smith

7 The Polish Minority in Germany: Marginal or Marginalised?   83
   Karl Cordell

8 Between Two Kin-States: The Round Table Meetings on the German
   Minority in Poland and the Poles in Germany 2010–2019   96
   Sławomir Łodzinski

9 Relations Between Polish Immigrant Organisations in Germany and
   Institutions of the Polish and German States   109
   Michał Nowosielski

CONTENTS

10 Does Polish Origin Matter? The Integration Challenges of Polish Card
Holders in Poland — 123
Myroslava Keryk

11 Identities of and Policies Towards the Polish National Minority in Lithuania — 136
Diana Janušauskienė

12 National Bonds, Foreign Policy and the Future of Europe — 150
Jan Zielonka

Index — 157

Citation Information

The chapters in this book were originally published in the *Ethnopolitics*, volume 20, issue 1 (January 2021). When citing this material, please use the original page numbering for each article, as follows:

Chapter 1
Karta Polaka, *Poland and its Co-ethnics Abroad*
Andreea Udrea, David Smith and Karl Cordell
Ethnopolitics, volume 20, issue 1 (January 2021) pp. 1–11

Chapter 2
Karta Polaka—*New Wine in Old Bottles*
Dorota Pudzianowska
Ethnopolitics, volume 20, issue 1 (January 2021) pp. 12–24

Chapter 3
The Paradoxical Nature of Diaspora Engagement Policies: A World Polity Perspective on the Karta Polaka
Bastian Sendhardt
Ethnopolitics, volume 20, issue 1 (January 2021) pp. 25–38

Chapter 4
Divided Nationhood and Multiple Membership: A Framework for Assessing Kin-State Policies and Their Impact
Myra A. Waterbury
Ethnopolitics, volume 20, issue 1 (January 2021) pp. 39–52

Chapter 5
Pragmatic Trans-Border Nationalism: A Comparative Analysis of Poland's and Hungary's Policies Towards Kin-Minorities in the Twenty-First Century
Magdalena Lesińska and Dominik Héjj
Ethnopolitics, volume 20, issue 1 (January 2021) pp. 53–66

Chapter 6
Minority Protection and Kin-State Engagement: Karta Polaka *in Comparative Perspective*
Andreea Udrea and David Smith
Ethnopolitics, volume 20, issue 1 (January 2021) pp. 67–82

viii CITATION INFORMATION

Chapter 7

The Polish Minority in Germany: Marginal or Marginalised?
Karl Cordell
Ethnopolitics, volume 20, issue 1 (January 2021) pp. 83–95

Chapter 8

Between Two Kin-States: The Round Table Meetings on the German Minority in Poland and the Poles in Germany 2010–2019
Sławomir Łodzinski
Ethnopolitics, volume 20, issue 1 (January 2021) pp. 96–108

Chapter 9

Relations Between Polish Immigrant Organisations in Germany and Institutions of the Polish and German States
Michał Nowosielski
Ethnopolitics, volume 20, issue 1 (January 2021) pp. 109–122

Chapter 10

Does Polish Origin Matter? The Integration Challenges of Polish Card Holders in Poland
Myroslava Keryk
Ethnopolitics, volume 20, issue 1 (January 2021) pp. 123–135

Chapter 11

Identities of and Policies Towards the Polish National Minority in Lithuania
Diana Janušauskienė
Ethnopolitics, volume 20, issue 1 (January 2021) pp. 136–149

Chapter 12

National Bonds, Foreign Policy and the Future of Europe
Jan Zielonka
Ethnopolitics, volume 20, issue 1 (January 2021) pp. 150–156

For any permission-related enquiries please visit:
http://www.tandfonline.com/page/help/permissions

Contributors

Karl Cordell University of Plymouth, UK.

Dominik Héjj Cardinal Stefan Wyszynski University in Warsaw, Poland.

Diana Janušauskienė Lithuanian Social Research Center, Lithuania.

Myroslava Keryk 'Our Choice' Foundation/Institute of Philosophy and Sociology of Polish Academy of Sciences, Poland.

Magdalena Lesińska University of Warsaw, Poland.

Sławomir Łodzinski University of Warsaw, Poland.

Michał Nowosielski Centre of Migration Research, University of Warsaw, Poland.

Dorota Pudzianowska University of Warsaw, Poland.

Bastian Sendhardt German Institute of Polish Affairs, Germany.

David Smith University of Glasgow, UK.

Andreea Udrea University of Glasgow, UK.

Myra A. Waterbury Ohio University, Athens, USA.

Jan Zielonka University of Venice, Italy; University of Oxford, UK.

Karta Polaka, Poland and its Co-ethnics Abroad

ANDREEA UDREA ⑩, DAVID SMITH ⑩ AND KARL CORDELL

One of the most contentious features of European politics in recent years, particularly in Central and Eastern Europe (CEE), has been the increased engagement of many states with their kin-minority groups.[1] In many cases, such engagement has found legal expression in domestic legislation as a trans-sovereign special duty of care vis-à-vis such groups. The tumultuous process of nation—and state-rebuilding that CEE experienced in the aftermath of the Cold War anchored kin-state politics strongly in the security paradigm, and the inherent potential for inter-state conflict arising from kin-state engagement is still routinely emphasised today (Vollebaek, 2009; OSCE High Commissioner on National Minorities (OSCE HCNM), 2020). Involvement by kin-states has indeed proved destabilising, as shown by Albania's intervention in Kosovo and Macedonia in the 1990s (Koinova, 2008) and the Russo-Georgian war in 2008 (Shevel, 2015), or disintegrative, as seen in the case of Russia's occupation of Crimea in 2014 (Shevel, 2015). A review of the broader European picture, however, shows that kin-state engagement can also have a positive societal impact. Where such engagement responds effectively to the claims formulated by co-ethnics abroad, it can help to improve their life chances (Csergő & Liebich, 2019) by ensuring the flourishing of their communities. Good examples are the case of the Danish minority in Germany (EURAC, 2007) or Germany's actions to support the cultural preservation of German minorities in CEE (Cordell & Wolff, 2007). Overall, it is acknowledged in the literature that involvement by a kin-state may help to maintain and promote the ethno-cultural, linguistic and/or religious identity of its co-ethnics abroad (Defeis, 2011).[2]

Kin-state politics has been conceptualised in the scholarly literature as sitting between irredentism and diaspora politics (Alonso & Mylonas, 2017; Mylonas, 2012; Saideman & Ayres, 2015; Waterbury, 2020) and remains embedded in an international regime that affirms a strong relationship between state, territory and citizenship rights.[3] From an international relations perspective, kin-state politics is currently considered to oscillate between two different functions: maintaining the location of borders and bridging the relations between states (Adamson & Demetriou, 2007; Klatt, 2017; McGarry & O'Leary, 2013).

Such views, however, fail to acknowledge the elusiveness of the ideal-type congruence between nation and state on which modern conceptions of sovereignty are built. This assumed congruence is especially prevalent in the justifications for kin-state politics that address co-ethnic communities that have been forcibly deprived of belonging to the national state through deportation or border changes. Such historical circumstances have fuelled a sense of national historic injustice and the idea that states bear a moral responsibility and should assert a right to take remedial action.[4] This phenomenon was highly prominent in inter-war Central and Eastern Europe, and became a revived feature of the region during the 1990s following the end of communism and the demise of the Soviet Union and Yugoslavia. The sometimes violent conflicts that accompanied the latter process also meant that kin-state engagement with minorities was again cast in securitised terms, as something likely to encourage political mobilisation by co-ethnics living as marginalised minorities within neighbouring—similarly ethnoculturally defined—'nationalising states'.[5] For all of the theoretically sophisticated thinking contained in Rogers Brubaker's (1996) work *Nationalism Reframed*, this was the central message it imparted: politics in the region would be shaped by a 'triadic nexus' comprising three competing inter-relational fields of ethnocultural nationalism. According to Brubaker, this dynamic was likely to become 'a locus of refractive and potentially explosive ethnic conflict' in the years to come (Brubaker, 1996). The involvement of international organisations, such as the Council of Europe (CoE) and the Organisation of Security and Co-operation in Europe (OSCE) in the early 2000s made kin-state politics the object of an expanded 'Quadratic Nexus' (Smith, 2002, 2020). Rather than devising new and innovative approaches in this area, however, the organisations in question have attempted to contain kin-states' engagement through the prism of state sovereignty and international security, thereby reaffirming and strengthening the convergence between state, territory and citizenship rights.

Kin-states' trans-sovereign involvement has challenged home-states' exclusive obligations under international law to protect their minority ethno-cultural groups.[6] Many scholars have persuasively argued that kin-state politics is in fact identity politics and have highlighted its role in maintaining the ethnocultural identity of co-ethnics abroad (Csergő & Goldgeier, 2004; Horváth, 2008, pp. 137–211; Pogonyi, 2017). Yet, despite the acknowledgement that kin-state engagement may impact positively on the fate of co-ethnics abroad by affording better protection against cultural assimilation, examinations of kin-state politics within multiculturalism have been rather marginal (Hatvany, 2006; Udrea, 2014). A state's responsibility towards its minority ethnocultural groups has been a prominent focus of liberal democratic political theory in the last 25 years, offering important insights into and solutions to the challenges of accommodating such groups in ways which are consistent with liberal justice (Crowder, 2013). Nonetheless, such accounts have focused exclusively on the responsibility of the home-state, and have therefore overlooked the nature, scope and impact of kin-state policies.

Furthermore, there has been little engagement in legal and political theory with the normative significance (and normative *limitations*) conferred to Hungary's Act LXII of 2001 on Hungarians Living in the Neighbouring Countries. Often referred to as the 'Hungarian Status Law', Act LXII remains the piece of legislation that first placed kin-state policies firmly on the agenda of international organisations and which continues to hold normative prominence in Europe, having been at the centre of the only evaluation to date of the legitimacy of kin-state involvement.[7] This was carried out by the Council of Europe's Venice Commission, whose resultant 2001 Report on the Preferential Treatment of National

Minorities by their Kin-state concludes that 'the emerging of new and original forms of minority protection, particularly by the kin-States, constitutes a positive trend insofar as they can contribute to the realisation of this goal' (Council of Europe, 2001). At the same time, it is clear that kin-states have increasingly instrumentalised their engagement with their co-ethnics abroad to achieve goals that are at odds with minority protection, such as superseding historical injustice through trans-sovereign nation-building (e.g. Hungary, Romania), tackling domestic demographic crises by encouraging immigration to the kin-state (e.g. Poland, Hungary, Bulgaria, or Czechia), and/or seeking to achieve influence by using kin minorities' disenchantment with home-states' minority accommodation as a pretext to engage in forms of hybrid intervention (e.g. Russia, Romania). Overall, the evolution of kin-state policies has challenged their defence as forms of minority protection and made it increasingly difficult to frame them as such.

The current volume offers new insights into these recent developments in kin-state politics, taking as its central focus Poland's fast-evolving relationship with Polish communities living beyond its borders.[8] Poland is among the most recent European countries to introduce legislation on kin-minorities. First adopted in 2007, and most recently amended on 12 April 2019, the Act on the Polish Card (Ustawą z dnia 7 września 2007 r. o Karcie Polaka—also known as *Karta Polaka* and hereafter referred to as such in this volume) has received only limited attention within the growing academic literature on kin-state—kin minority relations. *Karta Polaka* has been mainstreamed as the dominant policy approach of the Polish state towards its co-ethnics abroad. In fact, it is but one component of a policy package that includes two more policies specifically targeting the *Poles in the East*,[9] and it is supplemented by a diaspora policy first adopted in 1989 and continuously modified since (Nowosielski & Nowak, 2018), addressing Polish emigrants and people of Polish descent worldwide. Preceded by the Repatriation Act of 9 November 2000 (amended several times, most recently in 2017), and then followed by the Act on Polish Citizenship of 2009 which came into force in 2012, the foundation of all these policies is Article 6.2 of Poland's 1997 constitution, which states that '[t]he Republic of Poland shall provide assistance to Poles living abroad to maintain their links with the national cultural heritage'.[10]

According to the text of *Karta Polaka*, the Card offers a confirmation of belonging to the Polish nation without affecting the nature of such belonging or recognising it in a legally binding manner (Pudzianowska & Jagielski, 2008; quoted in Ładykowski, 2018, p. 115).[11] *Karta Polaka* and the other policies described here above are about far more than simply reaffirming a cultural affinity between Poland and its co-ethnics abroad. These policies are legitimised by a prevalent historical discourse centred upon highlighting the injustice of past border changes and population resettlement and stressing a need for redress (Ładykowski, 2018). As well as offering a form of partial reparation for past harm, such policies have also been justified as a way of preventing the mass emigration of Poles from neighbouring historically Polish territories while protecting and promoting the Polish identity of co-ethnics abroad (Hut, 2019; Mikołajczyk, 2015). Barbara Mikołajczyk notes that *Karta Polaka* was initially also thought of as a measure aiming to encourage young people of Polish origin to study in Poland and, in this way, to contribute to strengthening the elites of the Polish minority groups living in the East (2015).

In a similar vein, *Karta Polaka* has also been seen as an instrument of soft power projection for the Polish state, understood as an 'ability to exert influence on other international players to further the state's own interest' (Marczuk, 2019, p. 25). According to Paweł Karolewski (2015), the Act aimed to neutralise the effects of the Schengen border control regime on the one hand, and to increase the salience of the Polish language and culture in the bordering states on the other. By solidifying the Polish identity of the designated kin-minority groups and strengthening their relations with Poland, the Act has impacted negatively on Poland's inter-state relations, in particular with Lithuania and Belarus. The relations between Poland and Lithuania had already become highly contentious following the accession to the EU of both countries and remained as such until 2019. In this period, Poland made any progress in the bilateral relations between the two countries strictly conditional upon improvements in the accommodation of the Polish national minority, at issue being the unwillingness of the Lithuanian government to adopt special provisions which would protect and promote the culture and identity of national minority groups (Kuzborska, 2013). Relations with Belarus also deteriorated following Poland's accession to the EU (Minority Rights Group International, n.d.). The rights of the Polish minority have since been eroded, in particular the right to education (Weselowsky, 2019). *Karta Polaka* allowed ethnic Poles in Belarus to travel to and study in Poland, to maintain and develop social connections with Polish citizens (Wallace & Patsiurko, 2017). However, despite the high number of Polish cards awarded to Belarusian citizens,[12] *Karta Polaka* appears not to have changed the Belarusian government's stance that there are no Poles in Belarus, but only polonised Belarusians (Weselowsky, 2019).

As Pudzianowska observes in this volume, the idea that Polish governments have a responsibility towards Poles resident outside of Poland has been shared by virtually all political actors that emerged from the ruins of communism. This perceived responsibility has been heightened by the renewed wave of large-scale migration from Poland that began during the 1990s and accelerated with its accession to the EU in 2005 following the gradual opening to Polish citizens of the national labour markets in Europe. In this context, *Karta Polaka* became a particular flagship for Law and Justice (*Prawo i Sprawiedliwość*—PiS), which introduced the initial legislation while in government during 2005–2007 and later attached growing importance to the policy after it returned to power as Poland's major party in 2015. For the conservative-nationalist right, strategies linking Poles abroad to the motherland have been especially important, forming part of a set of values and commitments that elevate 'nation' above all other forms of identity. In this regard, *Karta Polaka* has been couched as a means of addressing historical injustices while at the same time protecting Poles abroad from the threat of cultural assimilation. More broadly, in the course of 2015–2019 the policy became strongly embedded in a strategy aimed at strengthening the rule of PiS, characterised by patronal politics, party state capture and exclusionary identity politics directed at minorities, refugees, international organisations and political opponents and other critics (Sata & Karolewski, 2020; Szczerbiak, 2017).

There remain, however, many questions regarding the nature, scope and impact of Poland's kin-state policies, especially given the extent and pace of recent developments. Drawn from the joint academic-practitioner conference on 'Poland's Kin-state Policies: Opportunities and Challenges', held at the University of Warsaw in May 2019,[13] this volume engages comprehensively with the 'what?', the 'why?' and the 'for whom?' of Poland's kin-state engagement. Thus, the collected papers variously trace the policymaking process in this area and analyse the underlying political agendas that have shaped it (contributions by Pudzianowska, Cordell and Łodziński); situate *Karta Polaka* in relation to broader conceptual and normative debates around kin-state and diaspora politics (contributions by Sendhardt, Waterbury, Udrea, & Smith and Lesińska & Héjj); and explore how kin-state engagement has been received in the neighbouring states and what implications it has had for the Polish communities in these countries (contributions by Keryk, Janušauskienė and Nowosielski).

Polish communities in the East obviously figured prominently in the discussions at the May 2019 conference, given that they provided the initial focus for *Karta Polaka*. This is reflected in the contributions by Keryk, who explores the perspectives and experiences of Polish Card holders with particular attention to those from Ukraine, and Janušauskienė, who factors kin-state engagement into a discussion of Polish national minority identity in Lithuania. Among other issues, these papers raise important questions about the 'belonging to the Polish nation' imputed to bearers of the Polish Card, and how this belonging is actually understood and practised in a contemporary setting. Not least, the authors highlight the complex and multi-layered identities that exist within minority communities and which do not fit readily with the imagined 'canon of Polishness' at the heart of *Karta Polaka*. This disjuncture carries multiple implications for Polish Card holders, both within their societies and origin and—as Keryk shows—within Poland itself.

The May 2019 discussions in Warsaw also underlined the important place that Germany continues to occupy within Poland's politics of external engagement, all the more so in a contemporary context where the previous line between 'kin-minority' and wider 'diaspora' policy is becoming increasingly blurred.[14] This is reflected in the contributions to the volume by Cordell, Łodzinski and Nowosielski, all of whom discuss the place of kin-minorities within Polish-German relations. In so far as Germany's contemporary Polish community consists primarily of people with a migration background, it differs in important respects from the more historically rooted Polish minorities found in the countries to Poland's east. As Łodziński describes in his paper, however, successive Polish governments have sought to blur this line of distinction, insisting that both the German and the Polish state bear historical and moral obligations towards Germany's Poles in a manner analogous to those which Poland carries towards ethnic Poles detached from Poland and subjected to Soviet rule after World War Two.[15] In part, at least, this stance can be seen to reflect the complex and often difficult historical relationship between Poland and Germany, which has kept minority issues on the agenda of inter-state relations even after the 1991 Treaty on Friendship and Good Neighbourliness and Poland's subsequent accession to the European Union. By providing the longer-term background to the entangled kin-state and minority politics of the two countries, Cordell's paper sets the scene for Łodziński's analysis of the 2010–2019 Round Table meetings and the question of whether Polish minority representatives in Germany and their German counterparts in Poland have actually been able to influence the policies of their respective kin-states. This feeds logically into Nowosielski's analysis of how Germany's multi-layered and highly heterogeneous Polish community has negotiated its relationship with both home and kin-state. In different ways, all of these papers raise interesting questions concerning the identity and capacity for agency of those categorised as belonging to kin-minorities.

A central conclusion to emerge from the volume is that, increasingly, *Karta Polaka* instrumentalises the issue of co-ethnics abroad for the purposes of attracting labour migrants to resolve the demographic crisis in Poland, with significant and rather negative implications upon the fate of Polish minorities in their home-states. In saying this, we recognise that all kin-state policies are instrumental to some extent. Following the theoretical approach of Brubaker (1996) and other authors (Schulze, 2018; Waterbury, 2010), state policies towards co-ethnics abroad can be conceived as the product of contested and contingent domestic politics shaped by different understandings and 'strategic framings' (Schulze, 2018) of those groups, of their identities and of the nature of the relationship between them and the kin-state. This approach helps to explain the significant ambiguity and differing interpretations that continue to surround *Karta Polaka* and Poland's kin-state politics more broadly.

By exploring the different rationales of this instrumentalisation, the volume situates *Karta Polaka* more firmly within broader European political developments. In particular, the contributions suggest that Poland's kin-state engagement sits at the confluence of two major and interrelated political trajectories shaping European politics—national conservatism and neoliberalism. As Cordell highlights in his essay and Zielonka reiterates in his concluding remarks, longer-term effects of neoliberal globalisation and the fallout from the 2008 economic crisis have prompted a generalised Europe-wide backlash from what have been described as ethnopopulist movements (Jenne, 2018).[16] Lesińska and Héjj show how the current 'extraordinary pan-European ... populist conjuncture' (Brubaker, 2017, p. 1191) has been a common denominator in the evolution of Hungarian and Polish policies following the arrival in power of Fidesz and PiS. While the two governments have had different agendas in the sphere of engagement with their co-ethnics abroad, Lesińska and Héjj note that both have pursued a 'pragmatic transborder nationalism' that views kin-minorities primarily as a resource. This can be seen in a further instance of diffusion between the two cases—namely, the growing importance conferred to citizenship acquisition as kin-state policy. In fact, facilitated access to a kin-state's citizenship has become the dominant policy approach of many European states vis-à-vis their co-ethnics abroad (Dumbravă, 2014; Pogonyi, 2017). In a similar way to Poland, other states including Hungary and Bulgaria have recently engaged in an active process of encouraging the immigration and permanent settlement of their co-ethnics abroad through facilitated citizenship acquisition in order to respond to labour shortages on their domestic markets. All of these cases exemplify what Mavelli calls a neoliberal political economy of belonging and is defined as a process of economisation, in which '[s]tates ... approach prospective or existing citizens as capital that may enhance not just their economy but their cultural, emotional and reputational value' (2018, p. 485).

As noted above, the volume also discusses the instrumentality of *Karta Polaka* in relation to existing European normative standards on minority protection, and to this end, Poland's engagement with its co-ethnics abroad is widely compared to that of Hungary. In essence, *Karta Polaka* has been—and remains—very different, in that it has territorialised its duties within the boundaries of the Polish state. Lesińska and Héjj thus question the extent to which *Karta Polaka* aligns with Hungary's Act LXII of 2001 and its subsequent kin-state policies, discussing the similarities and differences. Waterbury stresses that the situation of kin-minority groups is most accurately captured by the concept of divided nationhood and defined as a condition of multiple membership. Again reflecting on the cases of Hungary and Poland, she further examines the impact of kin-state policies on their ethnic kin, discussing the advantages as well as the disadvantages. Udrea and Smith in their contribution inquire whether the European norms and standards of minority protection adequately capture the relationship between Poland and its co-ethnics abroad as it is articulated in *Karta Polaka* and defend the necessity of sharing sovereignty as a safeguard against the instrumentalisation of kin-state engagement. As shown here, *Karta Polaka* has evolved into an immigration policy which does not cohere with the European norms and standards of minority protection. Distinctively, minority protection is pursued through bilateral treaties on the bases of reciprocity and cultural cooperation (Marczuk, 2019, pp. 25–40), and its delivery is complemented by the action of local and Polish transnational non-governmental organisations.

All in all, this set of papers shows that *Karta Polaka* has the capacity to illuminate wider contemporary debates on the phenomenon of kin-state—kin minority relations and—by extension—on issues of state, territory, citizenship, minority rights and European integration. By July 2020, when this introduction was completed, some evidence had emerged regarding the effects of the Covid-19 pandemic on kin-state engagement. The crisis, which unfolded in Europe during the first six months of 2020, limited kin-state engagement and carried consequences likely to last for many years ahead. In an analysis of the impact of the Covid pandemic on the German-Danish border region, Martin Klatt notes that border closure profoundly damaged the relations between Germany's Danish minority and its kin-state and anticipates that the 'Danish-German cross-border region might have to start from anew' (Klatt, 2020, p. 47). Similar conclusions are very likely to be reached for CEE where the relations between kin-states and kin minorities are more precariously institutionalised and strongly politicised. At the same time, scholars and practitioners raised serious concerns over a political trajectory shaped by the pandemic and quickly diffused worldwide, namely a renationalisation of the state characterised by reduced or suspended democratic freedoms and a weakened commitment to minority rights (Bieber, 2020; Chandra, 2020; EURAC, 2020). As noted by Joseph Marko, these developments suggest that segregation and assimilation will become normalised (EURAC, 2020), but according to the UN Assistant Secretary-General for Human Rights Ilze Brands-Kehris and the OSCE High Commissioner on National Minorities Lamberto Zannier they also highlight that the need for multilateralism has become very acute and the only way forward (EURAC, 2020).

Acknowledgements

This volume grew out of a two-year project entitled 'Poland's Kin-state Policies: Opportunities and Challenges' and led by David Smith and Andreea Udrea at the University of Glasgow. Given that the final preparation of the articles took place during the first months of the Covid pandemic, the editors would like to thank the contributors for their efforts and dedication in bringing this volume to completion despite the overwhelming personal and work commitments during the spring lockdown. Their gratitude, too, to the project partners whose enthusiastic involvement made this enterprise possible: Sławomir Łodziński, Dorota Pudzianowska, Paweł Hut, Ireneusz Paweł Karolewski, Magdalena Dembinska, Myra Waterbury, Zsuzsa Csergő and Zoltán Kántor. They would also like to thank the participants in the two events organised under this project for very enriching and insightful discussions: the international conference 'Poland's Kin-state Policies: Opportunities and Challenges' held at the University of Warsaw in May 2019, and the workshop 'Integration in a Transnational World: Poland, Scotland and Polish Communities Abroad' organised in Glasgow in November 2019. Finally, their gratitude to Sławomir Łodziński and Paulina Trevena for co-organising the events in Warsaw and in Glasgow respectively. The editors would also like to thank Jan Zielonka for his helpful comments and insightful suggestions on this paper.

Funding

The editors would like to thank the Noble Foundation Programme on Modern Poland (Poland's Kin-state Policies: Opportunities and Challenges - pomp.com.pl/en/programy-2017/polands-kin-state-policies-opportunities-and-challenges/ - administered under University of Glasgow project code 300460-01), the College of Social Sciences of the University of Glasgow and the Institute of Sociology of the University of Warsaw for their generous financial support which led to the publication of this volume.

Notes

1. The term 'kin-minority' refers specifically to groups which identify culturally with titular groups in another state described as a 'kin-state'. Often because of arbitrary territorial border shifts or population transfers, members of such groups and/or their ancestors became citizens of their current state against their wishes, for example as a result of the disintegration of the European empires, the peace settlements after both World Wars, and more recently the breakdown of the Soviet Union and Yugoslavia. Increasingly, however, the evolution of policies across Europe has blurred the distinction between diaspora and kin-minority groups. Poland and Hungary, the two cases widely discussed in this volume, are no exception to this.
2. These were highlighted as the most important benefits of Poland's engagement with its diaspora from Scotland at the workshop 'Integration in a Transnational World: Poland, Scotland and Polish Communities Abroad' (Glasgow, 14 November 2019) which brought together representatives of the Scottish Government, practitioners and academics. The workshop was organised by the University of Glasgow and funded by the Noble Foundation Programme on Modern Poland with additional support from the College of Social Sciences of the University of Glasgow (project code 200278-01). See: https://www.gla.ac.uk/research/az/crcees/research/kinpol/projects/.
3. On the relationship between kin-state policies and broader 'diaspora engagement policies', see also Sendhardt's contribution in the current volume.
4. As Erika Harris observes, nationalism—'a strategy for the attainment and preservation of political legitimacy'—always couches its claims 'in the name of justice (redressed or not yet addressed) and the **"right of the people"**. The general aim of nationalism is that **"the people"** be in charge of their collective identity' (Harris, 2009, p. 4).
5. This is the concept coined by Rogers Brubaker, to denote states that are themselves shaped by remedial projects of addressing historic injustice towards their 'titular' ethno-cultural majority populations.
6. On the question of responsibility for minority protection, see Udrea and Smith's contribution to the current volume.
7. See the contributions by Waterbury, Udrea, & Smith and Lesińska and Héjj in this volume for detailed discussions of the normative, political and theoretical importance of Hungary's Act LXII of 2001 on Hungarians Living in the Neighbouring Countries.
8. The volume arises out of the research project 'Poland's Kin-state Policies: Opportunities and Challenges', led by David Smith and Andreea Udrea at the University of Glasgow from 2018–2020 and funded by the Noble Foundation Programme on Modern Poland. See: https://www.gla.ac.uk/research/az/crcees/research/kinpol/projects/.
9. The Polish legislation differentiates between two categories of co-ethnics abroad: the Polish diaspora, generally referred to as *Polonia,* and the Poles living on the territory of the former Soviet Union, designated *Poles in the East* (Polacy na Wschodzie). According to the last census in the Soviet Union from 1989, 1,126,334 Soviet citizens of Polish nationality resided there (Sendhardt, 2017). Originally, the *Poles in the East* were those who were deported to, exiled or persecuted in the Soviet Union (Preamble) and/or their descendants, and are permanent residents of Armenia, Azerbaijan, Georgia, Kazakhstan, Kyrgyzstan, Tajikistan, Turkmenistan, Uzbekistan and the Asian part of the Russian Federation (Polish Sejm, 2000, Art 9(1)). *Karta Polaka* expands the category to include citizens of or stateless people registered in Armenia, Azerbaijan, Belarus, Estonia, Georgia, Kazakhstan, Kyrgyzstan, Lithuania, Latvia, Moldova, Russia, Tajikistan, Turkmenistan, Ukraine and Uzbekistan (Polish Sejm, 2007, Art. 2(2)). The latest amendment of *Karta Polaka* from 16 May 2019 has further enlarged the group of beneficiaries and now includes all people of Polish descent worldwide.

10. The constitutionality of *Karta Polaka* was challenged in the Supreme Court. In its ruling from 5 December 2013, the Supreme Court defined the Poles living abroad as being those who have a document which certifies their Polish citizenship as well as all foreigners of Polish ethnicity, thus removing the necessity of holding Polish citizenship to justify the trans-sovereign reach of the such legislation (Ładykowski, 2018, p. 114).
11. According to the text of the Act on the Polish Card, it is also neither a proof of Polish descent or citizenship (Art 7.1), nor does it entitle its holder to cross borders to or settle in Poland (Art 7.2). The Act provides a number of benefits to the card holders, including access to the labour market on a par with Polish citizens, education and cultural benefits on the territory of Poland, and access to health care. However, recent amendments from May 2016 (Polish Sejm, 2016) and November 2016 (Polish Sejm, 2016) have changed the aim of this policy by including provisions which facilitate the holders' settlement in Poland and their access to Polish citizenship (EFHR, 2016). These amendments exempt the Polish Card holders from any consular fees regarding their applications for a national visa or citizenship, entitle those who settle in Poland to receiving cash benefits that cover their costs of living, and most importantly, facilitate their access to Polish citizenship after one year of permanent residence on the territory of Poland and upon obtaining a language certificate. For further details see Pudzianowska's contribution in this volume.
12. According to the Ministry of Foreign Affairs, between 2008 and 24 September 2019 131,770 citizens of Belarus received Polish cards (Szoszyn, 2019).
13. This conference was co-organised by the School of Social and Political Sciences (University of Glasgow) and the Institute of Sociology (University of Warsaw) and funded by the Noble Foundation Programme on Modern Poland and the Institute of Sociology (University of Warsaw). See: https://www.gla.ac.uk/research/az/crcees/research/kinpol/projects/activitiesconferenceuniversityofwarsaw23-24may2019/.
14. This blurring of policy boundaries also inspired the theme of a follow-up event to the Warsaw conference ('Integration in a Transnational World: Poland, Scotland and Polish Communities Abroad'). See note 2 above.
15. In this respect, he cites previous work by Nowosielski and Nowak (2017).
16. Following Jenne, ethnopopulist movements are defined as those which '[propagate] narratives whereby enemies from beyond (migrants, immigrants, ethnic minorities) couple or even conspire with enemies from above (the EU, UN, IMF, "global elites" or foreign powers) to undermine or even de-nationalize the nation-people' (2018, p. 549).

ORCID

Andreea Udrea ⓘ http://orcid.org/0000-0002-3763-5216
David Smith ⓘ http://orcid.org/0000-0002-3346-3824

References

Adamson, F. B., & Demetriou, M. (2007). Remapping the boundaries of 'state' and 'national identity': Incorporating diasporas into IR theorizing. *European Journal of International Relations*, *13*(4), 489–526. https://doi.org/10.1177/1354066107083145

Alonso, A. D., & Mylonas, H. (2017). The microfoundations of diaspora politics: Unpacking the state and disaggregating the diaspora. *Journal of Ethnic and Migration Studies*, *45*(4), 473–491. https://doi.org/10.1080/1369183X.2017.1409160

Bieber, F. (2020). Global nationalism in times of the COVID-19 pandemic. *Nationalities Papers*, 1–13. https://doi.org/10.1017/nps.2020.35

Brubaker, R. (1996). *Nationalism reframed. Nationhood and the national question in the new Europe*. Cambridge University Press.

Brubaker, R. (2017). Between nationalism and civilizationism: The European populist moment in comparative perspective. *Ethnic and Racial Studies*, *40*(8), 1191–1226. https://doi.org/10.1080/01419870.2017.1294700

Chandra, K. (2020, May 7). [talk]. In Association for the Study of Nationalities (host). *Nationalism and the pandemic* [Webinar]. Facebook. https://www.facebook.com/Nationalities/videos/328120788161054/

Cordell, K., & Wolff, S. (2007). Germany as a kin-state: The development and implementation of a norm-consistent external minority policy towards Central and Eastern Europe. *Nationalities Papers, 35*(2), 289–315. https://doi.org/10.1080/00905990701254367

Council of Europe. (2001, October 22). *Report on the preferential treatment of national minorities by their kin-states.* https://www.venice.coe.int/webforms/documents/?pdf=CDL-INF(2001)019-e

Crowder, G. (2013). *Theories of multiculturalism. An introduction.* Polity.

Csergő, Z., & Goldgeier, J. (2004). Nationalist strategies and European integration. *Perspectives on Politics, 2*(1), 21–37. https://doi.org/10.1017/S153759270400060X

Csergő, Z., & Liebich, A. (2019, May 23–24). *Kin-state engagement and minority political agency in the sphere of education* [Paper presentation]. Poland's Kin-state: Opportunities and Challenges, Warsaw, Poland.

Defeis, E. F. (2011). Minority protection, bilateral mechanisms and the responsibility to protect. In W. Kemp, V. Popovski, & R. Thakur (Eds.), *Blood and borders. The responsibility to protect and the problem of the kin-state* (pp. 63–89). United Nations UP.

Dumbravă, C. (2014). *Nationality, citizenship and ethno-cultural belonging: Preferential membership policies in Europe.* Palgrave Macmillan.

EFHR. (2016, November). *Parliament of RP amended Polish Charter.* http://media.efhr.eu/2016/11/16/parliament-rp-amended-polish-charter/

EURAC. (2007). *Competence analysis: National minorities as a Standortfaktor in the German-Danish border region.*

EURAC (host). (2020). *Episode 1: Covid-19 and its effects on minorities* [Webinar]. http://www.eurac.edu/en/research/autonomies/minrig/services/Pages/Webinars.aspx

Harris, E. (2009). *Nationalism: Theories and cases.* Edinburgh University Press.

Hatvany, C. (2006). Legitimacy of kin-state politics: A theoretical approach. *REGIO. A Review of Studies on Minorities, Politics, and Society, 9*(1), 47–64. http://epa.oszk.hu/00400/00476/00006/pdf/Regio_2006_eng.pdf

Horváth, E. (2008). *Mandating identity. Citizenship, kinship laws and plural nationality in the European Union.* Kluwer Law International.

Hut, P. (2019). Relations of polish authorities with the polish diaspora in the (Post-) Soviet space. In K. P. Marczuk (Ed.), *Good neighbourhood treaties of Poland. Political, security and social relations* (pp. 163–177). Palgrave Macmillan.

Jenne, E. (2018). Is nationalism or ethnopopulism on the rise today? *Ethnopolitics, 17*(5), 546–552. https://doi.org/10.1080/17449057.2018.1532635

Karolewski, P. (2015). The polish charter. Extraterritorial semi-citizenship and soft power. In T. Agarin & P. Karolewski (Eds.), *Extraterritorial citizenship in postcommunist Europe* (pp. 65–87). Rowman & Littlefield.

Klatt, M. (2017). Minorities as secondary foreign policy agents in peacebuilding and reconciliation? The case of Denmark and Germany. *Regional & Federal Studies, 27*(3), 239–259. https://doi.org/10.1080/13597566.2017.1350651

Klatt, M. (2020). What has happened to our cross-border regions? Corona, unfamiliarity and trans-national borderland activism in the Danish-German border region. In C. Wille & R. Kanesu (Eds.), *Bordering in pandemic times. Insights into the Covid-19 lockdown* (pp. 43–48). Borders in Perspective, 4, 43–48. https://doi.org/10.25353/ubtr-xxxx-b825-a20b.

Koinova, M. (2008). Kinstate intervention in ethnic conflicts: Albania and Turkey compared. *Ethnopolitics, 7*(4), 373–390. https://doi.org/10.1080/17449050802243384

Kuzborska, E. (2013). The protection of Lithuania's polish minority: Bone of contention in bilateral Polish-Lithuanian relations. *European Yearbook of Minority Issues Online, 12*(1), 122–157. https://doi.org/10.1163/9789004306134_006

Ładykowski, P. (2018). 'National belonging' in legal and diplomatic formulas: The pole's card as a legacy of Poland's colonial past. *Baltic Journal of European Studies, 8*(2), 92–120. https://doi.org/10.1515/bjes-2018-0017

Marczuk, K. P. (2019). Good neighbourhood treaties and public diplomacy: Polish activities in neighbouring states (2007–2014). In K. P. Marczuk (Ed.), *Good neighbourhood treaties of Poland. Political, security and social relations* (pp. 25–40). Palgrave Macmillan.

Mavelli, L. (2018). Citizenship for sale and the neoliberal political economy of belonging. *International Studies Quarterly, 62*(3), 482–493. https://doi.org/10.1093/isq/sqy004

McGarry, J., & O'Leary, B. (2013). Introduction. In T. J. Mabry, J. McGary, M. Moore, & B. O'Leary (Eds.), *Divided nations and European integration* (pp. 1–32). University of Pennsylvania Press.

Mikołajczyk, B. (2015). Historical heritage in contemporary polish law relating to foreigners. *Immigrants & Minorities*, *33*(3), 279–300. https://doi.org/10.1080/02619288.2015.1047677

Minority Rights Group International. (n.d.). *World directory of minorities and indigenous peoples*. Belarus—Poles. https://minorityrights.org/minorities/poles/

Mylonas, H. (2012). *The politics of nation-building. Making co-nationals, refugees, and minorities*. Cambridge University Press.

Nowosielski, M., & Nowak, W. (2017). Między Wschodem a Zachodem—geograficzne ukierunkowanie polityki polonijnej i jego przemiany w latach 1989–2017. *Rocznik Instytutu Europy Środkowo-Wschodnie*, *15*, 139–158.

Nowosielski, M., & Nowak, W. (2018). Polish diaspora policy—directions of changes and fields of constants. *Spotlight. Newsletter of Centre of Migration Research*, *3*(3).

OSCE High Commissioner on National Minorities. (2020, April 21). *Streamlining diversity: Covid-19 measures that support social cohesion*. https://www.osce.org/hcnm/450433

Pogonyi, S. (2017). *Extra-territorial ethnic politics, discourses and identities in Hungary*. Palgrave Macmillan.

Polish Sejm. (2000, November 9). *Ustawa z dnia 9 listopada 2000 r. o repatriacji*. http://prawo.sejm.gov.pl/isap.nsf/DocDetails.xsp?id=WDU20001061118

Polish Sejm. (2007, September 7). *Ustawa z dnia 7 września 2007 r. o Karcie Polaka*. http://prawo.sejm.gov.pl/isap.nsf/DocDetails.xsp?id=WDU20180001272

Polish Sejm. (2016, May 13). *Ustawa z dnia 13 maja 2016 r. o zmianie ustawy o Karcie Polaka oraz niektórych innych ustaw*. http://isap.sejm.gov.pl/isap.nsf/DocDetails.xsp?id=WDU20160000753

Polish Sejm. (2016, November 15). *Ustawa z dnia 15 listopada 2016 r. o zmianie ustawy o Karcie Polaka oraz ustawy o cudzoziemcach*. http://isap.sejm.gov.pl/isap.nsf/DocDetails.xsp?id=WDU20160002066

Saideman, S. M., & Ayres, R. W. (2015). *For kin or country. Xenophobia, nationalism, and war*. Columbia University Press.

Sata, R., & Karolewski, I. P. (2020). Caesarean politics in Hungary and Poland. *East European Politics*, *36*(2), 206–225. https://doi.org/10.1080/21599165.2019.1703694

Schulze, J. L. (2018). *Strategic frames: Europe, Russia, and minority inclusion in Estonia and Latvia*. University of Pittsburgh Press.

Sendhardt, B. (2017). Theorizing the *Karta Polaka*. Debordering and rebordering the limits of citizenship, territory and nation in the EU's eastern neighbourhood. *The Journal of Power Institutions in Post-Soviet Societies*, *18*. https://doi.org/10.4000/pipss.4348

Shevel, O. (2015). Russia and the near abroad. *Great Decisions 2015, Topic 1*, 5–16.

Smith, D. J. (2002). Framing the national question in central and Eastern Europe: A quadratic nexus? *Global Review of Ethnopolitics*, *2*(1), 3–16. https://doi.org/10.1080/14718800208405119

Smith, D. J. (2020). The 'quadratic nexus' revisited: Nation-building in Estonia through the prism of national cultural autonomy. *Nationalities Papers*, *48*(2), 235–250. https://doi.org/10.1017/nps.2018.38

Szczerbiak, A. (2017). An anti-establishment backlash that shook up the party system? The October 2015 Polish parliamentary election. *European Politics and Society*, *18*(4), 404–427. https://doi.org/10.1080/23745118.2016.1256027

Szoszyn, R. (2019, September 26). Karta Polaka: Droga do Polski. *Rzeczpospolita*. https://www.rp.pl/Bialorus/309269893-Karta-Polaka-Droga-do-Polski.html

Udrea, A. (2014). A kin-state's responsibility: Cultural identity, recognition, and the Hungarian status law. *Ethnicities*, *14*(2), 324–346. https://doi.org/10.1177/1468796812472145

Vollebaek, K. (2009, June 30). *Address by Knut Vollebaek OSCE high commissioner on national minorities to the general committee on political affairs and security at the 18th annual session of the OSCE Parliamentary Assembly*. https://www2.osce.org/hcnm/38120

Wallace, C., & Patsiurko, N. (2017). Relational identities on EU borderlands: The case of Poles in Belarus and Belarusians in Poland. *Ethnic and Racial Studies*, *40*(1), 77–95. https://doi.org/10.1080/01419870.2016.1201582

Waterbury, M. A. (2010). *Between state and nation: Diaspora politics and kin-state nationalism in Hungary*. Palgrave.

Waterbury, M. A. (2020). Kin-state politics: Causes and consequences. *Nationalities Papers*, 1–10. https://doi.org/10.1017/nps.2020.3

Weselowsky, T. (2019, September 29). Stand up and be counted: Ethnic Poles in Belarus gear up for census. *RFE/RL's Belarus Service*. https://www.rferl.org/a/ethnic-poles-belarus-census-remember-who-i-am/30190010.html

Karta Polaka—New Wine in Old Bottles

DOROTA PUDZIANOWSKA

ABSTRACT   The *Karta Polaka* was adopted by the Polish parliament in 2007. Its main aim at the time was to facilitate the maintenance of cultural links between Poland and the Polish kin-minorities living in the former Soviet Union. This paper discusses the international context and long legislative history of the statute on the *Karta Polaka*, and illustrates the evolution of its provisions. The main argument is that the function of the *Karta Polaka* has evolved from one of maintaining links with the kin-minority abroad to facilitating emigration to Poland by people of Polish ethnic origin or cultural affinity.

The *Karta Polaka* in Regional Context

In the wake of the transition of the Central and Eastern European (CEE) countries during the early 1990s, maintaining contacts with and supporting kin minorities became an important political issue. After the collapse of the Soviet Union 'the region witnessed a renaissance of nations and national emotions (…) which had previously been reserved or at times even oppressed. In this period, these feelings also regained their political legitimacy' (Halász, 2006, p. 256). In most CEE countries this issue quickly became regulated by newly adopted constitutions which include provisions on supporting members of kin-minorities. These provisions are formulated in a very general manner, usually mentioning the need (and/or obligation) to support the diaspora.[1] Some regulations provide mainly for national identity to be maintained while others seem to go further. For example, Article 12 of the Constitution of Ukraine of 1996 states that 'Ukraine provides for the satisfaction of national and cultural, and linguistic needs of Ukrainians residing beyond the borders of the State'.[2] Article 7a of the Constitution of the Slovak Republic of 1992 states that: 'The Slovak Republic supports the national awareness and cultural identity of the Slovaks living abroad; it supports their institutions established to achieve this purpose and their relations with the mother country'.[3] This issue is regulated similarly in the Polish Constitution of 1997 in Article 6 (2): 'The Republic of Poland shall provide assistance to Poles living abroad to maintain their links with the national cultural heritage'.[4] In all three examples, providing assistance to members of the kin-minorities is limited to the function of maintaining national and cultural (linguistic) links.

In some constitutions, however, there are different approaches to the needs and goals of supporting national communities scattered around the world and the scope of support is not only limited to maintaining cultural ties. Examples include regulations contained in the Croatian, Albanian, Macedonian and Hungarian constitutions. Article 10 (2) of the Constitution of Croatia of 1991 states that: 'Parts of the Croatian nation in other states shall be guaranteed special concern and protection by the Republic of Croatia'.[5] In a similar manner, Article 8 (1) of the Constitution of Albania of 1998 states that 'The Republic of Albania protects the national rights of the Albanian people who live outside its borders'.[6] Article D of the Hungarian Constitution of 2011 states that 'Hungary shall bear responsibility for the fate of Hungarians living beyond its borders, and shall facilitate the survival and development of their communities'. Moreover, Hungary

> shall support their efforts to preserve their Hungarian identity, the assertion of their individual and collective rights, the establishment of their community self-governments, and their prosperity in their native lands, and shall promote their cooperation with each other and with Hungary.[7]

CEE constitutional provisions inspired the adoption of detailed solutions in ordinary legislation. In this sense, the CEE countries show a certain consistency in the connection of constitutional and statutory regulations.[8] Statutes aimed at supporting and maintaining contacts with kin-minorities were adopted in Hungary (2001), Slovakia (2005), Slovenia (2006), Romania (first in 1998 and then in 2007), Bulgaria (2000), Russia (1999) and Ukraine (2004). In Poland the statue was passed by the parliament in 2007, but the first bill on the *Karta Polaka* was introduced to parliament in April 1999, i.e. less than two years after the Polish Constitution of 1997.[9]

Motivating Factors Behind the First Bill on the *Karta Polaka*

The first bill on the *Karta Polaka* (Bill no 1206)[10] was linked to a broader legislative initiative, constituting part of a so-called 'package of three laws' alongside a new Act on Citizenship (Bill no 1222) and the Act on Repatriation (Bill no 1204). The idea behind the *Karta Polaka* was to facilitate frequent visits to the country for people who did not intend to return to Poland permanently but wanted to maintain cultural links with the country. The matter of immigration was relegated to the Act on Repatriation, which was aimed at facilitating permanent settlement in Poland by people of Polish origin. In turn, the new Act on Citizenship sought to replace the 1962 law and to dissociate post-communist Poland from the practices of totalitarian regimes based on deprivation of citizenship.[11]

The first and most important motivating factor behind the Bill was of a moral nature. The justification of the three laws referred to a 'moral obligation' imposed on Poland towards members of the Polish nation living abroad. The three laws were therefore intended as an attempt to regulate comprehensively the attitude of the Polish state towards Poles who, as a result of a turbulent history, found themselves outside the borders of the country often against their will.[12]

The argument of a 'moral obligation' builds on the history of Poland mainly during and after the Second World War. Due to the deportations during the war and border changes in its aftermath, an important part of the Polish population found itself outside the newly established borders. The residual ethnically Polish population that remained in former territories annexed by the Soviet Union was forcibly deprived of Polish citizenship and acquired Soviet citizenship (Czaplinski, 1991, p. 12). However, under the repatriation agreements (officially called evacuation agreements) signed in the years 1944–1945[13] and 1957[14] people of Polish origin who had held Polish citizenship before 17 September 1939 were permitted to return to Poland and regain Polish citizenship. The repatriation action in the years 1944–1948 covered about 1.5 million people from the Soviet Union, with the following wave in the second half of the 1950s covering almost 260,000 people (Hut, 2002, pp. 11–12). According to the Soviet population census of 1970 there were still 1.167 million people of Polish origin living in the Soviet Union (Hut, 2002, pp. 11–12). Even though not all of these people had been forced to remain, the argument of a 'moral obligation' focuses on those who could not relocate due to the narrowing of the scope of repatriation. First, it is claimed that the authorities underestimated the number of people who were interested in repatriation and that logistics were poorly organized; as a result, not everyone who wanted to leave could do so in the short time frame available (Wyszyński, 2013, p. 126). Second, the information about repatriation did not reach all interested parties. For example, evidence shows that in rural areas people were intentionally denied access to evacuation: registration points were scarce and set up late (Wyszyński, 2013, p. 117). Third, the bilateral agreements provided for the evacuation of people of Polish national origin (*narodowość*[15]) who were Polish citizens before 17 September 1939 and had expressed their wish to resettle. The intention at this initial stage was to restore citizenship not to everyone who had held a Polish passport before September 1939, but only to those who could demonstrate Polish (including Jewish) national origin.

Referring to the abovementioned restrictions, Tadeusz Jasudowicz wrote emotionally that the People's Republic of Poland '(…) did not turn out to be (…) a "good mother" and willingly agreed to an unacceptable narrowing (…) of the scope of evacuation in the years 1944–1945, as well as in the repatriation agreement of 1957' (Jasudowicz, 1996, p. 95). This narrowing of scope gave rise to arguments that post-communist Poland had a 'duty of special diligence and determination to restore the citizenship of the Polish state from before the war and to enable them [its former citizens] to return to their homeland' (Jasudowicz, 1996, p. 95). It was emphasized that pre-1989 Polish authorities did not show enough diligence in the implementation of this moral obligation and did not conduct negotiations aimed at granting Polish citizenship and enabling the return of Polish citizens from outside the territory of the Second Polish Republic to the homeland (Jasudowicz, 1996, pp. 97–98).

Although the way in which the moral obligation was formulated referred primarily to the Poles in the East, initially both the *Karta Polaka* and the Bill on Repatriation were addressed to former Polish citizens and their descendants throughout the world. Policymakers accepted that a 'moral obligation' also existed towards Poles who emigrated in the post-war period as a result of persecution on political, national, religious or economic grounds and who renounced or were deprived of their citizenship. Yet, in the end, the personal scope of both these Bills was narrowed down to the Poles in the East. Because of the costs involved, this restriction was linked to the conclusion that it was not possible to make up for the harm done to all former Polish citizens. It was considered that the first and most important group to be compensated were Poles in the former Soviet Union (justification of Bill no 1206 (1999), p. 10).

Work on the *Karta Polaka* was also accelerated for pragmatic reasons linked to Poland's anticipated accession to the European Union (EU) and the Schengen Area. This argument was voiced in the parliamentary debates in 1999. MPs were aware that the planned accession to the EU and the Schengen Area imposed an obligation on border states, such as

Poland, to tighten their frontiers. This was linked among other things with the necessity to introduce a unified visa system, to significantly increase visa fees, to introduce strict verification of the purpose of travel and funds available for subsistence. From the perspective of maintaining contacts with the diaspora in the East, this was perceived as an unfavourable phenomenon, as it made contacts with the homeland more difficult (Jagielski & Pudzianowska, 2008, p. 53).

These two different ways of justifying the need for this statute show that from the beginning two competing paradigms existed: the 'romantic' paradigm based on moral arguments mainly about cultivating 'Polishness' in the East, and the 'pragmatic' one which underlined the need to ease travel to Poland for a special category of foreigners. The first prevailed in the beginning, however the second has replaced it, as will be shown in this paper.

Karta Polaka's Legislative Vicissitudes

Prior to the enactment of the *Karta Polaka* of 2007, there had been three other bills that had sought to regulate the issue. The first was Bill no 1206 initiated by the members of the *Senate*, which constituted part of the 'package of three laws' (see above). The initiators were mainly senators of the conservative party Solidarity Electoral Action (AWS), but the draft law was presented in the *Sejm* (lower house of the Polish parliament) also thanks to the votes of senators from the Democratic Left Alliance (SLD). After the bill was introduced in the *Sejm* on 28 April 1999 it underwent many amendments, eventually being retitled Bill no 2641. On 20 February 2001 the *Sejm*'s commissions recommended that the Bill 2641 be adopted. After its second reading in the *Sejm* on 19 June 2001, the latter Bill was sent for further work in parliamentary committee, from where it was not returned to the parliament for a third and final reading before the end of term of the parliament in October 2001. After the 2001 elections won by the left-wing coalition SLD—Labour Union (UP), there were no new initiatives in this area for several years. The second and the third bills on the *Karta Polaka* came under discussion only after the victory of Law and Justice (PiS) in the elections of 2005. The first of these (hereafter 'Government Draft Bill of 2006') was never submitted to the *Sejm*. The second (Bill no 1957)—which was adopted into law—was introduced in the *Sejm* in July 2007. Before I discuss the *Karta Polaka* and its evolution, it is worth mentioning some of the solutions which made each of the earlier three proposals unique.

The *Senate* bill in its original version (no 1206) and the version changed by the *Sejm* (no 2641) were similar in scope. Both versions of the bill concerned persons of Polish origin who were not citizens of Poland and resided abroad. In other words, the draft laws concerned the Polish diaspora worldwide. They differed in the way the relations between the concepts of 'national origin' and 'citizenship' were defined. In the original *Senate* bill, having had Polish citizenship in the past was the most important condition, while in a version modified by the *Sejm* the basic condition became 'Polish origin'. Changes were introduced to the original bill also in respect of rights for holders of the Polish Card. In Bill no 2641 access to rights for a holder of the Card depended on whether s/he was in possession of a settlement permit. Only the latter category of Card holders had access to the full range of rights.

As explained above, Bill 1206 proposed by the *Senate* in 1999 evolved during the parliamentary process in the *Sejm* into Bill no 2641 of 2001 and since the work on this Bill had not been completed before the end of the parliament term (October 2001), it was lost. The length of time spent on the project—and its ultimate failure—were due to two factors: first, the negative opinion of the Secretary of the Committee for European Integration (KIE); and second, the critical position of the Council of Ministers (RM) in relation to the Bill. The KIE's objections mainly concerned visa issues. Bill no 2641 envisaged a special 'visa allowing for entry in order to settle'. As a result of the Convention implementing the Schengen Agreement,[16] long-stay visas are issued by the Member-States on the basis of their own internal regulations. However, the Convention precisely regulates short-term visas issued for a period of stay not exceeding three months. The problem raised by the KIE was that the bill did not clearly specify that a 'visa allowing for entry in order to settle' was a long-term visa. Even though its name suggested that it was issued for periods longer than three months, other provisions of the bill suggested it could also be issued for a short-term visit (KIE, 2001, point IV, pp. 2–3). Thus, if a visa allowing for entry in order to settle could have been issued as a short-term visa, this would have been considered incompatible with European standards (KIE, 2001, point IV, pp. 2–3).

In the opinion of the RM, other types of legal problems arose. Here, reservations concerned the granting of special rights to foreigners because of their Polish origin. According to the RM, there may have been a lack of compliance with Articles 32 and 37 of the Constitution of the Republic of Poland, which stipulate the necessity of equal treatment of all foreigners on the territory of Poland (RM, point I.3, p. 2). Concerns were also expressed that these regulations were contrary to regulations in international law concerning non-discrimination (RM, point I.3, p. 2). Furthermore, it was argued that the bill gave discretionary power to the Polish authorities to decide if someone is of Polish origin; this is contrary to international law, under which the national origin of a person is a matter of individual choice. It was feared that such provisions might have adverse political consequences, leading to the weakening of the position of Polish minorities abroad, as states where these minorities live might try to question the self-identification of people as Polish (RM, 2001, point I.2 pp. 1–2). Moreover, in the opinion of the RM, such a version of the bill would only serve the assumed objectives to a limited extent, as many rights granted were related to the possession of a settlement permit (see above) and the condition for obtaining such a permit was that the applicant should be provided with accommodation and subsistence. The number of people using these rights would therefore be negligible, which could cause frustration and dissatisfaction within the Polish diaspora (RM, 2001, point II, p. 3).

An important argument against the Bill was its cost, which, in the opinion of the government, was impossible to estimate (RM, 2001, I.4, p. 3). As an alternative, the government pointed to a different strategic approach. Instead of adopting a statute such as the *Karta Polaka*, the RM pointed to the need to invest to a greater extent in supporting Polish identity abroad (*e.g.* increasing expenditure on repatriation, helping the Poles living in Lithuania, Ukraine and Belarus by offering scholarships 'to support education of Polish youth in their country of residence' and establishing a Fund to Support Entrepreneurship of the Polish Community). According to the RM, the 'moral and symbolic' dimension of the bill could be fulfilled by introducing an 'Honorary Pole's Badge' (*Honorowa Odznaka Polaka*) which could be given to anyone who 'feels links with Poland and desires to cultivate and develop them' (RM, 2001, p. 5). As explained in the document, this solution would overcome the legal and political difficulties inherent in requiring the authorities to determine Polish origin.

As mentioned above, the second (Government Draft Bill of 2006) and the third bill (Bill no 1957) on the *Karta Polaka* came under discussion only after the victory of Law and Justice in the elections of 2005. Curiously, even though both bills were prepared by the Inter-Ministerial Team for the Polish Diaspora and Poles Abroad there was—as its former secretary Michał Dworczyk describes—'a resistance in the central administration to proceed with this bill'.[17]

The Government Draft Bill of 2006 was never introduced in the *Sejm*. The draft introduced a category of 'foreign Pole' (*Polak zagraniczny*), defined as a person in relation to whom a decision on the determination of Polish origin was issued. Such a person would be entitled to receive the Polish Card. A foreign Pole who was a holder of the Card was to have the same rights as those who had a settlement permit. The personal scope was broad and members of the worldwide diaspora were targeted. However, some privileges provided for in the Bill were only available to persons living permanently in the countries of the former Soviet Union. This was the case with rights such as the reduction of fees for public transport and free-of-charge entrance to museums.

Bill no 1957 was introduced to the Sejm on 6 July 2007 by Prime Minister Jarosław Kaczyński (PiS). In many respects it was similar to Bill no 1206 of 1999. However, this time great determination was visible on the part of the government to finish work. This mobilization was due to the approaching parliamentary elections (October 2007) and planned accession to the Schengen Area (December 2007). Such mobilization was made possible by the departure from office of the main opponent of the Karta Polaka, Minister of Administration and Internal Affairs Ludwik Dorn (PiS).[18] However, Dorn then became Speaker of the *Sejm* and he did not intend to proceed with the bill, which was evident when he did not include it on the list of bills to be discussed before the end of the parliamentary term. With the approval of J. Kaczyński, Michał Dworczyk helped to organize a protest in front of the *Sejm*.[19] The support expressed for the Act by members of kin-minority organizations from the East helped to mobilize wide political support. In August 2007, around 200 representatives of organizations from Ukraine, Belarus, Lithuania, Russia and Kazakhstan came to Poland to show their support for the Act (see photo below; Masalska, 2007). When they appeared in front of the *Sejm*'s building they were invited in by Dorn, who then publicly declared that the project would be discussed in the *Sejm* before the end of the term (Masalska, 2007). The legislative process took just two months, and on 22 September 2007 the bill was signed by the President.[20] There was almost unanimous support for the Act within the *Sejm*: 431 MPs voted in favour, only three MPs from the SLD voted against, and nobody abstained. This wide support in parliament was explained by the framing of the Act as a moral obligation, as well as the mostly symbolic list of rights granted to its beneficiaries. The broad moral justification was therefore linked with the thinness of the statute's material provisions as will be shown below (Figure 1).

The Original Version of the *Karta Polaka*

The original version of *Karta Polaka* of 7 September 2007 created a special legal status for citizens of the former Soviet republics. The preamble to the Act very specifically mentions that its rationale is to fulfil 'a moral obligation towards Poles in the East, who, as a result of the changing fate of our homeland, lost their Polish citizenship' and points to one of the aims of the statute which is to 'strengthen the ties between Poles in the East and the

Figure 1. A banner in front of the *Sejm* declaring 'Compatriots! Do not renounce us' (24 August 2007), Masalska (2007)

Motherland and to support their efforts to preserve the Polish language and cultivate the national tradition' (Journal of Laws no. 180 item 1280). In so doing, this version of *Karta Polaka* follows the logic of the Act on Repatriation already adopted in 2000. Furthermore, the fact that *Karta Polaka* was later complemented by the Act on Citizenship of 2009 (in force since 2012) shows that the original logic of the 'package of three laws' from the initial works has been preserved.

There are several conditions that have to be fulfilled by a person who wants to obtain the Polish Card, some of which are straightforward. It may be issued to a person who, at the time of application, is a citizen of a state formerly belonging to the Soviet Union (Art. 2.2), is not a Polish citizen or does not possess a leave to settle in Poland (Art. 2.4). Such a person has to declare affinity to the Polish nation and has to make a written declaration of belonging to the Polish nation (Art. 2.1(2)).

There are two other conditions which are more complex and serve to assess cultural and/or ethnic belonging to the Polish nation. First, a person has to show his/her connection to the Polish nation and state by demonstrating at least a basic knowledge of the Polish language (which the applicant has to acknowledge as his/her mother tongue) as well as a 'knowledge of and cultivation of Polish traditions and customs' (Art. 2.1(1)). This provision was criticized in the literature because it introduces a condition which is difficult to assess objectively (Jagielski & Pudzianowska, 2008, pp. 78–79). There is a risk it could be applied in a way that amounts to religious discrimination. Persons belonging to non-Catholic religious denominations may be discriminated against, as many Polish customs and traditions are in fact Catholic. Secondly, a person has to demonstrate that at least one parent or grandparent, or two great-grandparents, are/were of Polish national origin or were Polish citizens, or has to present a certificate from an authorized Polish organization in the home country confirming active involvement of the applicant in activities promoting the Polish language and culture, or otherwise assisting the Polish national minority for a period of at least three last years (Art. 2.1(3)). This means that in order to obtain Polish Card a person does not need to have ancestors of Polish national origin or ancestors who were Polish citizens, as it suffices to present a certificate of an authorized organization confirming that the conditions are met (Jagielski & Pudzianowska, 2008, p. 81).

The Card certifies belonging to the Polish nation. It neither certifies Polish citizenship, nor is it a residence permit. In its form it is similar to the national ID card. It certifies the entitlement to rights and privileges enumerated in the statute. Initially, the bill on the *Karta Polaka* mostly referred to rights which were symbolic in nature and had as their direct aim maintaining cultural links with Poland. According to the early version of the bill, holders had to apply for a visa and whilst on Polish territory they could: (1) access the Polish education system at higher level on the same terms as Polish citizens, while also being able to apply for scholarships and other assistance available to aliens learning and studying in Poland; (2) access health care in emergencies on the same terms as Polish citizens; (3) enjoy a 37% reduction on the cost of rail travel on Polish territory; (4) visit national museums in Poland free of charge; (5) have priority when applying for funding from the Polish state budget or the local authorities budget in Poland intended to support Poles abroad (Art. 6.1 (3–7)).[21]

At the last stage of parliamentary deliberation, two additional rights were added. These have a different character in that they serve the aim of maintaining cultural links only indirectly: the right to take up employment in Poland without the requirement to possess a work permit, and the right to carry out business activities in Poland on the same terms as Polish citizens (Art. 6.1 (1–2); Jagielski & Pudzianowska, 2008, p. 62). This is a clear illustration of the competing paradigms that have defined the scope of the statute from its inception. The 'romantic' aspect of the legislation was used instrumentally to gain support within the government. However, during the parliamentary debates there was the push for a more pragmatic approach which would have been blocked at the stage of inter-ministerial consultations.[22]

It follows from the above discussion that *Karta Polaka* was initially an instrument aimed at Poles in the East. However, *Karta Polaka* cannot be perceived easily as an instrument of ethnopolitics. From the wording of the statutory provisions it can be concluded that one does not need to have ancestors of Polish ethnic origin in order to be eligible for a Polish Card. Therefore, it should not be surprising that, according to available data, over 11% of holders officially declare a national origin other than Polish (Kowalski, 2015, p. 36). There is no available data showing what proportion of those who received Polish Cards without having ancestors of Polish national origin had ancestors with Polish citizenship. Possibly it is a majority of this group. Nevertheless, according to the law every citizen of the former Soviet Union who is sufficiently motivated (e.g. learns basic Polish and gets involved in the activities of Polish kin-minority organizations according to the conditions specified for in the statute) can obtain a Polish Card regardless of national origin or even the citizenship of his/her ancestors.[23] In other words, an applicant does not need to have a claim to pre-war Polish citizenship or to have ancestors of Polish national origin.

The Evolution of the *Karta Polaka*

The intended main function of *Karta Polaka* has evolved over time. Initially the idea was that it would serve as an instrument enabling people who live abroad on a permanent basis to maintain cultural links with Poland, while the Act of Repatriation was intended as an instrument encouraging immigration to Poland of the Poles from the East. Over time, this legislative idea has changed even though, as was mentioned above, indications of the more pragmatic approach to *Karta Polaka* were visible from the beginning.

The evolution of the *Karta Polaka* towards an instrument of encouraging immigration to Poland is not only visible from the Act itself but also from changes made to other statutes. Firstly, the Act on Citizenship of 2009 introduces the possibility of applying for Polish citizenship after two years of residence on the basis of a permanent residence permit obtained on the basis of Polish origin, for which the holders of the Polish Card could apply. Since 2013, a holder of the Polish Card has the right to a permanent residence permit (Art. 195.1 (9) of the Law on Foreigners of 2013). He or she has to apply for it, but in legal terms it is an entitlement. Next, in 2016, an explicit provision concerning the holders of the Polish Card was added to the Act on Citizenship and the period after which such a person can apply for Polish citizenship was shortened to one year (Art. 30.1 (7) of the Act on Citizenship). Further provisions introduced during the same year stipulate that visas can now be obtained by close family members of a person living in Poland who obtained permanent residence as a holder of a Polish Card (Art. 60.1 (19a) of Law on Foreigners of 2013). Additionally, since 2016 in cases where a holder files an application for a permanent residence permit, there is a right to obtain (for a period no longer than nine months) financial assistance intended for foreigners and their immediate family members residing with them in Poland (Art. 8a of *Karta Polaka*).

The abovementioned amendments were clearly aimed at encouraging migration to Poland from the East. It is interesting that the changes which took place in 2016 were criticized by some kin-minority organizations in the East, which claim that the new law will result in the 'depolonisation' of what are nostalgically called the historical 'Polish borderlands' (*Kresy*), whereas previously the aim of the Act was to strengthen 'Polishness' in these regions (Kresy.pl, 2016). The amendment concerning the possibility to receive financial assistance was even portrayed as a form of bribery—namely, payment in return for immigration to Poland (Kresy.pl, 2016). This critique shows that the reason why the 'romantic' paradigm dominated the articulation of the *Karta Polaka* in the beginning was not only to overcome the lack of support in the government to such policy, but also to cohere with the views articulated by some NGOs from the East underlining the importance of maintaining and promoting the Polish culture and language in the region.

Other amendments to the Act are more of a symbolic nature. First, since 2019 the Act applies to the Polish diaspora not only in the East, but worldwide (amendments were introduced to Art. 2 of the Act). During discussions in parliamentary commission it was claimed that there is an interest in the Polish Card on the part of people of Polish descent in South America (e.g. Brazil, Argentina). Nevertheless, it seems that this return to the original idea of targeting the diaspora worldwide is mostly symbolic.[24] Secondly, the list of rights and privileges in the *Karta Polaka* was widened to add consular protection for holders. This is the only right which is given to the holders when abroad. According to Art. 6 (8), a holder has a right to 'the assistance of the consul, within the framework of his competence and with due regard for custom and international law, in a situation of threat to life or safety'.[25] Thirdly, the amendment of 2017 changed the original wording of the condition for applying for the Polish Card, which stipulated that:

> a person has to demonstrate that at least one parent or grandparent, or two great-grandparents, are or were of Polish national origin or <u>were Polish citizens</u> or has to present a certificate from an authorized organization of Poles living abroad in the country of the alien's residence (...)

so as to eliminate the citizenship criterion 'were Polish citizens' (Art. 2.1 (3) of the amended version of *Karta Polaka* from 2017). MP Małgorzata Wypych (PiS) explained that following this amendment, in the case of each applicant 'there must be something that comes from the blood, not from the act of an official' (Anannikova, 2017). However, even though this change in law can be seen as a move towards ethnicization, individuals can still obtain a Polish Card simply by engaging in the activities of Polish organizations abroad and learning basic Polish (see Above).

The reasons for the change in the function of *Karta Polaka* towards an instrument of encouraging migration are not clear from the parliamentary debates, publicly available documents or public enunciations by government officials. The official justification of the recent changes was that the original legislative idea was verified by social reality, as applying for the Polish Card became more popular than making use of the lengthy procedure for repatriation (PAP, 2015). This 'success story' of *Karta Polaka* was presented in the media as the main argument behind recent changes in law which modify this instrument in important ways. Even though people do not obtain Polish citizenship the moment they cross the border and are not guaranteed housing and financial support for 12 months (as is the case with repatriation), the process of obtaining a Polish Card is quicker and the status permits the holder to work.

Nevertheless, there were also other reasons that were never expressed officially. As Dworczyk explains, first of all, he and a close group of people who worked on the Act have with time understood that:

> maintaining Polishness in the East is not possible and that such an assumption back in 2007 had been a bit 'romantic'. People either assimilate or leave for other countries. If they were to emigrate elsewhere, it is better they emigrate to Poland.[26]

Secondly, the expectations of the members of the Polish diaspora in the East have changed and willingness to emigrate to Poland has gained force. Dworczyk said that the amendments were intended to give them the choice of whether to stay or to emigrate to Poland. Thirdly, the demographic situation of Poland was also a factor in deciding about recent amendments, but it was 'the least important one'. Fourthly, 'resistance within the government' at the time of adoption of the original version of the Act has subsided. Therefore, it was possible for example to widen the scope of the Act to the diaspora worldwide.[27]

Conclusion

It has been shown that, from the beginning, two paradigms of thinking about the function of *Karta Polaka* might be detected—'romantic' and 'pragmatic'. The romantic paradigm based on moral grounds was used instrumentally to gain wide political support for the Act. In the beginning, the statute was mainly presented as an instrument of symbolic reparations for wrongs incurred by people who were forced to remain in the Soviet Union after the Second World War. Its main aim was to strengthen the Polish identity of kin-minorites in the countries where they lived by allowing them to maintain links with Poland. However, in recent years there has been a clear shift in the scope of the *Karta Polaka* which is consistent with the pragmatic paradigm. The series of legal changes that took place since 2013 demonstrates that the *Karta Polaka* has evolved into an instrument for encouraging permanent emigration to Poland.

Acknowledgements

The author deeply indebted to Karl Cordell, David Smith, Andreea Udrea, Piotr Korzec and Bastian Sendhardt for their comments and Michał Dworczyk for an interview.

Notes

1. I use the terms 'kin-minority' and 'diaspora' interchangeably.
2. Ukraine's Constitution of 1996 with amendments, English version available at: www.constituteproject.org.
3. Slovakia's Constitution of 1992 with amendments, English version available at: www.constituteproject.org.
4. Polish Constitution of 1997 with amendments, English version available at: www.constituteproject.org.
5. Croatian Constitution of 1991 with amendements. English version available at: www.constituteproject.org.
6. Albanian Constitution of 1998 with amendements. English version available at: www.constituteproject.org.
7. Hungarian Constitution of 2011 with amendements. English version available at: www.constituteproject.org.
8. Constitutions contain the basic principles and laws of a state that determine the powers and duties of the government and guarantee certain rights to the people in it. The statute is a law enacted by the legislative branch of a government as under the Constitution.
9. The statutes cover, inter alia, the creation of rights for members of the kin-minorities. It should be noted, however, that in the legislation of many countries, the aforementioned rights are also granted in other types of Acts, for example, in Acts on citizenship. These laws often provide for solutions that make it easier for a person of a given national (ethnic) origin to acquire citizenship by naturalization. These regulations may exist separately or in parallel to special statutes regulating rights and privileges of the diaspora (Jagielski & Pudzianowska, 2008, pp. 12–13).
10. Bill no 1206 entitled 'Draft Act on the Polish Card and the procedure for determining the belonging to the Polish Nation of persons of Polish citizenship or national origin'.
11. The principle that a Polish national cannot be deprived of citizenship was included in the Polish Constitution of 1997 (Art 34 (2)).
12. Cf. official justification of the Bill no 1206, available http://orka.sejm.gov.pl/Rejestrd.nsf/wgdruku/1206/$file/1206.pdf (accessed 29 December 2019).
13. First in 1944 evacuation agreements were signed between Polish National Liberation Committee and governments of three Soviet republics—Belarus, Lithuania and Ukraine—and in 1945 an evacuation agreement was signed with the Soviet Union.
14. Agreement between the Polish People's Republic and USSR of 25 II 1957.
15. The word 'narodowość' is used in Polish in a non-legal sense and means membership of a nation sharing a common history, culture, language or origin or it refers to membership of a national minority living within a state which may be culturally linked to an external kin-state. I will use the term 'national origin' as an equivalent of the Polish 'narodowość'.
16. Convention implementing the Schengen Agreement of 14 June 1985 between the Governments of the States of the Benelux Economic Union, the Federal Republic of Germany and the French Republic on the gradual abolition of checks at their common borders.
17. Author's interview with Michał Dworczyk, Head of the Chancellery of the Prime Minister, April 2020, Warsaw, Poland.
18. Author's interview with Michał Dworczyk, Head of the Chancellery of the Prime Minister, April 2020, Warsaw, Poland.

19. Author's interview with Michał Dworczyk, Head of the Chancellery of the Prime Minister, April 2020, Warsaw, Poland.
20. *Karta Polaka* entered into force after six months (29 March 2008).
21. Some of these rights give holders of the Polish Card a privileged position in comparison to Polish citizens and in this sense these rights can be qualified as privileges. Such is the nature of rights such as reduction on railway travel or free of charge entry to the museums.
22. It was possible at this stage because MPs' amendments do not necessitate inter-ministerial consultations. Author's interview with Michał Dworczyk, Head of the Chancellery of the Prime Minister, April 2020, Warsaw, Poland.
23. *Karta Polaka* can be also granted to a person whose Polish descent was validly certified in accordance with the provisions of the Act of 9 November 2000 on Repatriation.
24. Author's interview with Michał Dworczyk, Head of the Chancellery of the Prime Minister, April 2020, Warsaw, Poland.
25. The addition of this right, even though it is worded carefully, is surprising. Following the report of the Venice Commission on the Act of 19 June 2001 on Hungarians living in neighbouring countries (Venice Commission, 2001), it is clear that rights which have the effect on the territory of other countries are problematic in view of international law.
26. Author's interview with Michał Dworczyk, Head of the Chancellery of the Prime Minister, April 2020, Warsaw, Poland.
27. Author's interview with Michał Dworczyk, Head of the Chancellery of the Prime Minister, April 2020, Warsaw, Poland.

References

Anannikova, L. (2017, December 11). Obywatelu, Karta Polaka nie dla ciebie [The Polish Card not for citizens]. Gazeta Wyborcza.
Czaplinski, W. (1991, November 26). Obywatelstwo zagrabione [Stolen citizenship]. Gazeta Wyborcza.
Halász, I. (2006). Models of Kin minority protection in central and eastern Europe. In O. Ieda (Ed.), *Beyond sovereignty: From status law to transnational citizenship?* (pp. 255–279). Slavic Research Center, Hokkaido University. Slavic Euroasian Studies 2006, no 9.
Hut, P. (2002). *Warunki życia i proces adaptacji repatriantów w Polsce w latach 1992–2000* [Living conditions and adaptation process of repatriates in Poland in 1992–2000]. Oficyna wydawnicza ASPRA.
Jagielski, J., & Pudzianowska, D. (2008). *Ustawa o Karcie Polaka. Komentarz* [The act on the Polish Card. A commentary]. Wolters Kluwer.
Jasudowicz, T. (1996). Powrót do obywatelstwa polskiego odebranego przez Związek Sowiecki w czasie lub w związku z II wojną światową [Return to Polish Citizenship Taken Away by the Soviet Union during or in connection with World War II]. In P. Bajda (Ed.), *Obywatelstwo w Europie Środkowo-Wschodniej, Materiały z konferencji „Prawo do posiadania obywatelstwa w Europie Środkowo-Wschodniej* [Citizenship in central and eastern Europe, conference materials, 'Right to citizenship in central and eastern Europe'] (pp. 83–108). Fundacja im. Stefana Batorego.
Justification to the Bill no 1206. (1999). Justification of the draft act on the *Karta Polaka* and the procedure for determining the belonging to the Polish nation of persons of Polish citizenship or national origin (Bill no 1206). *Sejm* of the III term, materials. http://orka.sejm.gov.pl/Rejestrd.nsf/wgdruku/1206/$file/1206.pdf
KIE. (2001). *Opinia Sekretarza Komitetu Integracji Europejskiej do sprawozdania Komisji Administracji i Spraw Wewnętrznych oraz Łączności z Polakami za granicą o senackim projekcie ustawy o Karcie Polaka i trybie stwierdzania przynależności do Narodu Polskiego osób narodowości polskiej lub polskiego pochodzenia* [Opinion of the secretary of the committee for European integration on the report of the committee of administration and home affairs and liaison with poles abroad on the senate draft act on the Polish Card and the procedure for determination of national affiliation of persons of polish citizenship and Polish national origin].
Kowalski, M. (2015). Raport z badań na temat posiadaczy Karty Polaka [Research report on holders of Polish Card]. In M. Dworczyk (Ed.), *Odkryte Karty Historii. Podsumowanie ustawy o Karcie Polaka* [The discovered cards of history. summary of the act on Karta Polaka] (pp. 25–60). Fundacja Wolność i Demokracja.
Kresy.pl. (2016). https://kresy.pl/wydarzenia/projekt-nowelizacji-ustawy-o-karcie-polaka-w-sejmie-kresowianie-zglaszaja-watpliwosci/
Masalska, I. (2007). Rodacy nie wyrzekajcie się nas [Compatriots! Do not renounce us]. *Kurier Galicyjski nr, 2* (44), 31. sierpnia 2007.

PAP. (2015, August 5). Polish press agency (PAP), MSZ: spada zainteresowanie wizami repatriacyjnymi, rośnie Kartą Polaka [MFA: Interest in repatriation visas is decreasing, while the interest in *Karta Polaka* is growing].

RM. (2001, June 19). *Stanowisko Rządu wobec senackiego projektu ustawy o Karcie Polaka i trybie stwierdzania przynależności do Narodu Polskiego osób narodowości polskiej lub polskiego pochodzenia* [The government's position towards senate draft act on the Polish card and the procedure for determination of national affiliation of persons of Polish citizenship and Polish national origin]. druk sejmowy nr 1206-2641-x.

Venice Commission. (2001, October, 19–20). Report on the preferential treatment of national minorities by their kin-state adopted by the Venice commission at its 48th plenary meeting (Venice).

Wyszyński, R. (2013). Przesiedlenia ludności polskiej z ZSRR w latach 1920–1960 [Resettlement of the Polish population from the USSR between 1920 and 1960]. *Studia BAS Nr, 2*(34), 107–130.

The Paradoxical Nature of Diaspora Engagement Policies: A World Polity Perspective on the *Karta Polaka*

BASTIAN SENDHARDT

ABSTRACT   This paper uses the example of the *Karta Polaka* to develop a more general argument about the place of diaspora engagement policies in the global political order. Specifically, I address the paradoxical nature of these policies, which are concomitantly undermining and reaffirming the nation-state form as a model for organising political communities. By combining insights from the literature on state-diaspora relations and world polity theory with empirical perspectives yielded from the example of the *Karta Polaka*, it is argued that diaspora engagement policies challenge an ideal model of the nation-state by reconfiguring citizenship, territory and national belonging as the basic tenets of this model. In this way, diaspora engagement policies such as the *Karta Polaka* can be understood as a reconfiguration of the nation-state model, which is not indicative of an erosion of state sovereignty but rather, on the contrary, of the resilience and adaptability of the nation-state form to challenges posed by globalisation.

Introduction

State-diaspora relations are on the rise. Particularly since the end of the Cold War, we are witnessing a sharp increase in the number of states that maintain ever closer relations with and, in fact, engage 'their' diasporas. Even at a cursory glance, we find examples of such 'diaspora engagement policies' (Gamlen, 2006) in more than half of the United Nations member states, ranging from Albania to Zimbabwe (Gamlen et al., 2019). Diaspora engagement policies (DEP), in other words, are a genuinely *global* phenomenon. These state-driven policies are aimed at recognising diaspora communities as a constituent element of the 'global nation' (Smith, 2003a, p. 726) and at institutionalising this transborder relationship.[1] The content of these 'global nation policies' (Levitt & de la Dehesa, 2003, p. 588) varies and may include state-run and public television and radio broadcasting, national holidays commemorating the diaspora, the convening of congresses, the (sometimes extraterritorial) extension of rights and privileges usually reserved to citizens and (legal long-term) residents, but also repatriation and return laws as well as 'diaspora institutions', that is, 'formal offices of state dedicated to emigrants and their descendants' (Gamlen, 2014, p. 184; see also Ragazzi, 2014, p. 75).

Recent decades have seen the emergence of a vast interdisciplinary body of scholarship on DEP, with an exponentially growing interest among the International Relations (IR) community. Central to the literature on state-diaspora relations is the question of *why* states engage with their diasporas (Gamlen, 2008b). The answers, often based on individual case studies, have been manifold. In analysing the relationship between states and diasporas, scholars have focused on issue areas such as economic and political remittances (Kunz, 2011; Levitt & de la Dehesa, 2003), external (Bauböck, 2009) and transnational citizenship (Padilla, 2011), international conflicts (Koinova, 2013; Shain, 2002), the role of diasporas for both irredentism (Saideman & Ayres, 2008) and conflict mediation (Kocadal, 2016) well as on 'the role of kin-state nationalism in domestic policy contestation' (Waterbury, 2010, p. 17).

But also the question of *how* state-diaspora relations bear on central principles of global political order has become a recurrent trope in the literature (Adamson & Demetriou, 2007; Délano, 2014; Délano & Gamlen, 2014; Gamlen, 2008a; Levitt & de la Dehesa, 2003; Ragazzi, 2009). Here the focus is on how state-diaspora relations 'are re-inventing the role of states outside of territorial boundaries and in this way reconfiguring traditional understandings of sovereignty, nation and citizenship' (Levitt & de la Dehesa, 2003, p. 606) and how they are 'questioning the traditional understanding of the Westphalian configuration of International Relations' (Ragazzi, 2009, p. 380). More specifically, this scholarship investigates how state-diaspora relations and DEP, in particular, relate to the nation-state form as a model for organising political communities. Sharpening this argument, particularly the IR scholarship on DEP has highlighted that, in fact, these policies pose something of a 'paradox' (Brand, 2006, p. 26; Varadarajan, 2010, p. 7). *On the one hand*, by extending rights and privileges beyond the boundaries of territory and, at times, citizenship, these policies reflect a form of transborder nationalism that appears to be *undermining* basic aspects of national sovereignty and the nation-state model itself. *On the other hand*, however, by addressing diasporas as constitutive elements of the nation, these policies reflect a form of 'transsovereign nationalism' (Csergo & Goldgeier, 2004, p. 26) which is (re-)emphasising the nation as an 'imagined political community' (Anderson, 2006, p. 6), thus *reaffirming* the nation-state form (see also Varadarajan, 2010, p. 32, 36–37).

So far, the paradox of state-diaspora relations has remained unresolved. There are two reasons for this. First, the existing scholarship has failed to systematically unpack the nature and functioning of the nation-state form and how DEP relate to it. More specifically, this scholarship has taken the nation-state for granted, thus failing to explicate in the first place, the ways in which the nation-state form serves as a global model for organising political communities. But, as I argue in this paper, we first need to unpack the nature of the nation-state form and only in a second step can we specify and analyse how DEP reconfigure this form by concomitantly undermining and reaffirming it. Second, although most research on state-diaspora relations acknowledges that DEP are a global phenomenon, the globality of these policies is not adequately incorporated into theory-building. Furthermore, this research is unable to explain how both the nation-state model itself and DEP that are concomitantly undermining and reaffirming this model, can be considered legitimate and thus persist and diffuse.

This paper's central argument is twofold, addressing conceptual and theoretical questions. In conceptual terms, this paper draws on insights from the literature on the relations between states and (accidental) diasporas. In contrast to the literature on DEP, which largely focuses on migrant diasporas, scholars researching accidental diasporas, or kin-state legislation, have dealt at much greater length with the question of how these policies relate to the principle of national sovereignty and the nation-state form (Brubaker, 2010; Fowler, 2004). In a first step, these authors have defined the nation-state form as the ideal congruence of citizenship, territory and national belonging as the basis of the ideal of the national resident citizen. In a second step, these approaches help us explain how DEP bear on the ideal model of the nation-state by reconfiguring its basic tenets of citizenship, territory and national belonging.

In theoretical terms, this paper draws on selected elements of world polity theory (WPT) in sociological neo-institutionalism, the so-called Stanford School. WPT sees nation-states as embedded in a world culture, that is, a global institutional environment that exogenously prescribes models for what a state should look like and how it should act. While these world-cultural scripts provide nation-states with legitimacy, nation-states are faced with the challenge of adapting these models to actual political circumstances on the ground and vice versa. In particular, WPT helps us address two lacunae in the literature on state-diaspora relations. First, WPT provides a theoretical perspective to analyse DEP as a genuinely global phenomenon. Second, WPT provides a compelling argument for why DEP are concomitantly undermining and reaffirming the nation-state form. For this, WPT uses the concept of decoupling and recoupling. From a world polity perspective, world-cultural scripts such as the principle of national sovereignty provide states with legitimacy. On the other hand, circumstances on the ground require states to adapt world-cultural models to realities on the ground (decoupling), such as the fact that a significant portion of the Polish nation is outside the boundaries of both Polish citizenship and territory. But also the resulting political practices need to be re-adapted to the model in order to ensure legitimacy (recoupling).

To illustrate this line of argument, I use the example of the *Karta Polaka*, a Polish diaspora engagement policy, as a heuristic device to analyse how such policies are concomitantly undermining and reaffirming the nation-state form by reconfiguring the ideal congruence of citizenship, territory and national belonging. The *Karta Polaka* is a form of diaspora engagement policy, originally addressing solely the Poles in the East,[2] that is, members of the Polish diaspora in the successor states of the Soviet Union.[3]

With the *Karta Polaka*, this paper adds an example of the 'Global East' (Müller, 2018) to the debate on DEP that so far has focused on cases from the Global North and South. And while the Global East does not represent a world of its own, the kin-state policies of Central and Eastern European countries can be seen as a specific variant of DEP. In contrast to the policies of sending states addressing emigration diasporas, kin-state laws address 'accidental diasporas' (Brubaker, 2000), which come into existence not as a result of 'the movement of people over borders, but by the movement of borders over people' (Brubaker, 2010, p. 69). This also applies to the Poles in the East, a diaspora that emerged as a result of border changes and deportations in the course of the Second World War. In this way, *accidental diaspora* engagement policies such as the *Karta Polaka* markedly differ from the DEP of sending countries, which usually address their '*citizens* abroad' (Brand, 2006; my emphasis).

What makes the *Karta Polaka* thus noteworthy from an IR perspective is the fact that it grants these rights and privileges to individuals who are neither citizens nor residents of Poland. In other words, the Polish state extends rights and privileges usually reserved for its own citizens and legal residents on its territory to *non-resident non-citizens* on the basis of their *belonging to the Polish nation* (Sendhardt, 2017).

On the other hand, in its 2007 version, the *Karta Polaka* does not address the global Polish diaspora in its entirety. Originally, eligibility was restricted to the Poles in the East, that is, to individuals who, first, declare and give evidence of their belonging to the Polish nation, who, second, are citizens of one of the successor states of the USSR and, third, whose permanent place of residence is outside Poland. In other words, the Polish state, via the *Karta Polaka*, establishes a direct relationship to *non-resident non-citizens* based on mutual rights and obligations that states had originally restricted to their own citizens and only since the second half of the twentieth century began to extend to legal residents. In this way, kin-state policies such as the *Karta Polaka*, just as similar phenomena such as dual citizenship, external citizenship or denizenship, are reconfiguring complex global patterns of inclusion and exclusion.

The aim of this paper is, thus, to address the need for further theorisation of diaspora-state relations (see Délano & Gamlen, 2014, p. 50) and provide answers to the following questions: How do DEP relate to the model of the nation-state and the global political order as a system of nation-states? How can we make sense of the observation that these policies are undermining and strengthening this model at the very same time? How can we make sense of the fact that states go to great lengths to institutionalise a relationship with non-resident (non-)citizens and thus incorporate foreigners residing outside their territories into their domestic structures? In order to address these lacunae, I propose the empirical example of the *Karta Polaka* as a heuristic device to theorise and systematise the ways in which kin-state laws as a specific variant of DEP relate to the nation-state form as a model for organising political communities. I will proceed as follows. First, I will present a problem statement explaining the paradoxical nature of state-diaspora relations and pointing to the conceptual and theoretical shortcomings of existing approaches. Second, drawing on the literature on the relations between states and accidental diasporas, I will unfold the paradox. Third, drawing on selected elements of world polity theory, I will theorise the paradox.

Problem Statement: The Paradoxical Nature of Diaspora Engagement Policies

In the transnationalism literature of the 1990s, diasporas were primarily seen as harbingers of 'deterritorialized nation-states' (Basch et al., 1994, p. 20) in a 'postnational political order' (Appadurai, 1996, p. 22) and as emblematic of an erosion of national sovereignty. In a similar vein, diasporic transnational communities were labelled as 'the paradigmatic Other of the nation-state' (Tölölyan, 1991, p. 5). Diasporas, from this perspective, were celebrated as a new form of transnational community that would challenge and eventually overcome the hegemonic system of nation-states. At the same time, however, these celebrations of diasporas as an alternative to the nation-state model tended to obfuscate the role of the state in fostering transborder relations with diaspora communities (Brand, 2006, p. 10; Varadarajan, 2010, p. 6).

But the works of Brand and Varadarajan can also be read as a response to another stream of literature dealing with the relations between diasporas and the nation-state as a model of global political order. This stream contents itself with stating that the static model might be in itself coherent but does not correspond with the dynamic (diasporic) reality on the ground. Shain and Sherman (1998, p. 339), for example, argue that the 'nationalist ideal' of a congruence of nation and state 'fails to capture the *dynamics* of a reality in which political loyalties and national identities are constantly undergoing change'. This understanding of the nation-state model as being merely an inadequate perspective for political realities on the ground was vehemently rebuffed by Smith (2003a, p. 725):

> We can, of course, criticize the standard notion of political community as the nation-state, wherein the 'nation' (in the sense of 'a people') is coterminous with the territorial boundaries of the state. Citizenship in the state institutionalizes this relationship legally [...]. Such coterminousness has always been a myth, but it merits critique because it has organized much political and academic discourse. Yet most early transnational research raises questions of political community, citizenship and membership only in critiquing this coterminous myth, not as a substantive issue to be worked out in the current context.

National sovereignty based on the coterminousness of exclusive notions of citizenship, territory and national belonging has always been an ideal, a myth, although a powerful one. In the words of Krasner (1999), national sovereignty has always been an 'organized hypocrisy', but a hypocrisy that, until today, has structured politics on a global scale. Building on Krasner, Brand (2006, p. 34) argues that states' efforts to tend to and promote the welfare of the entire/global nation—including those parts abroad in the diaspora—as the source of national sovereignty, can be read as part of the 'script of modernity[,] [...] something that a modern state does' to be considered legitimate (Krasner, 1999, p. 33).

Developing such lines of argument, a more recent stream in diaspora studies refocused attention back onto the state, both as an actual driving force in engaging diasporas and as a model for organising politics on a global scale. This new focus on state-diaspora relations and DEP (see, e.g. Délano, 2014; Délano & Gamlen, 2014) particularly challenges the abovementioned notion of diasporas as being fundamentally opposed to the principle of national sovereignty and the nation-state. At the same time, this scholarship recognised that in a '*world of nation-states*, diasporas can be considered a problem because they do not fit into the equation of [collective] identity with territory, which underpins that *global order*' (Barabantseva & Sutherland, 2011, p. 5; my emphasis). From this perspective, what needs to be explained is not so much the alleged erosion of national sovereignty, but rather how sovereignty has remained relevant, given conceptual challenges such as the transborder relations between states and 'their' diasporas.

Scholars such as Brand (2006) and Varadarajan (2010) have highlighted this *paradoxical nature of state-diaspora relations*. As Brand argues, globalisation implies various transborder dynamics that are undermining national sovereignty but states, nevertheless, remain the central actors in the global political order (2006, p. 26). Through DEP, 'states manifest one aspect of their robustness by attempting to renegotiate their role, thereby reshaping and reasserting sovereignty' (ibid, p. 26). These policies 'should be seen as a part of their efforts to assert or maintain authority in the ongoing processes of redefining and reconfiguring sovereignty in the international system' (ibid, p. 33). From this perspective, these new relations between states and their diasporas are not emblematic of the erosion of national sovereignty but rather 'indicators of state resilience' (ibid, p. 26).

Varadarajan addresses the paradoxical nature of state-diaspora relations in a similar way. On the one hand, these policies reflect a transborder understanding of the nation as a political community, which is usually depicted as a decline of national sovereignty by the transnationalism literature (Appadurai, 1996; Basch et al., 1994). On the other hand, however, DEP are 'propelled by the state itself and reaffirm its authority' (Varadarajan, 2010, p. 7). And she concludes: 'The task we are faced with is then to make sense of a process that in some respects reinforces the modern nation-state system and the territorial nation-state as its constitutive unit, while in others strikes at its very foundations' (ibid, p. 7).

And while this stream of scholarship convincingly explains *that* DEP are undermining and reaffirming the nation-state form as a model for organising political communities, they are much less interested in theorising and systematising *how* these policies are concomitantly undermining and reaffirming this model. What is lacking is a theoretical perspective that is able to make sense of this paradox.

Unfolding the Paradox: The *Karta Polaka* as a Diaspora Engagement Policy

As argued above, the literature on state-diaspora relations failed to define and systematise the model of the nation-state to which DEP apparently relate. But the attempt to unravel the paradoxical nature of state-diaspora relations does not need to start from zero. In fact, a great deal of scientific spadework has been done already. Interestingly, however, these foundations have been laid not by IR accounts of states' relations with their migration diasporas but by scholars studying kin-state legislation such as the *Karta Polaka* (Brubaker, 2010; Fowler, 2004). In the following, using the *Karta Polaka* as a heuristic device and based on the insights of Brubaker and Fowler, I unpack the nature and functioning of the nation-state form in order to analyse how DEP relate to it.

Following Brubaker, the diaspora phenomenon reflects 'a deep tension inherent in the nation-state *as a model* of political organization' (1996, p. 112; my emphasis). The 'conceptual model of the nation-state' asserts 'the congruence between nation and state' (Brubaker, 2010, p. 62). Similarly, Fowler argues that DEP pose a challenge to the model of modern statehood that is based on the 'assertion that territory and citizenship can be the only bases for a relationship between the state and individuals, and that the state's territory, citizenry and nation must be coterminous' (2004, p. 197). More precisely, according to this model each and every individual is connected to a state (but only one) on the basis of singular citizenship, territorial residence and national belonging. From this perspective, as Fowler maintains, these policies are a 'deviation from "modern" norms of statehood—of absolute territorial sovereignty, singular national identities, and an exclusive citizenship as the only possible legal and political relationship between states and individuals' (2004, p. 182) (see Figure 1).

However, I argue that by focusing on the ways in which DEP undermine the nation-state model, Fowler overlooks the paradoxical nature of these policies, which at the same time reaffirm the nation-state form. As argued by Brubaker (2010, p. 71), DEP

cannot be understood as disturbing the congruencies that are central to the idealized conceptual model of the nation-state. More precisely, they can be understood from an atemporal, *logical* perspective as deviating from the conceptual model, but they cannot be understood in *historical* perspective as departing from or disturbing a previous condition of congruence. These are not new incongruencies; they have characterized nation-states from their inception.

Territory	Citizenship	
(Residence)	Citizen of state A	Foreigner to state A
Domestic (State A)	Resident citizen	Resident non-citizen (e.g. denizen)
	Member of state A's titular nation National resident citizen	Member of state A's titular nation National resident non-citizen
Abroad	Member of state A's titular nation National non-resident citizen	Member of state A's titular nation National non-resident non-citizens (*Karta Polaka*)
	Non-resident citizen (expatriate)	Non-resident non-citizen (foreigner)

Figure 1. Citizenship, territory and national belonging (the latter included in the grey box) as bases for inclusion. *Source*: Adapted from Fowler (2004, p. 238, Figure 1).

Consequently, Brubaker continues, DEP 'do not presage the transcendence of the nation-state; they indicate, rather, the resilience and continued relevance of the nation-state model' (2010, p. 77). As forms of 'external membership' in the state, based on national belonging, DEP 'are neither trans-state nor transnational; as forms of transborder nationalism, they represent an extension and adaptation of the nation-state model, not its transcendence' (p. 78).

The *Karta Polaka* clearly illustrates this line of argument. By evoking the basic tenets of the nation-state model—citizenship, territory and national belonging—, the *Karta Polaka* is both undermining and reaffirming this model in complex ways. It is undermining this model because it extends rights and privileges to non-resident non-citizens, that is, persons who are neither residents nor citizens of Poland. Furthermore, the *Karta Polaka* evokes the notion of a transborder nation that is neither bound by territory nor by citizenship. However, the *Karta Polaka* is also a state-driven policy, which functions *within* the categories of the nation-state model, thus reaffirming it. More precisely, the *Karta Polaka* reconfigures the basic tenets of nation-statehood but it does not render them obsolete. It is not a 'post-national citizenship' (Soysal, 2012) because national belonging is a central criterion for eligibility. Neither is the *Karta Polaka* a 'post-territorial citizenship' (Ragazzi, 2017, p. 144). Territory remains a central aspect in two respects. First, according to the law's 2007 version, persons having a permanent residence permit in Poland were not eligible for the card. Second, the vast majority of rights and privileges (e.g. the right to work, schooling, healthcare, financial assistance and other benefits) can be enjoyed only while on Polish territory. Finally, while the *Karta Polaka* is not the same as Polish citizenship, it is a 'quasi-citizenship' (Bauböck, 2007, p. 2396) because it creates a legal status defining a relationship between state and individual based on rights and obligations (Fowler, 2004, p. 183). From this perspective, DEP such as the *Karta Polaka* point to the fact that '[n]ationalism', understood as the rationale underlying the nation-state form as model for organising political communities, 'is a remarkably flexible and adaptable idiom' (Brubaker, 2010, p. 77).

Theorising the Paradox: A World Polity Perspective on the *Karta Polaka*

While the insights provided by Brubaker and Fowler are tremendously useful in conceptually framing the paradoxical nature of state-diaspora relations, they do not provide *theoretical* perspectives. To develop such a theoretical perspective, I draw on selected elements from the Stanford School's world polity theory. While, so far, WPT has not been employed systematically for theorising DEP, the yet untapped potential of this approach has not gone unnoticed. As Gamlen explains, a world polity perspective presents an 'unexplored avenue' for understanding the global diffusion of diaspora institutions and DEP (2014, p. 195). While Gamlen finds the theory particularly useful in explaining processes of policy diffusion, this paper uses this theory to discuss the notion of the nation-state form as a global model. As I argue in this paper, WPT is a promising candidate for theorising state-diaspora relations, and this for two reasons. First, as a theory of globalisation, WPT offers an adequate framework for analysing state-diaspora relations as a global phenomenon, while avoiding the pitfalls of methodological nationalism (Wimmer & Glick Schiller, 2002). Second, WPT's concepts of isomorphism, world-cultural or global models as well as decoupling (and recoupling) help us understand *how* DEP such as the *Karta Polaka* concomitantly undermine and strengthen the global model of the nation-state.

WPT begins with a puzzle. Nation-states all over the world, despite fundamental historical and regional differences, display a good deal of isomorphism. They reveal striking structural similarities. States serve similar 'collective purposes' (McNeely, 1995, p. 19) and pursue similar policies to attain goals such as social justice, equality, economic growth and human development. These goals are often enshrined in national constitutions, defining the main purpose and institutions of the state as representing the nation (that is, the people) and promoting its welfare (Boli, 1987). Finally, and particularly important for the line of argument in this paper, nation-states are based on the notion of national sovereignty and the related concepts of citizenship, territory and national belonging (Jacobson, 1997, pp. 4–5; Meyer et al., 1997, p. 160). In other words, based on constructivist epistemologies, every nation-state refers to a nation (as a communicative instance, not a primordial entity), has a territory and the institution of citizenship.

From the perspective of WPT, this 'universality' (Meyer et al., 1997, p. 158) and 'globalization of the nation-state form' (Boyle & Meyer, 1998, p. 214) is a direct result of the embeddedness of states in a world culture, that is, a set of rules and norms that exogenously defines 'the primacy of nation-states as organizational forms [in world politics; B.S.], and the obligations of these organizations to pursue modern "progress" on behalf of their populations' (Meyer, 1987, p. 50). More precisely, world culture as a global structure provides models for modern nation-statehood based on scripts prescribing what modern states should look like and how they should work in order to be considered legitimate actors in world society (Meyer et al., 1997). Thus, rather than being primordial self-interested entities, states are exogenously structured through world-cultural universalist models (Meyer, 2009, p. 49). One of the core ideas put forward by WPT is that world-cultural principles, such as the principle of national sovereignty, function as myths. These myths provide ideal models underpinned by 'a rational theory of how' organisations, such as nation-states, should work (Meyer & Rowan, 1977, p. 342). Of course, as even a cursory glance at the world of politics reveals, more often than not the idealised world-cultural models of nation-statehood are not fully translated into political practice. However, WPT is particularly interested in the tensions that emerge between legitimising but utterly unrealistic models and necessarily imperfect political practices.

This, too, is applicable to the case of Poland, where the ideal congruence of citizenship, territory and national belonging underlying the nation-state form is, of course, constantly disrupted. The Preamble of the Polish Constitution (1997) shows that the notion of the Polish nation is torn between a civic conception of membership and an ethnicised understanding of the nation. The latter is exemplified by the case of the *Karta Polaka*. Here, a sizeable portion of the Polish nation is outside of the boundaries of both Polish territory and Polish citizenship.

WPT frames this incongruency between theoretical models and political practices as *decoupling*. As I argue in this paper, two related, yet different, notions of decoupling can be distinguished. The first, and by far the most prominent, refers to inconsistencies 'between formal policies and actual practices' (Meyer, 2009, p. 50). Decoupling is thus not so much a sign of a lack of political will or incompetent governments, but rather a result of marked inconsistencies between highly legitimate but, at the same time, utterly unrealistic models on the one hand and limited capacities of states (historic path dependencies, local interests, lack of authority) on the other. A typical example is the ratification of international treaties by states in order to gain legitimation in the world polity, however, without introducing the relevant mechanisms to actually enforce the treaty provisions (Hafner-Burton & Tsutsui, 2005, pp. 1382–1383). As argued by Meyer, 'global models are elaborated as ideals to solve global problems of legitimation, not only to be useful in practice' (2009, p. 51). But why, then, do states conform to world-cultural principles and go to great lengths to enact global models that eventually might curtail national sovereignty? The answer is legitimacy.

However, as argued by scholars of organisational institutionalism (from which WPT emerged), decoupling appears not only 'as a response to save internal organizational efficiency' but also, in a second sense, as 'a result of heterogeneous organizational fields with multiple and often contradictory pressures on the organization' (Boxenbaum & Jonsson, 2008, p. 86). In other words, decoupling may also arise from 'internal contradictions and inconsistencies in world-cultural models' (Meyer et al., 1997, pp. 168–169).

One of these contradictions is inherent in the nation-state model itself. On the one hand, the principle of sovereignty 'holds that each state constitutes the locus of ultimate authority [...]. No state has sovereignty over any other' (Boli, 1999, p. 277). As Boyle and Meyer argue: 'The idea of sovereignty itself emanates not from each nation independently but from the global recognition of the nation-state form' (1998, p. 215). On the other hand, as states *of and for* the nation, nation-states are organised around 'collective purposes' (McNeely, 1995, p. 19) and are expected to promote the welfare of the nation as a whole.

Again, the *Karta Polaka* is a case in point. It is an adaptation of the world-cultural model of the nation-state to actual political realities on the ground. While, as stated in the Polish Constitution, the Polish state is to cater for the welfare of the entire Polish nation, a good portion of this nation is living abroad in the diaspora (Art 6 (2)). Members of the diaspora are definitely outside the borders of Polish territory but also, as in the case of the *Karta Polaka*, outside the boundaries of Polish citizenship. From a world polity perspective,

DEP such as the *Karta Polaka* are thus political practices that are decoupled from the ideal nation-state model. They are adaptations of this model to local circumstances. DEP, in this context, constitute a state response to the tension between the requirement to promote national welfare and the existence of global nations transcending the jurisdictional limits of individual states.

Consequently, and here this paper goes beyond the central core of WPT, states cannot simply content themselves with decoupling actual political practices from the expectations held by world-cultural models, however unrealistic they might be. Put differently, as argued by Boxenbaum and Jonsson, '[i]t is not always possible to sustain a purely ceremonial myth' (2008, p. 88). Drawing from organisational theorists in sociological neo-institutionalism, we can complement the concept of *decoupling* with the concept of *recoupling*. Recoupling describes the observation that institutional myths and actual political practices that had been linked only loosely, become tightly coupled (Hallett, 2010, p. 53). From an organisational theory perspective, Meyer and Rowan argue: 'Organizations must not only conform to myths but must also maintain the appearance that the myths actually work' (1977, p. 356). The notion of recoupling, in other words, is a relinking of official, declaratory policies and actual political practices, thus emphasising that world-cultural myths indeed are 'myths that matter' (Espeland, 1998, p. 93).

As the *Karta Polaka* illustrates, DEP also reflect a recoupling of these practices to the legitimating world-cultural models. More precisely, while the *Karta Polaka* challenges the ideal congruency of citizenship, territory and national belonging that underlies the nation-state form, it does not do away with these constitutive concepts or create something entirely new. While cardholders must not possess Polish citizenship in order to be eligible, citizenship still plays a role. The *Karta Polaka* provides for a one-year short track to acquire Polish citizenship. Furthermore, it provides cardholders with rights and privileges on a par with Polish citizens, which is why this legislation rightfully has been termed 'semi-' or 'quasi-citizenship'. As for the concept of territory, one of the central benefits of the *Karta Polaka* is facilitated access to national multiple-entry visas. This is so because the vast majority of rights and privileges arising from the *Karta Polaka* can be enjoyed solely when on Polish territory. National belonging, finally, forms the centrepiece of the *Karta Polaka*. Being Polish is the supreme requisite for eligibility. Regarding the development of the card to include now the entire diaspora and to encourage permanent residence in Poland by means of financial assistance and help with integrating and adapting in Poland as well as offering a fast-track to Polish citizenship, it can be said that the *Karta Polaka* is steering towards re-establishing the ideal model of the nation-state (recoupling).

Conclusion

The aim of this paper was to make a contribution to the theorisation of DEP, using the example of the *Karta Polaka* as a heuristic device. By combining insights from studies on (accidental) diasporas and world polity theory, the paper developed a conceptual and theoretical framework to address the paradoxical nature of these policies, which are concomitantly undermining and reaffirming the model of the nation-state. DEP such as the *Karta Polaka* are thus a response by nation-states to tensions inherent in the world-cultural principle of national sovereignty, given the dispersal of global nations. DEP serve to reconcile respect for other states' territorial integrity with the requirement to promote the nation's welfare. Through decoupling and recoupling processes, nation-states attempt to serve both masters. On the one hand, we can thus observe an undermining of the nation-state model based on the principle of national sovereignty. Globalisation challenges states with human rights obligations such as the integration of immigrants and ethnic minorities on their territories. But globalisation is not a one-way street that only works from the outside in. As the example of the *Karta Polaka* shows, it also works from the inside out. In other words, kin-state policies reflect a 'globalization of domestic politics' (Koslowski, 2005). In the terminology of WPT we could say that what we observe—the incorporation of non-resident non-citizens into the institutional structures of the Polish state—is a decoupling of nation-states' policies from the world-cultural model of the nation-state. At the same time, we can also observe forms of recoupling the *Karta Polaka* policy to the nation-state model based on the congruence of citizenship, territorial residence and national belonging. In the course of the past ten years, the *Karta Polaka* has been amended to encourage the permanent return of cardholders through immediate residence permits, financial assistance during an integration period and a short-track procedure to Polish citizenship.

Therefore, it can be argued that states pursue DEP of the *Karta Polaka*-type in order to '"renegotiate" their place in the world' by drawing on 'global categories, global standards, and global institutions' (Lechner, 2007, p. 357) such as the concepts of citizenship, territory and national belonging, enshrined in the world-cultural principle of national sovereignty. From this perspective, kin-state laws such as the *Karta Polaka* as well as other forms of DEP are not so much a 'deviation from "modern" norms of statehood' (Fowler, 2004, p. 182), but rather an adaptation of statehood to challenges posed by globalisation. Therefore, rather than heralding the beginning of a postnational era, these policies highlight the resilience of the principle of national sovereignty and the nation-state form in the global political order.

Acknowledgements

I would like to thank the anonymous reviewers, the journal's editors, and the participants of the conference 'Poland's Kin-state Policies: Opportunities and Challenges' held in Warsaw on 23–24 May 2019 for their comments on earlier versions of this paper.

Notes

1. The term 'global nation' implies more than a mere description of a nation's worldwide dispersal. Rather, global nations are the outcomes of specific state policies defining (parts of) the diaspora as constitutive elements of the nation (see Smith, 2003b). From this perspective, I argue that global nations are part of states' constant efforts at nation-building which now, under conditions of globalisation, have become global themselves.
2. This paper mainly deals with the 2007 version of the *Karta Polaka* that focused solely on the diaspora in the post-Soviet space. Important later amendments extended the scope of the law to all persons of Polish origin regardless of citizenship (2019) and increased the rights and benefits side by granting an immediate right of residence as well as financial assistance and a quasi-diplomatic protection status (2016).
3. These are Armenia, Azerbaijan, Belarus, Estonia, Georgia, Kazakhstan, Kyrgyzstan, Lithuania, Latvia, Moldova, Russia, Tajikistan, Turkmenistan, Ukraine and Uzbekistan.

References

Adamson, F. B., & Demetriou, M. (2007). Remapping the boundaries of 'state' and 'national identity': Incorporating diasporas into IR theorizing. *European Journal of International Relations, 13*(4), 489–526. https://doi.org/10.1177/1354066107083145

Anderson, B. (2006). *Imagined communities: Reflections on the origin and spread of nationalism.* Verso.

Appadurai, A. (1996). *Modernity at large: Cultural dimensions of globalization.* University of Minnesota Press.

Barabantseva, E., & Sutherland, C. (2011). Diaspora and citizenship: Introduction. *Nationalism and Ethnic Politics, 17*(1), 1–13. https://doi.org/10.1080/13537113.2011.550242

Basch, L. G., Glick Schiller, N., & Szanton Blanc, C. (1994). *Nations unbound: Transnational projects, postcolonial predicaments, and deterritorialized nation-states.* Gordon and Breach.

Bauböck, R. (2007). Stakeholder citizenship and transnational political participation: A normative evaluation of external voting. *Fordham Law Review, 75*(5), 2393–2447. http://ir.lawnet.fordham.edu/flr/vol75/iss5/4

Bauböck, R. (2009). The rights and duties of external citizenship. *Citizenship Studies, 13*(5), 475–499. https://doi.org/10.1080/13621020903174647

Boli, J. (1987). World polity sources of expanding state authority and organization, 1870–1970. In G. M. Thomas, J. W. Meyer, & J. Boli (Eds.), *Institutional structure: Constituting state, society, and the individual* (pp. 71–91). Sage.

Boli, J. (1999). Conclusion: World authority structures and legitimations. In J. Boli & G. M. Thomas (Eds.), *Constructing world culture: International nongovernmental organizations since 1875* (pp. 267–301). Stanford University Press.

Boxenbaum, E., & Jonsson, S. (2008). Isomorphism, diffusion and decoupling. In R. Greenwood, C. Oliver, K. Sahlin, & R. Suddaby (Eds.), *The SAGE handbook of organizational institutionalism* (pp. 78–98). Sage.

Boyle, E. H., & Meyer, J. W. (1998). Modern law as a secularized and global model: Implications for the sociology of law. *Soziale Welt, 49*(3), 213–232.

Brand, L. A. (2006). *Citizens abroad: Emigration and the state in the Middle East and North Africa.* Cambridge University Press.

Brubaker, R. (1996). *Nationalism reframed: Nationhood and the national question in the new Europe.* Cambridge University Press.

Brubaker, R. (2000). *Accidental diasporas and external "homelands" in Central and Eastern Europe: Past and present* (Political Science Series No. 71). Institute for Advanced Studies.

Brubaker, R. (2010). Migration, membership, and the modern nation-state: Internal and external dimensions of the politics of belonging. *Journal of Interdisciplinary History, 41*(1), 61–78. https://doi.org/10.1162/jinh.2010.41.1.61

Csergo, Z., & Goldgeier, J. M. (2004). Nationalist strategies and European integration. *Perspectives on Politics, 2*(1), 21–37. https://doi.org/10.1017/S153759270400060X

Délano, A. (2014). The diffusion of diaspora engagement policies: A Latin American agenda. *Political Geography, 41*, 90–100. https://doi.org/10.1016/j.polgeo.2013.11.007

Délano, A., & Gamlen, A. (2014). Comparing and theorizing state–diaspora relations. *Political Geography, 41*, 43–53. https://doi.org/10.1016/j.polgeo.2014.05.005

Espeland, W. N. (1998). *Language and legal discourse. The struggle for water: Politics, rationality, and identity in the American Southwest.* The University of Chicago Press.

Fowler, B. (2004). Fuzzing citizenship, nationalising political space: A framework for interpreting the Hungarian 'Status Law' as a new form of kin-state policy in Central and Eastern Europe. In Z. Kántor, B. Majtényi, O. Ieda, B. Vizi, & I. Halász (Eds.), *The Hungarian Status Law: Nation building and/or minority protection* (pp. 177–238). Slavic Research Center, Hokkaido University.

Gamlen, A. (2006). *Diaspora engagement policies: What are they, and what kinds of states use them?* (Working Paper No. 62). University of Oxford: Centre on Migration, Policy and Society.

Gamlen, A. (2008a). The emigration state and the modern geopolitical imagination. *Political Geography, 27*(8), 840–856. https://doi.org/10.1016/j.polgeo.2008.10.004

Gamlen, A. (2008b). *Why engage diasporas?* (Working Paper No. 63). University of Oxford: ESRC Centre on Migration, Policy and Society.

Gamlen, A. (2014). Diaspora institutions and diaspora governance. *International Migration Review, 48*(1_suppl.), 180–217. https://doi.org/10.1111/imre.12136

Gamlen, A., Cummings, M. E., & Vaaler, P. M. (2019). Explaining the rise of diaspora institutions. *Journal of Ethnic and Migration Studies, 81*(3), 1–25. https://doi.org/10.1080/1369183X.2017.1409163

Hafner-Burton, E. M., & Tsutsui, K. (2005). Human rights in a globalizing world: The paradox of empty promises. *American Journal of Sociology, 110*(5), 1373–1411. https://doi.org/10.1086/428442

Hallett, T. (2010). The myth incarnate: Recoupling processes, turmoil, and inhabited institutions in an urban elementary school. *American Sociological Review, 75*(1), 52–74. https://doi.org/10.1177/0003122409357044

Jacobson, D. (1997). *Rights across borders: Immigration and the decline of citizenship.* Johns Hopkins University Press.

Kocadal, Ö. (2016). A conceptual typology of kin-state mediation. *Negotiation Journal, 32*(3), 171–189. https://doi.org/10.1111/nejo.12158

Koinova, M. (2013). *National and ethnic conflict in the twenty-first century. Ethnonationalist conflict in postcommunist states: Varieties of governance in Bulgaria, Macedonia, and Kosovo.* University of Pennsylvania Press.

Koslowski, R. (Ed.). (2005). *International migration and the globalization of domestic politics.* Routledge.

Krasner, S. D. (1999). *Sovereignty: Organized hypocrisy.* Princeton University Press.

Kunz, R. (2011). *The political economy of global remittances: Gender, governmentality and neoliberalism.* Routledge.

Lechner, F. J. (2007). Redefining national identity: Dutch evidence on global patterns. *International Journal of Comparative Sociology, 48*(4), 355–368. https://doi.org/10.1177/0020715207079535

Levitt, P., & de la Dehesa, R. (2003). Transnational migration and the redefinition of the state: Variations and explanations. *Ethnic and Racial Studies, 26*(4), 587–611. https://doi.org/10.1080/0141987032000087325

McNeely, C. L. (1995). *Constructing the nation-state: International organization and prescriptive action.* Greenwood Press.

Meyer, J. W. (1987). The world polity and the authority of the nation-state. In G. M. Thomas, J. W. Meyer, & J. Boli (Eds.), *Institutional structure: Constituting state, society, and the individual* (pp. 41–70). Sage.

Meyer, J. W. (2009). Reflections: Institutional theory and world society. In G. Krücken & G. S. Drori (Eds.), *World society: The writings of John W. Meyer* (pp. 36–63). Oxford University Press.

Meyer, J. W., Boli, J., Thomas, G. M., & Ramirez, F. O. (1997). World society and the nation-state. *American Journal of Sociology, 103*(1), 144–181. https://doi.org/10.1086/231174

Meyer, J. W., & Rowan, B. (1977). Institutionalized organizations: Formal structure as myth and ceremony. *American Journal of Sociology, 83*(2), 340–363. https://doi.org/10.1086/226550

Müller, M. (2018). In search of the Global East: Thinking between North and South. *Geopolitics, 22*(2), 1–22. https://doi.org/10.1080/14650045.2018.1477757

Padilla, B. (2011). Engagement policies and practices: Expanding the citizenship of the Brazilian diaspora. *International Migration, 49*(3), 10–29. https://doi.org/10.1111/j.1468-2435.2011.00694.x

Ragazzi, F. (2009). Governing diasporas. *International Political Sociology, 3*(4), 378–397. https://doi.org/10.1111/j.1749-5687.2009.00082.x

Ragazzi, F. (2014). A comparative analysis of diaspora policies. *Political Geography, 41*, 74–89. https://doi.org/10.1016/j.polgeo.2013.12.004

Ragazzi, F. (2017). *Governing diasporas in international relations: The transnational politics of Croatia and former Yugoslavia.* Routledge.

Saideman, S. M., & Ayres, R. W. (2008). *For kin or country: Xenophobia, nationalism, and war.* Columbia University Press.

Sendhardt, B. (2017). Theorizing the *Karta Polaka*: Debordering and rebordering the limits of citizenship, territory and nation in the EU's eastern neighbourhood. *The Journal of Power Institutions in Post-Soviet Societies, 18.* http://journals.openedition.org/pipss/4348

Shain, Y. (2002). The role of diasporas in conflict perpetuation or resolution. *SAIS Review, 22*(2), 115–144. https://doi.org/10.1353/sais.2002.0052

Shain, Y., & Sherman, M. (1998). Dynamics of disintegration: Diaspora, secession and the paradox of nation-states. *Nations and Nationalism, 4*(3), 321–346. https://doi.org/10.1111/j.1354-5078.1998.00321.x

Smith, R. C. (2003a). Diasporic memberships in historical perspective: Comparative insights from the Mexican, Italian and Polish cases. *International Migration Review, 37*(3), 724–759. https://doi.org/10.1111/j.1747-7379.2003.tb00156.x

Smith, R. C. (2003b). Migrant membership as an instituted process: Transnationalization, the state and she extraterritorial conduct of Mexican politics. *International Migration Review, 37*(2), 297–343. https://doi.org/10.1111/j.1747-7379.2003.tb00140.x

Soysal, Y. N. (2012). Post-national citizenship: Rights and obligations of individuality. In E. Amenta, K. Nash, & A. Scott (Eds.), *The Wiley-Blackwell companion to political sociology* (pp. 383–393). Wiley-Blackwell.

Tölölyan, K. (1991). The nation-state and its others: In lieu of a preface. *Diaspora*, *1*(1), 3–7. https://doi.org/10.1353/dsp.1991.0008

Ustawa z dnia 7 września 2007 r. o Karcie Polaka [Act from the 7th of September 2007 on the *Karta Polaka*].

Varadarajan, L. (2010). *The domestic abroad: Diasporas in international relations*. Oxford University Press.

Waterbury, M. A. (2010). *Between state and nation: Diaspora politics and kin-state nationalism in Hungary*. Palgrave Macmillan.

Wimmer, A., & Glick Schiller, N. (2002). Methodological nationalism and beyond: Nation-state building, migration and the social sciences. *Global Networks*, *2*(4), 301–334. https://doi.org/10.1111/1471-0374.00043

Divided Nationhood and Multiple Membership: A Framework for Assessing Kin-State Policies and Their Impact

MYRA A. WATERBURY ⓘ

ABSTRACT This article uses an expanded notion of *divided nationhood* and the framework of *multiple membership* to assess the impact of kin-state policies on national minority communities in the European neighbourhood. Drawing upon the key cases of Hungary and Poland, the article presents the challenges faced by states that position themselves in relation to a multifaceted set of external populations within and outside of Europe that can claim national membership, including recent emigrants, older diasporas, as well as kin minorities in neighbouring states. The second aspect of this framework focuses on the impacts of kin-state policies made by the governments representing divided nations on the national minority communities that are their target. This is done by conceptualizing minorities as embedded within the condition of *multiple membership*, which highlights the opportunities and the pitfalls in having access to the political, economic, and cultural community of the kin-state while striving to maintain the coherence of the minority community and assert minority rights at home.

An increasingly rich and robust literature has developed over the past few decades detailing the largely domestic factors that shape kin-state policies (Koinova, 2008; Saideman & Ayres, 2008; Waterbury, 2010) and outlining the security and normative implications of kin-state policies in Europe (Kemp et al., 2011; Palermo & Sabanadze, 2011). However, recent developments within the European political and social landscape necessitate a rethinking of what we know about kin-state policies, particularly as relates to their impact on external populations that are the target of those policies. The first development is the shifting borders of European Union (EU) enlargement, which cut across and through kin-state—minority relations in Central and Eastern Europe, creating external kin communities with different struggles and needs. The second development relates to the changing rights and identity landscape of national minorities as they work to access the rights they have on paper and maintain their cultural distinctiveness while searching for political and economic advancement within a broader European space. The third development is the increasing salience of demography—emigration and declining birth rates—for both kin-states and national minority communities (Krastev, 2017).

This paper seeks to contribute to this project of rethinking kin-state policies and their impact on national minority communities by highlighting two conceptual frameworks. The first addresses the complicated context of kin-state policymaking in and around the borders of Europe. I argue that we should understand kin-state policy making and politics as defined by the condition of *divided nationhood*, a concept that encompasses not only cross-border minority communities, but other external and diaspora communities as well. The second addresses the multi-layered reality of national minorities in Europe. I argue that we need to see national minorities as embedded within and responding to the condition of *multiple membership*, which provides both opportunities and constraints. In the third section, I bring these two frameworks together to assess the ways in which kin-state policies either expand or constrain the possibilities for national minorities to flourish and enjoy the benefits of membership within a broader set of inter-related cultural and political communities: their home state community, their minority community, the kin-state community, and the larger regional or European community. I do so using examples taken from the cases of Hungary and Poland, both of which are widely recognized as active kin-states that have long-standing and complex relationships with national minority communities throughout the region. Applying the frameworks outlined here to these two cases demonstrates their applicability beyond the specificities of any one national context, and highlights the range of outcomes produced by divided nationhood and multiple membership for national minority communities.

The Kin-State Condition: Divided Nationhood

Divided nationhood has most often been used to describe cases in which nationally affiliated groups have been separated politically and territorially by the shifting of borders (McGarry & O'Leary, 2014), potentially triggering kin-state activism by states. In this vein, post-communist Hungary has made it a priority to maintain relations with Hungarians across the borders living in neighbouring Romania, Slovakia, Serbia, and Ukraine. To a lesser extent Poland has also fostered relations with Polish minority communities to the east in states such as Lithuania and Belarus. The 'complicated history' of Central and Eastern Europe, however, has generated numerous instances of population displacement and mobility, not all of which fall neatly into the category of kin-state—kin-minority relations (Grzymała-Każłowska, 2013). An expanded conception of divided nationhood helps us see how this complicated history impacts kin-states such as Hungary and Poland, which position themselves as staunch defenders of supposedly unified ethno-cultural nations that in reality comprise a multifaceted set of external populations within and outside of Europe (Waterbury, 2020). Older and more established diasporas are one example of this expanded community of divided nationhood, as are intra-EU migrants. In addition, the border that divides EU member states from non-member states creates another kind of potential division within the nation. National minorities affiliated with a kin-state will likely have more mobility and access to the kin-state depending on which side of that border they are on, as is the case for Hungarian minorities in Romania and Slovakia versus those in Serbia or Ukraine, or for Poles in Lithuania versus those in Belarus.

Finally, states such as Poland have also created policies to allow for the limited repatriation of co-nationals and their descendants that were exiled to farther-reaching parts of the former Soviet Union, creating yet another type of external kin community (Hut, 2019).

The challenges of divided nationhood for states the likes of Hungary and Poland have become increasingly apparent. On the level of policy, the challenge has been to determine how and to what extent the state can provide differential policies for different populations, and how to balance relations with external populations with the needs of the state's domestic population. This is particularly difficult when different external populations have varying legal, cultural, or historical relationships to the kin state. For example, intra-EU migrants have a clear legal relationship with the homeland through citizenship, but may be excluded from the full rights of citizenship, such as access to voting in national elections (Waterbury, 2018). National minorities in neighbouring states with cultural and historical connections to the kin-state may differ greatly in the collective and legal rights afforded to them at home and in relation to the kin-state. The kin-state may provide access to citizenship or other forms of preferential treatment for members of the external minority, but that legal connection to the kin-state may be constrained by the home state's position on the acquisition of dual citizenship or extraterritorial identity cards (Dumbrava, 2014). The practical nature of citizenship acquisition also differs greatly, based on whether kin-state citizenship can provide access to the EU's labour market that would otherwise not be available to co-ethnics in a non-member state. In addition, some countries such as Poland have more distant historical kin who were exiled or forcibly removed and are now subject to forms of privileged, yet conditional, kin-state naturalization through repatriation and preferential access policies. Different external populations also represent varying types and levels of political, economic, and symbolic resources for the kin-state. Recent migrants and older diaspora communities may offer access to economic or foreign policy lobbying resources, but may represent a more problematic symbolic politics for the homeland state. These nascent diaspora communities also offer more 'indirect' political remittances than kin minorities in that their organizations are likely to be less political and less well organized (Kovács, 2020).

There are political trade-offs for kin-state governments in protecting and promoting different external populations (Waterbury, 2018). For example, the governing Fidesz party in Hungary has long staked its nationalist credentials on being the primary advocate for and defender of the Hungarian minority communities in neighbouring countries, and has repeatedly argued that assimilation and out-migration from those communities are the biggest threats to the survival of the larger Hungarian nation. Yet, Hungary's governing party has arguably made it easier for ethnic Hungarian minorities to leave their homelands by offering them non-resident ethnic citizenship (Pogonyi, 2017; Sik & Surányi, 2015), and has done so during a period of population decline within Hungary. The migration of minority Hungarians from countries neighbouring Hungary can be seen, therefore, as part of a strategy for Hungary to minimize its own demographic and labour market problems by drawing in workers of Hungarian nationality (Bárdi, 2017; Papp, 2017).

Poland has traditionally been seen as an emigration state due to the large number of Poles in the global diaspora (the Polonia) but it also has kin-state ties with two significant groups of external Poles in the post-Soviet region. One group comprises Polish exiles, who were forcibly moved from Poland (or former Polish territories) to various parts of the Soviet Union after World War II, and a second group consists of the sizable Polish communities in neighbouring states residing on territory that was once controlled by Poland, making

Poland an ethnic kin-state with historical and cultural ties to the Poles across the border in Lithuania, Ukraine, and Belarus. Similar to Hungary, Poland's governing Law and Justice (PiS) party has made an effort to deal with demographic losses of domestic Poles going to Western Europe by encouraging Polish minorities from Ukraine—in addition to non-Polish Ukrainians—to migrate to Poland for work, while at the same time espousing a hardline anti-migrant policy for Poland and Europe in general (Walker, 2019). Policies instituted by previous governments, such as the liberalization of labour market access for foreign workers from select countries to the East and the privileged access to Poland for ethnic Poles through the *Karta Polaka*, have also contributed to the cross-border movement of Poles from Ukraine and Belarus (Lesińska, 2015). While Hungary and Poland are differently configured as divided nations, with Hungary having a more assertive kin-state commitment and Poland a more deeply institutionalized commitment to a global diaspora strategy, both can be seen as struggling to balance the protection and promotion of cross-border Hungarian or Polish minorities, the maintenance of ties with emigrant and diaspora communities, and the needs of their domestic populations in a time of demographic decline.

The Minority Condition: Multiple Membership

The main targets and recipients of kin-state policies—the national minorities living in countries bordering the kin-state—are also embedded within their own complicated political and policy environment, one that I describe as the condition of *multiple membership*. These national minorities must navigate membership in multiple, overlapping, and sometimes competing political and cultural communities, which include their home state community, their minority community, the kin-state community, and a broader transnational or supranational space, primarily the community tied to EU membership of their home and/or kin-state. As I explore below, while there are important benefits for national minorities in their overlapping memberships with the kin-state community, these benefits have to be weighed against the difficulties such external membership may create for the stability of the minority community within its state of residence, arguably still the most important communal membership in terms of rights and representation.

There are three sets of potential benefits to multiple membership for members of national minority communities. The first concerns the benefits of mobility and fluidity of identity at the level of individual choice. The ability to move easily between different communities through possessing citizenship or other legal rights of membership, crossing state borders if necessary, provides individuals with a wider array of economic and lifestyle choices. The ability to move between and within identity communities using knowledge of both the minority and majority languages and cultural practices also allows for more personal choice and opportunities in where one can work, who one can marry, and what kinds of social relations one can have. Second, multiple membership can provide the minority community access to a wider variety of resources, including financial support for the creation and maintenance of institutions, and opportunities to pool and share resources around common interests and projects. Third, on the level of political agency and mobilization, multiple memberships can offer individuals as well as the overall minority community access to a wider variety of arenas for claims-making, representation, and voice (Waterbury, 2017).

For our purposes, the key issue is to understand the bases of the multiple and overlapping memberships that connect kin-states and national minorities. The first, and perhaps most important, is membership in a shared cultural and linguistic community, which drives kin-state support for and coordination around minority claims on their own state regarding mother tongue education, representation of the minority language in public spaces and administration, and non-discrimination (Csergő, 2007; Horváth & Toró, 2018). A shared religious tradition, which culturally binds those in the kin-state with those in the national minority and marks the minority as different than the majority within their home state, is another key area for transnational coordination and cross-border support from the kin-state. It is this shared cultural and linguistic membership that justifies kin-state action to protect and promote the maintenance of these external communities as national minorities.

The second type of membership that binds together kin-states and national minorities is one based on shared resources, which can include formal and informal networks and institutions built upon cross-border economic, political, cultural, and personal ties. These networks and institutions can be more or less robust, more or less transparent, and more or less formalized in terms of the degree to which they are institutionalized and driven by state versus non-state actors (Csergő & Regelmann, 2017). They include cross-border financial resources and investment, institutions of shared deliberation and policymaking, political coordination and party ties, educational, church-based and religious networks, cross-border leisure and tourism regions, as well as shared knowledge-based and personal networks.

The third type of membership is based on shared political and legal rights, most clearly represented through citizenship ties and other forms of preferential access to the kin-state. Through more expansive kin-state citizenship regimes, members of the minority community become formal members of the kin-state political community (Dumbrava, 2014; Pogonyi, 2017). They can claim the same legal protections, have the opportunity to vote in the same elections, and access a similar degree of mobility as those resident members of the kin-state community. Preferential visas, identity-based cards offering special benefits to kin minorities (such as the *Karta Polaka*, and the identity cards issue through the Hungarian Status Law), and preferential labour market access also provide various degrees of legal membership in the kin-state community.

There are important differences among national minority communities in the degree to which their membership in these various communities are institutionalized or otherwise routinized. For example, the Hungarian minority in Romania is unique both in the high degree of institutionalization of its minority community (Kiss et al., 2018) and in its degree of embeddedness within a set of institutions and policies emanating from the Hungarian kin-state community (Waterbury, 2017). In contrast, the Polish minority in Belarus is not particularly ethnically institutionalized domestically nor transnationally embedded, and the use of the Polish language as a primary language is relatively rare, though language plays an important role in symbolic identification with Polish identity, as does the Catholic Church (Rotman et al., 2011). Poles in Belarus, however, rely on Poland's status as an EU member to provide both physical and economic mobility, and there are strong cross-border ties between Polish state and non-state actors and the minority community (Wallace & Patsiurko, 2017, p. 82). Poles in Lithuania are more institutionalized, politically organized, have higher levels of Polish language acquisition, and are less interested in the *Karta Polaka* as their ability to travel to Poland is already enshrined through EU membership

(Matulionis et al., 2011, pp. 9–10). However, Lithuanian Poles do rely on ties to Poland for the maintenance of their cultural and educational institutions, as well as for political mobilization in both the domestic and European Union arenas (Barwiński & Wendt, 2018; Waterbury, 2016).

Multiple Membership and Kin-State Policies

The remainder of the paper considers how we can assess the impact of kin-state policies on national minority political life given the realities of divided nationhood and multiple membership. States such as Hungary and Poland that take on the role of a kin-state must clearly balance that responsibility with the need to protect and promote other domestic and external populations that make up the larger nation. National minorities and their political leaders must balance and negotiate membership in competing and overlapping communities, attempting to reap the advantages of this condition while maintaining communal cohesion and advancing their rights and representation at home. Using the three categories of possible advantages from multiple membership that I outlined above—expanding individual choice and opportunities; expanding access to community-building resources; expanding political voice, influence, and representation—we can think about the conditions under which various kin-state policies and forms of membership might or might not allow for these outcomes. I argue here that although kin-state support can increase opportunities for minority communities, these extra-territorial policies can also have potential drawbacks. On one hand, kin-state policies can result in the hardening of boundaries between groups and reflect a project of homogenization that may conflict with the pursuit of flexible opportunities for individual mobility and collective inter-group bargaining. On the other hand, due to the broader tensions of divided nationhood and the expansion of cross-border citizenship and membership options, these policies may incentivize a degree of cross-border mobility that can undermine the political cohesiveness and leverage of the minority community. Finally, we can see that minorities are often caught between incomplete and partial memberships. They may not be treated equally as full members of the home state community due to discriminatory laws and practices, and are more vulnerable to changes in resource levels or access to institutions of cultural reproduction stemming from varying levels of kin-state support.

The Advantages of Overlapping Membership

At the level of individual choice, kin-state support and membership can foster opportunities for bi- or multi-lingualism, labour market and cross-border mobility, and the enjoyment and maintenance of minority identity. If there are strong assimilationist pressures coming from the minority's state of residence, kin-state support and resources for the teaching and use of the minority language can be particularly impactful in preventing the loss of minority language knowledge (Han, 2013). Kin-state support for minority language acquisition, maintenance, and everyday usage can give members of the minority the option to become bi- or multi-lingual, thereby expanding their economic, educational, and overall life opportunities. Yet to truly take advantage of multiple memberships, individuals must have a reasonable opportunity to also gain or maintain competence in the majority language; otherwise, they trade membership in one language community for another and lose the benefits of flexibility. This flexibility is key if labour market opportunities are closely tied to majority language knowledge. Under the right conditions, kin-state support might also induce some in the majority language community to also learn the minority language, creating a situation of 'symmetric bilingualism' that could benefit members of both communities by increasing the prospects for minority integration (Csata, 2016). However, it seems that where this is happening, it is not the amount of available resources from the kin-state that induces minority language acquisition by members of the majority, but the desire to acquire the citizenship of a country that would allow more mobility and economic opportunity. We can see this in reports from the Vojvodina area of Serbia and in Ukraine, where some non-Hungarians have learned Hungarian in order to gain Hungarian citizenship (Sik & Surányi, 2015; Stjepanovic, 2018 , pp. 180–190; Tátrai et al., 2017), or Polish in order to get preferential access to the Polish labour market (Lesińska, 2015).

The resources flowing through the networks and institutions connected to the kin-state play an important role in supplementing the resources coming from within the minority community and its state of residence, ideally strengthening minority institutions and organizations and incentivizing the commitment of individuals to maintain their linguistic and cultural identity. In the case of Hungary, its kin-state support has been key in supplementing and supporting the activities and mobilization of Hungarian minority communities throughout the region, even to the point of sustaining areas of 'ethnic parallelism' that allow minorities to maintain pockets of everyday autonomy (Kiss & Kiss, 2018). Strengthening and maintaining the identity and communal coherence of its kin-minority communities have been among the stated goals of Hungary's expansive policies of cross-border funding, which include support for minority language education, economic development, and vocational education programmes. For example, the policy justification for providing funds for economic and educational development in the minority Hungarian communities is that this will 'strengthen the identity of Hungarians living abroad' by creating jobs for Hungarians in businesses run by Hungarian entrepreneurs (Nemzetpolitikai Kutatóintézet, 2015, p. 4). In turn, this would incentivize parents to send their children to Hungarian language primary and secondary schools, and college-age Hungarians to choose Hungarian language vocational schools or universities, ultimately creating a stronger Hungarian community in which fewer people would choose to leave the territory or the linguistic community. A central justification for Hungary's extension of non-resident ethnic citizenship in 2011 was also to increase the value of and attachment to Hungarian identity (Papp, 2017; Waterbury, 2017).

Poland's kin-state support has also prioritized the maintenance of minority identity and institutions of cultural reproduction, but has not ventured as deeply into the economic life of minority communities. Poland has sent Catholic priests and Polish language teachers and has financially supported the Union of Poles and Polish Houses in Belarus, which has been crucial for the maintenance of that community in the face of a particularly non-democratic regime (Wallace & Patsiurko, 2017, p. 84). Poles in Lithuania have also looked to Polish diplomats to help press their dissatisfaction with education laws that discriminate against Polish schools (Barwiński & Wendt, 2018, p. 25.) In terms of the impact of Poland's kin-state support on minority identity, there is evidence that Poles in Belarus have responded to kin-state support and eased travel via the *Karta Polaka* and lessened visa restrictions by identifying more with Poland, and Europe as well, as an extension of their Polish identity. This has been the case particularly for younger people who travel between Poland and Belarus regularly, allowing them to construct 'a very fluid idea of what it means to be Polish' (Wallace & Patsiurko, 2017, pp. 83–84). We see here both the possibility of increased identity with the minority and kin-state identity, as well as the flexibility to create hybrid identities that bridge multiple communal memberships, including a broader identification with Europe. Multiple memberships based on kin-state connections are most beneficial, therefore, when they provide identity security, help to promote and sustain minority claims and projects, and offer flexibility to minority members.

The Disadvantages of Overlapping Membership

Despite the benefits of kin-state support, the condition of multiple membership can also serve to harden boundaries between and within groups in ways that might be problematic for national minorities. To be truly advantageous to individual members of the minority, membership in the kin-state community should not preclude or disincentivize other aspects of identity-based and personal choice, such as inter-marriage, temporary or long term emigration out of minority-majority regions, inter-ethnic economic association, and even integration (by choice) into the majority community. To help preserve and stabilize the minority community kin-state support should be relatively transparent, should focus on maintaining access to existing institutions of cultural reproduction, and should not diminish the ability of minority representatives to bargain and negotiate with local and national actors across ethnic or national boundaries. As the 2008 Bolzano Recommendations on National Minorities in Inter-State Relations highlighted, kin-state policies become problematic when they 'undermine the integration of minorities' (OSCE, 2008). Too many kin-state resources and highly politicized financial support, or support that frames bi- or multi-lingualism as a zero-sum 'loss' for the shared kin-state and minority language community, might in fact narrow the scope of individual choice and lead to the worsening of inter-ethnic relations.

We know from the broader literature on groups and identities that there is an inherent tension between the logic of boundary policing in order to maintain collective identity coherence and the logic of incentivizing identity hybridity and fluidity to cross-cut group identities and offer individual opportunities. We can see this tension playing out in the situation of national minorities navigating between their individual agency, their desire for collective voice and cultural maintenance, and their ties to a cross-border kin-state and its national community. Certain types of resources and networks that might be influenced by kin-state policies may be more or less divisive internally or inter-ethnically. As Pickering has shown in the case of post-conflict Bosnia, neighbourhoods, voluntary organizations, and workplaces that are at least somewhat interethnic and crosscutting in nature allow individuals to develop the type of 'weak' but bridging ties that promote 'cooperative interethnic behaviour' and 'mutual interdependence' (2006,, p. 81). In a multilingual environment, such as often exists in areas with national minorities, we can translate this idea to the situation of a non-ethnically bifurcated labour market and the promotion of bi- and multi-lingualism. If a kin-state attempts to use its resources in the national minority community to promote monolingualism or to create enclaves of mono-ethnic cultural, economic, or political activity, then the kin-state would be engaged more strongly in a project of homogenization and in-group policing that could increase ethnocentrism within the minority and the majority.[1]

From the perspective of the kin-state—and some minority political actors—this project of homogenization and boundary-policing may be seen as justified and necessary. In the context of a national minority group that has been historically disadvantaged and under-represented within its own state, and keeping in mind the condition of divided nationhood that drives kin-state actors to protect and preserve vulnerable and highly-symbolic external members of the nation, hybridity of identity may logically be understood as a 'debased' condition to be avoided at all costs (Wallace & Patsiurko, 2017, p. 79). As groups become smaller, declining through emigration, low birth rates, or assimilation, they may 'need to develop strong boundary policing institutions to maintain themselves as distinct groups' (Fearon & Laitin, 1996, p. 726). The kin-state will work to maintain and harden these boundaries in order to keep access to the symbolic and soft power resources that the minority communities represent, particularly if the kin-state government is of a more nationalist-populist character. In cases where there is competition for limited group resources (e.g. votes for an ethnic party or patronage from the state based on group status), there will likely be increased pressure from within the group as well to police group boundaries and restrict fluidity. We can see this in the case of the Democratic Alliance of Hungarian Romanians (the main Hungarian minority party in Romania—RMDSZ in Hungarian), the leadership of which has at times chosen to homogenize communal voice and police boundaries, even when this risks the demobilization of its own members, in order to have more bargaining leverage with its own government (Toró, 2020).

We have as an example of these dynamics the government controlled by the Fidesz party in Hungary, which has increased its funding for Hungarians in the region, re-establishing old and creating new patronage networks to maintain support for Fidesz throughout the Hungarian minority communities in neighbouring countries. Since 2010, the Hungarian kin-state significantly increased funding for economic development programmes in Hungarian minority communities, Hungarian language education, and religious and sports organization, and from 2015 on there was a significant spike in overall funding from Hungary that appears to support cross-border networks developed by Fidesz (see Bárdi, 2017; Culic, 2019; Kiss et al., 2018; Sik & Surányi, 2015; Sipos, 2017). The danger in such an approach is that once kin-state funding moves beyond supplementation to become a major financial driver of minority institutions, a home state such as Romania might respond by modifying its limited accommodation of minority claims and isolating the minority from access to state resources 'on the justification that those are catered for from other sources' (Kiss et al., 2018). Increased dependence on funding from the kin-state may also erode the willingness of minority elites to bargain with the majority centre and weaken the legitimacy of minority parties, such as the RMDSZ, as they struggle to bargain both with the kin-state government and their own government (Bárdi, 2017; Bodó, 2016, p. 62). The possible 'emergence of an ethnically defined enclave economy' (Csata, 2018) funded by the kin-state might also fragment society in the home state, as it lessens opportunities for flexible, everyday interactions with members of the majority community, as well as for more structured inter-ethnic interactions (Varshney, 2003). In addition, there is also an increasingly ethnic—and kin-state cantered—media world through which minority Hungarian youth, in particular, seem to be getting their news. Between the increasing funding of Hungarian media, and the increasing influence of Hungarian state media in the minority Hungarian community, the media space of the minority Hungarians is more and more 'a decisively Budapest product' with little presence of the majority nation's culture or political life (Bárdi, 2017). Hungary's kin-state policies have also come to dominate cross-border cooperation along the Hungary-Ukraine border, with many of those benefiting from what are meant to be broad regional projects tied directly to Hungarian 'quasi-diaspora networks'. Researchers assessing these programmes have worried that the ethnicization and politicization of these programmes 'may create inter-ethnic suspicion, decrease trust, and become a fertile soil for ethnicity-based cleavages' (Sik & Surányi, 2015, pp. 4–5). In addition, the lure and now increased ease of learning Hungarian in Ukraine due to kin-state support is likely to further decrease bilingualism, particularly among Hungarian Ukrainian youth in areas of Hungarian concentration near the border (Sik & Surányi, 2015, pp. 27–28).

The availability of kin-state citizenship and other forms of preferential access to the kin-state may also negatively impact minority political projects by orienting political attention in the minority community towards the kin-state, and by increasing mobility out of those communities. The ability to acquire Hungarian citizenship and vote in Hungarian elections, or to gain access to the Polish welfare state through the *Karta Polaka*, has the potential to hollow out institution building within the minority communities by offering a substitute to inter-ethnic bargaining without necessarily changing the structural realities of minority existence (Bárdi, 2017; Papp, 2017, p. 27). Even as non-resident ethnic citizenship from Hungary and the Polish *Karta Polaka* were both meant to compensate historically disadvantaged external communities and maintain minority identification, they may instead strengthen identification with the kin-state community and even increase migration out of the minority communities, which weakens the minority's potential for political mobilization (Waterbury, 2017). Ironically, the beneficiary of this out-migration may be the kin-state, which gains access to easily assimilatable migrants to fill holes in the domestic labour force. This shift towards even indirect acceptance of out-migration from the areas of Hungarian concentration is a significant departure from previous Hungarian state policy, which has traditionally seen the demographic decline of Hungarian minority areas as something to be avoided at all costs (Waterbury, 2010). In the case of Poland, there were also concerns from state policymakers in the 1990s and 2000s that massive emigration from the Eastern borderlands would be undesirable and unfeasible (Hut, 2019). However, emigration from minority areas may be politically palatable if there is evidence that minority members will confine their mobility to the kin-state, rather than continue on to other parts of Europe. This suggests that the commitment of the kin-state government to the maintenance of minority communities *in situ* may weaken as the need to protect the domestic population from demographic decline becomes more urgent.

We see these tensions and contradictions both in the case of Hungary and Poland. The extension of Hungarian citizenship seems to have increased the migration potential of Hungarians in the region, particularly those from non-EU member states, such as Ukraine and Serbia (Pogonyi, 2017; Tátrai et al., 2017). Ukraine in particular has been hit hard by the mobility offered by neighbouring kin-states. A 'strong and continuous emigration of the younger generations' has resulted from the expansion of Hungarian citizenship to Hungarians in Ukraine, including those with skills and higher degrees of education (Sik & Surányi, 2015, pp. 7–9). Repatriation as 'privileged ethnic migration' and the *Karta Polaka* have generated a good deal of migration to Poland from Ukraine, with 88% of the *Karta Polaka* holders coming from Ukraine and Belarus by 2011. This has led to a brain drain of Polish elites from those areas (Grzymala-Kazlowska & Grzymala-Moszczynska, 2014, pp. 603–604).[2] Recent changes in Poland's *Karta Polaka* policy, however, demonstrate a different challenge for Polish minorities in the East stemming from the partial and contingent terms of multiple membership. In the summer of 2019, the Polish government extended the *Karta Polaka* to foreigners of Polish descent throughout the world, making it a tool of global diaspora engagement in addition to one of minority maintenance for Polish communities to the East (Lesińska, 2019). This change continues a trend of shifting emphasis as Polish kin-minorities in the regional bordering Poland have had to struggle more for recognition and support from the kin-state while more attention goes to Poles with weaker cultural identification from farther-flung parts of Polonia or to more organized Polish diaspora organizations (Nowak & Nowosielski, 2018, pp. 167–168).

Conclusion

This paper has attempted to make sense of the increasingly complex nexus of identities, arenas, policies, and politics that shape what kin-states do and the effects their actions have on the national minority communities they are meant to benefit. I utilized an expanded understanding of the concept of *divided nationhood* as a way to see the challenges and trade-offs facing kin-state policymakers. I then offered *multiple membership* as a way to see the various communities of interest and identity in which national minorities are embedded and must negotiate. Finally, I brought these two frameworks together to think analytically and conceptually about the ways in which kin-state policies and the overlapping memberships they create can provide both advantages and disadvantages for members of national minority communities. Using examples from both the cases of Hungary and Poland—in relation to their kin-communities in neighbouring states—I hope to have demonstrated that these frameworks provide a useful way to think about kin-state—minority relations and their contradictions in a moment of mobility, uncertainty, and demographic change in Europe and at its borders.

These frameworks offer a way to normatively evaluate the possibilities and limits of kin-state policies in light of the opportunities they offer for national minority communities to reproduce and represent themselves over time. Ideally, kin-state policies should be made with the needs of specific minority communities in mind, reflecting the fact that minority communities differ in their ability to form and maintain their own institutions and to enjoy the benefits of multiple membership. Yet, the domestic political dynamics that shape kin-state politics—and the demands of divided nationhood—make it likely that kin-state policies may not always reflect what minority communities need to maintain coherence, stability, and political voice. Instead, these policies may be highly politicized and driven by specific kin-state projects. The homogenizing and totalizing tendencies of nationalist, populist governments in Hungary and Poland are also reflected in their approach to kin-state policies, as the governing parties see the minority communities as symbols of cultural strength that can be transformed into political and economic resources. Those in the minorities, however, struggle to maintain the flexibility to be found in inter-ethnic accommodation and cross-communal mobility while finding the resources to sustain communal coherence. Kin-state support can be a key resource in achieving these goals, but it can also narrow the path to both accommodation and coherence for kin minorities.

Notes

1. Fearon and Laitin (1996) famously argued that interethnic cooperation relied on strong intraethnic policing and sanctioning regimes that were weakened by 'too frequent' interethnic interactions (p. 723). However,

their model relied on a model assuming high and constant inter-group tensions, and the lack of inter-ethnic networks in everday life.
2. The liberalization of the EU visa regime for Ukraine in 2017 has also increased cross-border mobility.

ORCID

Myra A. Waterbury ⓘ http://orcid.org/0000-0003-1133-3575

References

Bárdi, N. (2017). Álságos Állítások a Magyar Etnopolitkában: A külhoni magyarok és a budapesti kormányzatok magyarsgpolitikája. In A. Jakab & L. Urbán (Eds.), *Hegymenet. Társadalmi és politikai kihívások Magyarországon* (pp. 130–155). Osiris Kiadó.

Barwiński, M., & Wendt, J. A. (2018). National minorities in Polish politics and its Eastern neighbors. *International Journal of Management Academy, 1*, 22–36. Retrieved August 18, 2020, from https://dergipark.org.tr/tr/download/issue-full-file/36781

Bodó, B. (2016). Minority civil society. *Acta Unis Sapientie, European and Regional Studies, 10*, 51–64. https://doi.org/10.1515/auseur-2016-0020

Csata, Z. (2016). Reflections on the economic aspects of multilingualism in Transylvania. *Belvedere Meridionale, 28*(2), 51–65. https://doi.org/10.14232/belv.2016.2.4

Csata, Z. (2018). Economy and ethnicity in Transylvania. In T. Kiss, I. G. Székely, T. Toro, B. Nándor, & I. Horváth (Eds.), *Unequal accommodation of minority rights. Hungarians in Transylvania* (pp. 345–379). Palgrave Macmillan.

Csergő, Z. (2007). *Talk of the nation: Language and conflict in Romania and Slovakia.* Cornell University Press.

Csergő, Z., & Regelmann, A. C. (2017). Europeanization and collective rationality in minority voting: Lessons from Central and Eastern Europe. *Problems of Post-Communism, 64*(5), 291–310. https://doi.org/10.1080/10758216.2017.1330659

Culic, I. (2019). Neoliberalism meets minority nationalism: The politics of Hungarian higher education in Romania. *East European Politics and Societies: and Cultures, 33*(2), 357–377. https://doi.org/10.1177/0888325418790364

Dumbrava, C. (2014). *Nationality, citizenship and ethno-cultural belonging: Preferential membership policies in Europe.* Palgrave Macmillan.

Fearon, J., & Laitin, D. (1996). Explaining interethnic cooperation. *American Political Science Review, 90*(4), 715–735. https://doi.org/10.2307/2945838

Grzymała-Każłowska, A. (2013). Migration and socio-demographic processes in Central and Eastern Europe: Characteristics, specificity and internal differences. *Central and Eastern European Migration Review, 2*, 5–11. Retrieved August 18, 2020, from http://www.ceemr.uw.edu.pl/vol-2-no-1-june-2013/editorial/migration-and-socio-demographic-processes-central-and-eastern-europe

Grzymala-Kazlowska, A., & Grzymala-Moszczynska, H. (2014). The Anguish of repatriation: Immigration to Poland and integration of Polish descendants from Kazakhstan. *East European Politics and Societies: and Cultures, 28*(3), 593–613. https://doi.org/10.1177/0888325414532494

Han, E. (2013). External cultural ties and the politics of language in China. *Ethnopolitics, 12*(1), 30–49. https://doi.org/10.1080/17449057.2011.621402

Horváth, I., & Toró, T. (2018). Language use, language policy and language rights. In T. Kiss, I. G. Székely, T. Toro, B. Nándor, & I. Horváth (Eds.), *Unequal accommodation of minority rights. Hungarians in Transylvania* (pp. 167–223). Palgrave Macmillan.

Hut, P. (2019). Relations of Polish authorities with the Polish diaspora in the (post)-Soviet space. In K. Marczuk (Ed.), *Good neighbourhood treaties of Poland* (pp. 163–177). Palgrave Macmillan.

Kemp, W., Popovski, V., & Thakur, R. (Eds.). (2011). *Blood and borders: The responsibility to protect and the problem of the Kin-state.* United Nations University Press.

Kiss, T., & Kiss, D. (2018). Ethnic parallelism: Political program and social reality. An introduction. In T. Kiss, I. G. Székely, T. Toro, B. Nándor, & I. Horváth (Eds.), *Unequal accommodation of minority rights. Hungarians in Transylvania* (pp. 227–247). Palgrave Macmillan.

Kiss, T., Toró, T., & Székely, I. G. (2018). Unequal accommodation. An institutionalist analysis of ethnic claim-making and bargaining. In T. Kiss, I. G. Székely, T. Toro, B. Nándor, & I. Horváth (Eds.), *Unequal accommodation of minority rights. Hungarians in Transylvania* (pp. 71–165). Palgrave Macmillan.

Koinova, M. (2008). Kinstate intervention in ethnic conflicts: Albania and Turkey compared. *Ethnopolitics*, 7(4), 373–390. https://doi.org/10.1080/17449050802243384

Kovács, E. (2020). Direct and indirect political remittances of the transnational engagement of Hungarian kin-minorities and diaspora communities. *Journal of Ethnic and Migration Studies*, 46(6), 1146–1165. https://doi.org/10.1080/1369183X.2018.1554315

Krastev, I. (2017). *After Europe*. University of Pennsylvania Press.

Lesińska, M. (2015). *Immigration of Ukrainians and Russians into Poland – inflow, integration trends and policy impacts*. INTERACT Research Report 06, Robert Schuman Centre for Advanced Studies. European University Institute.

Lesińska, M. (2019). *Pole's Card and related benefits to be available to wider group of foreigners*. European Web Site on Integration, Migrant Integration Information and good practices. Retrieved October 28, 2019, from https://ec.europa.eu/migrant-integration/news/poles-card-and-related-benefits-to-be-available-to-wider-group-of-foreigners

Matulionis, A., Beresnevičiūtė, V., Leončikas, T., Frėjutė-Rakauskienė, M., Šliavaitė, K., Šutinienė, I., Žilinskaitė, V., Heinrich, H.-G., & Alekseeva, O. (2011). *The Polish minority in Lithuania*. ENRI-East Research Reports 8. Retrieved January 9, 2020, from https://www.ceass-center.net/enri-east-2008-2011

McGarry, J., & O'Leary, B. (2014). Introduction. In T. J. Mabry, J. McGarry, M. Moore, & B. O'Leary (Eds.), *Divided nations and European integration* (pp. 1–32). University of Pennsylvania Press.

Nemzetpolitikai Kutatóintézet. (2015). *An economic base is necessary for the preservation of Hungarian identity*. Weekly Media Review of Hungarian Communities Abroad, 18. Retrieved October 28, 2019, from https://bgazrt.hu/wp-content/uploads/NPKI_sajtoszemlek/weekly_media_review/2015/Weekly%20Media%20Review%20201518.pdf

Nowak, W., & Nowosielski, M. (2018). The state, diaspora policy and immigrant organizations – lessons from the Polish case. *Yearbook of the Institute of East-Central Europe*, 16, 159–176. Retrieved August 18, 2020, from https://ies.lublin.pl/rocznik/riesw/2018/5

OSCE High Commissioner on National Minorities. (2008). *The Bolzano/Bozen recommendations on National minorities in inter-state relations*. Retrieved August 29, 2019, from https://www.osce.org/hcnm/bolzano-bozen-recommendations

Palermo, F., & Sabanadze, N. (Eds.). (2011). *National minorities in inter-state relations*. Brill, Nijhoff.

Papp, A. Z. (2017). Trickster logics in the Hungarian dual-citizenship offer. *Nationalism and Ethnic Politics*, 23(1), 18–32. https://doi.org/10.1080/13537113.2017.1273656

Pickering, P. M. (2006). Generating social capital for bridging ethnic divisions in the Balkans: Case studies of two Bosniak cities. *Ethnic and Racial Studies*, 29(1), 79–103. https://doi.org/10.1080/01419870500352397

Pogonyi, S. (2017). *Extra-territorial ethnic politics, discourses and identities in Hungary*. Palgrave Macmillan.

Rotman, D., Ivaniuto, O., & Veremeeva, N. (2011). *The Polish minority in Belarus*. ENRI-East Research Reports 4. Retrieved January 9, 2020, from https://www.ceass-center.net/enri-east-2008-2011

Saideman, S., & Ayres, R. W. (2008). *For kin or country: Xenophobia, nationalism, and war*. Columbia University Press.

Sik, E., & Surányi, R. (2015). *The Hungarian/Slovak/Ukrainian tri-border region*. EU External Borders and the Immediate Neighbors. Analysing Regional Development Options through Politics and Practices of Cross-Border Co-Operation.

Sipos, Z. (2017). Határon túli támogatások 1: a jobb kéz nem tudja, mit támogat a bal. *Erdély Átlátszó*. Retrieved October 28, 2019, from https://erdely.atlatszo.hu/2017/03/15/hataron-tuli-tamogatasok-1-a-jobb-kez-nem-tudja-mit-tamogat-a-bal/

Stjepanovic, D. (2018). *Multiethnic Regionalisms in Southeastern Europe*. Palgrave Macmillan.

Tátrai, P., Erőss, Á, & Kovály, K. (2017). Kin-state politics stirred by a geopolitical conflict: Hungary's growing activity in post-Euromaidan Transcarpathia. *Hungarian Geographical Bulletin*, 66(3), 203–218. https://doi.org/10.15201/hungeobull.66.3.2

Toró, T. (2020). Detached implementation: Discourse and practice in minority language use in Romania. *Language Policy*, 19(1), 5–29. https://doi.org/10.1007/s10993-018-9494-2

Varshney, A. (2003). Ethnic conflict and civil society: India and beyond. *World Politics*, 53(3), 362–398. https://doi.org/10.1353/wp.2001.0012

Walker, S. (2019, April 18). 'A whole generation has gone': Ukrainians seek a better life in Poland. *The Guardian*.

Wallace, C., & Patsiurko, N. (2017). Relational identities on EU borderlands: The case of Poles in Belarus and Belarusians in Poland. *Ethnic and Racial Studies*, *40*(1), 77–95. https://doi.org/10.1080/01419870.2016.1201582

Waterbury, M. A. (2010). *Between state and nation: Diaspora politics and Kin-state nationalism in Hungary*. Palgrave Macmillan.

Waterbury, M. A. (2016). National minorities and intra-ethnic coordination in the European Parliament: Evidence from Central and Eastern Europe. *Europe-Asia Studies*, *68*(3), 391–408. https://doi.org/10.1080/09668136.2016.1148663

Waterbury, M. A. (2017). National minorities in an era of externalization: Kin-state citizenship, European integration, and ethnic Hungarian minority politics. *Problems of Post-Communism*, *64*(5), 228–241. https://doi.org/10.1080/10758216.2016.1251825

Waterbury, M. A. (2018). Caught between nationalism and transnationalism: Responses to East-West emigration in Central and Eastern Europe. *International Political Science Review*, *39*(3), 338–352. https://doi.org/10.1177/0192512117753613

Waterbury, M. A. (2020). Populist nationalism and the challenges of divided nationhood: The politics of migration, mobility, and demography in post-2010 Hungary. *East European Politics and Societies and Cultures*, https://doi.org/10.1177/0888325419897772

Pragmatic Trans-Border Nationalism: A Comparative Analysis of Poland's and Hungary's Policies Towards Kin-Minorities in the Twenty-First Century

MAGDALENA LESIŃSKA ⓘ AND DOMINIK HÉJJ ⓘ

ABSTRACT This paper outlines the dynamic development of policies in Poland and Hungary towards kin-minorities and their outcomes under the rule of right-wing governments. The main aim is to provide a comparative analysis of kin-state policies targeting co-ethnics living beyond the countries' borders and point out possible explanations for common and different elements in these two cases. The similarities between Poland's and Hungary's policies towards kin-minorities are manifested in an official narrative about one existing nation across borders, and legal measures and political actions aimed at supporting minorities in neighbouring countries. At the same time, there are some important differences concerning, *inter alia*, ethnic preferential citizenship laws. The Hungarian authorities use preferential naturalisation as a means of strengthening the influence of non-resident ethnic Hungarians as voters in Hungary's elections. Non-resident Hungarians also play an important role in foreign policy towards neighbouring countries. For policymakers in Poland, ethnic Poles living abroad remain a demographic and economic reservoir. The changes in legal regulations, aimed at encouraging them to settle and work in Poland, are dictated by the constantly high demand for a labour workforce and expected severe demographic decline. Both Hungarian and Polish policies towards kin-minorities are examples of pragmatic trans-border nationalism, which is a concept also developed in the article.

Introduction

The process of building a national community across territorial boundaries—aimed at including diaspora members (emigrants and kin-minorities) living in other countries and at spreading among them the sense of belonging to the homeland—is variously referred to in academic publications as 'trans-border nationalism' (Brubaker, 1996, 2010), the policy of a global nation (Ragazzi, 2009), political incorporation (Collyer, 2014) and long-distance nationalism (Basch et al., 1994). Kin-minorities living in neighbouring countries play an important role in this process; this is particularly evident in the countries of Central and Eastern Europe which experienced major territorial and political changes in the twentieth century. In the light of those countries' diaspora policies, kin-minorities are treated as a priority group over non-kin migrants. Special benefits are offered to kin-minority members, such as fast-track citizenship procedures, external voting, preferential access to the state territory and repatriation schemes, etc. Furthermore, a sizeable element of public funds allocated to the diaspora policy is transferred to activities addressed to them (Kovács, 2020; Lesińska, 2019). Kin-minorities also have a superior position in governments' political narrative, which is dominated by an embracing perspective that assumes co-ethics abroad as an essential part of the nation; the goal of the kin-state's activities is to include its compatriots residing outside the country in the broadly understood national community (Gamlen et al., 2013).

The main goal of this paper is to present the findings of a comparative analysis of the development of Polish and Hungarian policies towards kin-minorities, with particular emphasis given to recent years, when both countries have been ruled by right-wing nationalist parties—the Fidesz-Christian Democratic People's Party (KNDP) coalition in Hungary since 2010 and Law and Justice (PiS) in Poland since 2015. Following the coming to power of these parties, there was an intensified phase of kin-state engagement. Trans-border nationalism has been evident in the official political narrative, which often refers to the national community existing beyond state borders, as well as in new regulations regarding preferential conditions of naturalisation and settlement in the country of origin addressed to kin-minority members. There are pragmatic grounds for the above-mentioned trans-border nationalism. For the Polish authorities, who have struggled with the consequences of mass emigration after the country's accession to the European Union (EU) and a predicted deep demographic decline, kin-minorities have begun to be perceived as a natural demographic reservoir of people who are of close cultural background and are ready to integrate rapidly upon settling in the country of origin. For the Hungarian government, ethnic Hungarians living in neighbouring countries have become a valuable resource as voters supporting the ruling party and as an important element of foreign policy conducted towards these countries.

There are two interlinked dimensions of trans-border nationalism: an essentialist one to build a common national community and identity beyond borders, and more pragmatic one, which serves political purposes such as gaining political support at election time or encouraging settlement in the country of origin to fill economic and demographic gaps. When analysing Hungarian and Polish government policy towards kin-minorities, one can only agree with Myra Waterbury (2014, p. 47), who argues that

> ethnic kin groups in Eastern and Southeastern Europe continue to represent important sources of cultural, moral, political, demographic, and even economic material for homeland state policy makers.

The analysis presented below focuses on the policies of Hungary and Poland as kin-states, in particular on the key legal and institutional solutions adopted there during the time when right-wing political parties assumed power and gave pragmatic justifications for the policies implemented. The paper assesses the characteristics of the dominant narratives on kin-minorities, along with common elements in both countries' policies, as well as those factors that differentiate between the two cases; it offers also possible explanations of the paths followed by Hungarian and Polish governments in this area.

Poland and Hungary as Kin-States and Their Policies Towards Kin-Minorities

When analysing the policies pursued by Hungary and Poland towards kin-minorities, three factors should be identified which, in our view, induce many parallels between them: similar historical experiences regarding the formation of kin-minority groups in surrounding countries, an ethnicised conception of the nation (relying on an ethnic rather than civic concepts of nationhood) and the ideological proximity of both ruling political parties.

In both cases, numerous kin-minorities in surrounding countries arose due to ground-breaking historical events and border changes. After the end of World War II, Poland's borders were moved westward and under the Yalta Agreement extensive population transfers took place—more than one million Poles were relocated from the Soviet Union to Poland just after the war—but many Poles inhabiting the border areas still remained within the frontiers of present-day Russia, Lithuania, Belarus and Ukraine. The collective term 'Poles in the East' is often used in official narrative to describe Polish minorities living beyond Poland's Eastern border. This includes both the Polish minorities in neighbouring countries as well as the descendants of Poles forcibly displaced in the nineteenth and early-twentieth centuries by the Tsarist and then Soviet authorities to the Asian part of Russia/the Soviet Union—i.e. the present-day territories of Kazakhstan and Uzbekistan (Grzymała-Kazłowska & Grzymała-Moszczyńska, 2014). The latter group became the target of a repatriation policy dating back to 2000, when the Law on Repatriation was implemented.[1]

The current number of ethnic Poles in the East is obviously difficult to count. The Ministry of Foreign Affairs (2015) estimates that there are around one million people of Polish origin inhabiting the former Soviet states, although other estimates go much higher. According to censuses carried out in recent years, the number of Poles in Lithuania numbers 200,000, with another 295,000 in Belarus and 144,000 in Ukraine (these numbers may be underesttimates as some people may not have disclosed their Polish nationality). There are also 34,000 Poles living in Kazakhstan, 46,000 in Latvia and 47,000 in Russia (*ibidem*).

Turning to Hungary, we may note that one of the most important events in the history of modern Hungary—which also has a special meaning for Hungarians' collective memory—is the Treaty of Trianon (signed in Versailles in 1920). The treaty resulted in the country's area being reduced by a third. About 10.6 million residents of the former Kingdom of Hungary remained outside the country's new borders—i.e. within the territories of present-day Romania, Slovakia, Serbia and Ukraine as well as Austria, Slovenia and Croatia (Rothschild, 1974, p. 155). According to 2011 estimates by the Hungarian Central Statistical Office, the population of Hungarians (people with Hungarian citizenship and ethnic Hungarians) in neighbouring countries amounted to around 1.22 million in Romania, 251,000 in Serbia, 459,000 in Slovakia and 141,000 in Ukraine (KSH, 2011). This historical event and its consequences were treated by Hungarians and the Hungarian authorities as a national trauma. The myth of Greater Hungary within the pre-Trianon Treaty borders remains, reproduced and used explicitly by right-wing parties. In Poland, resentment over the lost Eastern territories was also present but to a much lesser extent; currently, in the public sphere, it is mostly exploited by far-right movements.

Historical experiences common to Poland and Hungary can also be found in later decades. Throughout almost half a century following the end of World War II, state borders in the entire region of Central and Eastern Europe were almost completely closed. The possibilities of entry and exit were strictly controlled and therefore maintaining contacts with compatriots living in other countries was difficult and sometimes practically impossible. In turn, the beginning of the 1990s was framed by a tough period of political and economic transformation. It was, however, also a period that saw the first attempts to renew relations between kin-state governments and co-ethnics residing abroad and to develop state policies addressed towards them (Kovács, 2017; Pogonyi, 2017).

Another important element that is shared by both countries is an ethnic and cultural understanding of the national community. The feeling of belonging to the nation is understood in these two cases in essentialist terms, built upon a common history, language, memory and culture, along with strong symbolic elements (Brubaker, 1996; Greenfeld, 1992). Trans-border nationalism identifies and constitutes certain trans-border populations as members of the nation and justifies maintaining or re-establishing ties with them. This may be represented in various ways and can be oriented internally—by building bonds of loyalty and membership in the community across borders in order to consolidate national identity and cohesion—as well as externally, by using kin minorities as a 'tool' in foreign policy undertaken by the kin-state towards neighbouring countries (Brubaker, 2011; King & Melvin, 1999/2000; Waterbury, 2010).

Minority issues are traditionally one of the key areas of Hungarian government's activities in the international arena. Over the past few years, the Hungarian government has caused a deterioration of bilateral relations with Romania over the rights of Hungarian minorities living in this country and brought the dispute to the international level (by blocking Romania's membership in the OECD) (Szijjártó, 2017a). The most recent example is the strained relationship between Hungary and Ukraine since the government in Kyiv adopted a reform of the education system that introduced restrictions on the use of national minority languages in schools (Sadecki & Iwański, 2018). The Minister of Foreign Affairs and Trade has repeatedly stated that if the Ukrainian authorities do not abandon the new legislation, Hungary will block Ukraine's closer cooperation with the EU and NATO (Szijjártó, 2017b). In the case of Hungary and Poland, policy towards kin-minorities is also a tool of domestic policy. It serves to legitimise power that is further reinforced by referring to the ethnic vision of the nation. The idea of a nation as an ethnic and cultural community is strongly present in the official political narratives on kin-minorities in both countries. Reference to one nation across borders, a duty of care, a sense of commitment and compensation towards kin-minorities (ethnic Hungarians in neighbouring countries and Poles in the East, respectively) who deserve comprehensive support (legal, financial and moral) is commonly present in official documents and statements by government officials.[2]

Reference to kin-minorities can also be found in these countries' constitutions. The special role of Hungarians living in the Kingdom of Hungary's former territories is highlighted in the 2011 constitution's preamble as follow:

> We promise to preserve the intellectual and spiritual unity of our nation torn apart in the storms of the last century [a clear reference to the Treaty of Trianon].

In addition, Article D states:

> Bearing in mind that there is one single Hungarian nation that belongs together, Hungary shall bear responsibility for the fate of Hungarians living beyond its borders, shall facilitate the survival and development of their communities, shall

support their efforts to preserve their Hungarian identity (…) and shall promote their cooperation with each other and with Hungary.

On the other hand, in the Polish constitution (1997), only two short passages are devoted to Poles living abroad—there is a reference to the Polish nation bounded in community with its compatriots dispersed throughout the world in both the preamble and in Article 6, which notes that 'the Republic of Poland shall provide assistance to Poles living abroad to maintain their links with the national cultural heritage'. The moral obligation of the Polish state to Poles beyond the Eastern border is recalled, among other things, in the 2007 Act on the *Karta Polaka*. The very introduction of the *Karta* as a document confirming the fact that a person belongs to the Polish community is defined there as

> … fulfilling a moral obligation towards Poles in the East who have lost their Polish citizenship as a result of our homeland's changing fortunes [and] meeting the expectations of people who have never held Polish citizenship but, because of their feelings of national identity, wish to obtain confirmation of their Polish nationality. (*Karta Polaka* Act)

Similar phrases referring to the Polish state's moral duty towards kin-minorities are present in several other significant documents—which indicate policy measures aimed at these groups (irrespective of whether they were developed by the Senate, the Ministry of Foreign Affairs or the Chancellery of the President)—as well as in each annual exposé of the Minister of Foreign Affairs, whose speech partly relates to the state's policy towards Poles abroad (Lesińska, 2019).

The narrative on one nation beyond borders aimed at strengthening co-ethnics' awareness of their ties with the country of origin is propelled by various initiatives (Gamlen, 2006). One good example is the establishment of national holidays that refer to the memory of the diaspora. In 2002, 2 May was established as the Polish Diaspora and Poles Abroad Day. Since 2010, the Day of National Cohesion is celebrated in Hungary (*Nemzeti összetartozás napja*, where '*összetartozás*' means restoring unity or re-bonding —indirectly speaking—the nation), which signals the dissolution of historic Hungary and the existence of Hungarian kin-minorities in neighbouring countries. It is celebrated on 4 June, the anniversary of the Trianon Treaty. Furthermore, on 18 May 2019, the Hungarian National Assembly declared that 2020 would be the Year of National Unity, which aroused great emotions in countries bordering Hungary.[3] In both countries there are also dedicated TV channels (*Duna TV* in Hungary, *TVP Polonia* in Poland) which broadcast Hungarian- and Polish-language programmes addressed at emigrants and kin-minorities. Another example of a symbolic initiative stimulating the narrative of a national community across borders is the media campaign announced by the Polish authorities in 2019 with the slogan 'There are 60 million of us'. The goal of this initiative is to make Poles in Poland and abroad aware that 'there is a great number of us and we constitute a great community; the goal is also to take care of and to strengthen this community' (Polish Radio One, 2019). This theme is also present during football matches of the Hungarian national team when the slogan 'There are 15 million of us'—referring to the Hungarian community both at home and abroad—is chanted.

Political elites in Hungary and Poland have already referred to the narrative of one global nation in the past (during the political transformation at the turn of the 1980s and 1990s) and are again doing so nowadays in the era of increased inflows of migrants and fears concerning the erosion of national cohesion and the two countries' future demographic situation.[4] Both governments referred to the influx of refugees during the so-called 'migration crisis' in 2015 as supposedly threatening the national community. In Poland, the policy towards kin-minorities that is aimed at encouraging their members to settle in the country is presented as a positive counter-example for the migration policy of Western Europe, where —according to the Polish authorities—the policy of accepting foreigners from culturally distant countries and the integration policy based on multiculturalism have failed.[5]

Many countries in Central and Eastern Europe grant co-ethnics living outside their borders certain benefits in the homeland, preferential access to citizenship and/or a kind of certificate that proves their ethnic belonging to the nation (Dumbrava, 2019; Waterbury, 2014). Concerning the latter benefit, the *Karta Polaka* and the Certificate of Hungarian Nationality (*Magyar Igazolvány*) were introduced as documents guaranteeing the holder's adherence to the Polish or the Hungarian nation. The relevant legal acts were introduced under the rule of right-wing parties (Fidesz and PiS) in 2001 and 2007, respectively.[6] Table 1 presents a comparison of both legal measures.

Implementation of this solution, however, went in different directions in both investigated countries. While amendments to the *Karta Polaka* legislation in 2016 and 2019 extended its geographical scope and granted further rights to its holders, the significance of the Certificate of Hungarian Nationality in the Hungarian case has diminished with the adoption of the new naturalisation regulations in 2010 (see below). Evidently, the policy of the Hungarian government has focused on assisting trans-border Hungarians in their countries of residence rather than facilitating their arrival and settlement in the country of origin, which has been the main aim of Polish authorities.

One important common feature connecting both countries is the ideological closeness of their respective ruling parties, which have been described as an example of a 'radicalized conservative right' (Camus & Lebourg, 2017, p. 241). The success of Viktor Orbán and his party, Fidesz who, after eight years in opposition, took power in Hungary in 2010, made Polish right-wing politicians hope for a similar scenario.[7] These hopes were realised in 2015 with PiS's electoral success and the formation of a government by this party. Since then, the governments formed by Fidesz and PiS have followed similar conservative and nationalist trajectories (Dostal et al., 2018; Sata & Karolewski, 2020). They also went hand in hand in criticising the EU's refugee policy and the relocation scheme during the 2015 migration crisis and using exclusionary discourses directed at groups labelled as enemies (refugees, Muslims, ethnic and sexual minorities) (Zgut, 2020).

Shortly after the two parties took power, interest in the kin-minority issue intensified and new legal measures devoted to these groups were introduced, including ethnic preferential citizenship laws. During its first year in power, Fidesz established new rules for the acquisition of Hungarian citizenship by ethnic Hungarians living in surrounding countries. In Poland, the possibility of a fast naturalisation track for *Karta Polaka* holders was introduced by the government in 2016 for those who decided to settle in Poland. Shortly after, in 2017, the rules of repatriation policy were also modified, which accelerated and simplified procedures for people who would like to use the resettlement path to move to Poland.

New Dynamics of Kin-State Laws and Their Outcomes

After the election victory of the Fidesz–KDNP coalition in Hungary in spring 2010 Viktor Orbán's party initiated a number of activities designed to favour the position of kin-

Table 1. Comparison between the *Karta Polaka* and the *Certificate of Hungarian* Nationality

	Hungary	Poland
Legal act	Act on Hungarians Living in Neighbouring Countries, effective from 1 January 2002; amendments in 2011.	Act of 7 September 2007 on the *Karta Polaka*; amendments in 2016 and 2019.
People entitled to receive the Certificate/Card	Those of Hungarian origin who are citizens of Ukraine, Slovakia, Romania, Croatia, Serbia or Slovenia.	2007: people of Polish origin living in 15 countries formed after the collapse of the USSR. Since 2019, all people of Polish origin.
Conditions for obtaining the Certificate/Card	Declaration of belonging to the Hungarian nation and fulfilment of one of two conditions: • knowledge of the Hungarian language and/or • residence in one of the above countries.[a]	Knowledge of the Polish language and fulfilment of one of two conditions: • having Polish ancestors—one of the parents or grandparents or two great-grandparents, or • presenting a certificate of a Polish organisation operating in one of 15 countries confirming active involvement in activities that promote the Polish language and culture and the Polish minority for at least three years.
Certificate-/Card-holder's most important rights	• free entry into the territory of Hungary • free access to Hungarian schools and universities • free healthcare in Hungary • the right to modest financial support after arriving in Hungary.	In 2007: • free entry into the territory of Poland • free access to Polish schools/ universities • the right to work in Poland • the right to run a business in Poland Since 2016: • simplified procedure for obtaining a permanent residence permit • possibility to obtain Polish citizenship after a year of uninterrupted stay in Poland • financial assistance: cash benefit for 9 months on arrival; co-financing of rental for an apartment • possibility to attend Polish language and vocational courses

[a]Persons with Hungarian citizenship may also apply for the Certificate of Hungarian Nationality. This option is used by Hungarians living in countries that do not recognise dual citizenship (e.g. in Slovakia and Ukraine). They want to hide the fact of holding Hungarian citizenship from these countries' authorities and at the same time enjoy the privileges of having a certificate.

Source: Authors' elaboration.

minorities in countries bordering Hungary. Apart from the already mentioned establishment of the Day of National Cohesion, parliament began work on a preferential procedure of granting Hungarian citizenship to co-ethnics. The narrative around the relevant Act was full of symbolic references—it mentioned the restoration of Hungarians' dignity outside the country—whereas the new naturalisation regulations were to fulfil the obligations of the Hungarian state towards its compatriots (Hungarian Citizenship Act of 2010). The time of publication of the new Act was not accidental either: 20 August is celebrated as King Stefan's Day—a national holiday to commemorate the creation of the Hungarian state. The new regulations made it possible to obtain Hungarian citizenship without permanent residence in Hungary if two criteria were met: applicants had to prove that at least one of their ancestors was a citizen of Hungary and they had to have a basic command of the Hungarian language (the new law thus abolished the obligation to take an exam in Hungarian and to live in the territory of the country). Although the simplified naturalisation procedure was intended to be addressed to all people brought up in the Hungarian culture and speaking the Hungarian language (emigrants and their descendants as well as representatives of kin-minorities), in practice the main addressees were the inhabitants of the former Kingdom of Hungary (Héjj, 2018).

According to Fidesz's 2004 estimates, the number of Hungarians potentially interested in using the simplified procedure was as high as 800,000 (Bőhm, 2010). This goal was already achieved by 2015 and, two years later, the number had exceeded one million.[8] Statistics shows that, between 2011 and 2015, the overwhelming majority (95%) of these citizenship applications came from Hungary's neighbouring countries (KSH, 2017).[9] Naturalised Hungarians have the same rights as those living in the country, including free access to education, health care, social care and pension support. Interestingly, the results of a poll published in 2018 show that the majority of Hungarians do not support the granting of special rights to newly naturalised Hungarians abroad. Respondents opposed their active voting rights (57%), other voting privileges (76%), subsidies (60%) and social privileges (60%) provided. At the same time, the vast majority of respondents (68%) supported the possibility of granting citizenship to ethnic Hungarians abroad (Publicus Institute, 2018).

Hungarian citizens living abroad have the right to vote in national elections. Under the amendment to the Electoral System of 2011 and the Electoral Code in 2013, two groups can be distinguished: the first consists of emigrants who must possess a postal address in Hungary in order to vote while the second group are citizens living in surrounding countries who do not need to have a Hungarian postal address but are additionally granted the right to vote by post (the most numerous group are Hungarians from Transylvania). Other groups, for instance Hungarian emigrants residing in the United States and EU member-states not neighbouring Hungary, must cast their votes in person at diplomatic missions (Héjj, 2018).

The data indicate that Hungarians who voted abroad overwhelmingly support the Fidesz–KNDP coalition. In the 2018 parliamentary elections, 51,000 Hungarians voted at polling stations abroad. At the same time, the number of valid postal votes was 4.5 times higher and amounted to 225,000, including 216,000 votes (96%) cast for the Fidesz–KNDP (National Election Office, 2018). As a result of the naturalisation of several hundred thousand eligible ethnic Hungarians, it was expected that the number of votes cast would reach at least 600,000. In reality, however, the number was much lower: in 2018 around 380,000 people living outside Hungary were registered as voters. Despite the fact that the number of voters abroad was lower than expected, they still had a key impact on the election result. In the 2014 elections, the votes from abroad contributed to gaining the one extra seat necessary to secure a constitutional majority in parliament by the ruling party. In the elections of 2018, votes from neighbouring countries benefitted Fidesz in terms of 'winner compensation' (allocation of additional votes to the winning parties under the d'Hondt method), allowing it to maintain a constitutional majority (Róbert, 2018). The engagement of historic Hungarian minorities thus represents an example of direct political remittances for the kin-state (Kovács, 2020).

In the Polish case, the electoral power of kin-minorities is much more limited. Only a few co-ethnics living in neighbouring countries have Polish citizenship entitling them to participate in elections. Holders of the *Karta Polaka* do not have electoral rights either. The vast majority of votes gathered from abroad were cast by emigrants who settled in EU countries and North America. The interest of Poles living abroad in participating in elections is low, with the most votes from abroad cast in 2019—some 314,000, which represented 1.7% of all votes cast in the elections (PKW, 2019). The votes were also scattered among several major political parties. What is more, the system of converting votes into seats additionally marginalises the influence of votes from abroad: the so called 'assimilated representation' applies in Poland, which means that all votes cast abroad are compiled and assigned to one voting district in the country, namely Warsaw.

Unlike the politicians of the ruling parties in Hungary, policymakers in Poland do not see kin-minorities as influential voters. In recent years, however, they have started to be perceived as a demographic and economic reservoir—as potential residents and employees who can come and settle in the country (Zespół do Spraw Migracji, 2019). In consequence, as a result of the 2016 law amendment, preferential naturalisation paths for *Karta Polaka* holders were introduced (Act of 13 May 2016). The scope of entitlements of persons of Polish origin who decided to come and settle in Poland was also significantly expanded (see Table 1). The implemented changes undoubtedly contributed to the increase in the number of applications for the *Karta* Polaka[10] as did the permanent residence permits issued for their holders.[11] The *Karta* became an instrument of active migration policy. In total, 10,300 people of Polish descent and their family members moved to Poland from the territory of the former USSR in 2018, including over 9,000 holders of the *Karta Polaka* and only slightly more than 1,000 repatriates. Undoubtedly, the *Karta* has become an attractive 'entry ticket to Poland'—it is a simple and fast path to arrival and to taking up studies and/or work for people of Polish descent, especially for young citizens of Ukraine and Belarus.[12]

Apart from the changes to the *Karta Polaka* regulations, the PiS government also attempted to reactivate the repatriation policy but the number of people using this path of settlement in Poland and obtaining Polish citizenship was very low—about 8,000 were repatriated to Poland between 2001 and 2018 (Nowosielski & Stefańska, 2018). Several changes were made to the Act on repatriation in 2017, which opened new procedural paths for going to Poland and enlarged the scope of support after arrival; the possibility of granting Polish citizenship was also extended to non-Polish members of a repatriate's immediate family (Act of 7 April 2017).

These legal and political changes, noticeable in recent years in both countries' policies towards kin minorities, reflect the dominant narrative on the national community across borders, as well as the duty of care from the countries of origin for these groups. They expose the government's overarching goal of maintaining the identity relations of kin-minorities with the homeland and an awareness of belonging to the national community beyond the borders. At the same time, the different pragmatic rationale of the two countries should be emphasised. Ethnic Hungarians, especially those who took advantage of the possibility of naturalisation, are becoming a real electoral and political resource for the ruling party in Hungary; whether they decide to come to Hungary or to stay in their present country of residence is a secondary consideration. For the Polish authorities, the changes introduced to kin-minority regulations have a slightly different but also pragmatic purpose—encouraging ethnic Poles to settle in Poland, supplying its population and labour market, as well as, in the next step, formalising their relations with the state by applying for Polish citizenship.

In seeking possible explanations for the different paths followed by the two governments, one should examine the (more recent) history of laws adopted by these governments and take into account the official narrative of the past. In the case of Hungary, to have numerous clusters of Hungarian citizens living in neighbouring countries (resisting assimilation and remaining members of the Hungarian nation where they are, instead of moving to Hungary) is crucial to keeping alive the idea of a Greater Hungary, to which the government often refers. Whereas in Poland the tradition of 'returning to the homeland' from exile is deeply rooted in national history, and indeed in the wake of the democratic transition of 1989 when many Poles returned to the mother country. Consequently, there has been an expectation of and wide public support for a repatriation policy addressed to the descendants of people in the Soviet successor states, which has been widely perceived as a historical moral obligation for the Polish state (Grzymała-Kazłowska & Grzymała-Moszczyńska, 2014, p. 608).

Conclusion

Both in Hungary and in Poland, kin minorities were and are prioritised as part of state policies. When right-wing nationalist parties came to power in these countries, they devoted considerable effort to building formal and symbolic bonds with kin-minorities in surrounding states, including the narrative of a national community across borders of whom a considerable part are kin-minorities left outside the country as a result of historical events, and who should receive support and compensation from the kin-state. The narrative was accompanied by specific legal measures, such as the *Karta Polaka* in Poland and Hungary's Act LXII of 2001 on Hungarians Living in Neighbouring Countries, as well as preferential paths of settlement and naturalisation. The similarities are framed by analogous historical experiences regarding the formation of kin-minority groups in surrounding countries, convergence in perceiving the nation as an ethnic community across state borders, as well as the ideological proximity of the ruling governments.

At the same time, however, one should also pay attention to the differences visible in the two cases. The governments in Hungary and Poland both treat their kin minorities as human resources, although they are utilised in different ways. Hungary's approach represents a policy of ethno-demographic consolidation aimed at increasing the size and strength of the Hungarian nation beyond the borders, controlled by the kin-state via a naturalisation scheme open for co-ethnics living in neighbouring countries. On the other hand, the Polish authorities use various tools (such as the repatriation scheme or the *Karta Polaka*) to attract co-ethnics to settle on its territory and to quickly naturalise. While Hungary tends to make use of the demographic and political strength of the kin minority population abroad, mainly as voters, the goal for the Polish government is to encourage the inflow of new employees and new citizens—needed in the face of a constantly high demand for a labour force and an increasingly severe demographic decline. In both cases, the policy towards kin-minorities is an evident example of pragmatic trans-border nationalism.

Acknowledgements

This article is based on Research Project No. 2018/31/B/HS5/00913, funded by the National Science Centre, Poland.

Funding

This article is based on Research Project No. 2018/31/B/HS5/00913, funded by the National Science Centre, Poland.

Notes

1. The repatriation scheme was addressed to persons who declared Polish nationality and demonstrated a connection with Polishness through cultivation of the Polish language and customs and who had (or had in the past) at least one parent or grandparent or both great-grandparents of Polish nationality or citizenship. A person arriving in Poland with a repatriation visa acquired Polish citizenship at the moment of crossing the border to Poland. What was important was that the geographical scope of repatriation was restricted to the territory of the Asian parts of the former USSR and was not applicable for Poles in Ukraine or Belarus (**the Act of 9 November 2000 on Repatriation, No. 106, Item 1118).
2. The dominant tone in the Polish authorities' official narrative on the state's duties towards Polish minorities in the East could best be illustrated by the words of the Polish President regarding the rights of the harmed, multi-million part of our nation that remained behind the Eastern border of the country, in the territory of the Second Polish Republic painfully cut off by the decisions of the Allied powers in Yalta [and] the nation's commitment to compensate compatriots from the former Soviet Union for the harm suffered [...] This task is a priority and duty of state authorities towards the past, present and future generations of Poles (Ministry of Foreign Affairs, 2016, p. 3).
3. The Ministry of Foreign Affairs of Romania has described the introduction of the Day of National Cohesion as the act of revisionism (see: *România megalapozatlannak tartja, hogy 2020 a nemzeti összetartozás évének lett nyilvánítva* [Romania believes that 2020 has been declared the year of national cohesion]. Retrieved January 6, 2020, from https://magyarnemzet.hu/kulfold/romania-megalapozatlannak-tartja-hogy-2020-a-nemzeti-osszetartozas-evenek-lett-nyilvanitva-7049264/). The Slovak authorities have also expressed their criticism in this matter (see: *Szlovákia bírálja a nemzeti összetartozás évéről hozott magyar döntést* [Slovakia criticises the Hungarian decision on the year of national belonging]. Retrieved January 5, 2020, from https://www.m190-21-hp-nemzeti-osszetartozas-everol-hozott-Magyar-dontest).
4. Demographic perspectives are unfavourable in both countries, mostly as a consequence of low fertility and high emigration (noted especially after accession to the EU). The fertility rates in Poland and Hungary are amongst the lowest in Europe (1.4), while the number of Hungarian and Polish citizens of working age (20–64 years) in European countries in 2015 was 5 and 6% of these countries' populations respectively (European Commission, 2016).
5. According to Jan Dziedziczak (Secretary of State at the Polish Ministry of Foreign Affairs) conclusions should be drawn from the erroneous migration policy of France, Germany or the Benelux Countries and therefore 'an effective migration policy based on our compatriots should be led' (statement at the conference 'Repatriates or immigrants. Directions of Poland's and European Union's migration policy'/'*Repatrianci czy imigranci. Kierunki polityki migracyjnej Polski i Unii Europejskiej*', 18 April 2016. Retrieved January 7, 2020 from https://www.youtube.com/watch?v=41SgEYcRBoA.
6. The first attempt to establish the *Karta Polaka* was made in 1999 but it was not possible to adopt the relevant act before the end of the parliamentary term. It was finally adopted in 2007.
7. During the announcement of the results of the defeated 2011 election, the PiS chairman said: 'I am deeply convinced that the day will come when we shall succeed in having Budapest in Warsaw' (statement by Jarosław Kaczyński, 9 October 2011).
8. Although dual citizenship is not allowed in Slovakia and Ukraine, Hungarian consulates grant the citizenship, which entails many serious legal consequences in the event of disclosure of this fact, including deprivation of a person's citizenship of the country of residence.

9. Unfortunately, there are no current data on the number of ethnic Hungarians from neighbouring countries who settled in Hungary. Available data relate to 1985–2011 and indicate that their number could be as high as 173,000 (Péti et al., 2017).
10. According to data provided by the Ministry of Foreign Affairs (2010–2017), about 250,000 documents have been issued since the introduction of the *Karta Polaka* Act in 2007, including over 90% to citizens of Belarus and Ukraine.
11. Official estimates show that about 70% of all permanent residence permits issued in 2017–2018 were granted on the basis of holding the *Karta Polaka* (Zespół do Spraw Migracji, 2019).
12. In 2017, nearly 9,000 people were granted permanent residence permits based on the *Karta Polaka*, an increase of 107% over the previous year; in 2018 this number exceeded 9,600 permits (Office for Foreigners, 2018).

ORCID

Magdalena Lesińska ⓘ http://orcid.org/0000-0002-7520-3895
Dominik Héjj ⓘ http://orcid.org/0000-0002-3159-8936

References

Act of 13 May 2016 amending the *Karta Polaka* Act and some other acts, No. 2016, Item 753.
Act of 7 April 2017 amending the Repatriation Act and some other acts, No. 2017, Item 858.
Basch, N., Glick Schiller, N., & Blanc-Szanton, C. (1994). *Nations unbound: Transnational projects, postcolonial predicaments and deterritorialized nation-states.* Routledge.
Bőhm, A. (2010). Baloldali visszavágó – 2002 [Left rebound 2002]. In G. Földes & L. Hubai (Eds.), *Parlamenti választások Magyarországon 1920–2010* [Parliamentary elections in Hungary 1920–2010] (pp. 381–408). Napvilág Kiadó.
Brubaker, R. (1996). *Nationalism reframed: Nationhood and the national question in the new Europe.* Cambridge University Press.
Brubaker, R. (2010). Migration, membership, and the modern nation-state: Internal and external dimensions of the politics of belonging. *Journal of Interdisciplinary History, 41*(1), 61–78. https://doi.org/10.1162/jinh.2010.41.1.61
Brubaker, R. (2011). Nationalizing states revisited: Projects and processes of nationalization in post-Soviet states. *Ethnic and Racial Studies, 34*(11), 1785–1814. https://doi.org/10.1080/01419870.2011.579137
Camus, J.-Y., & Lebourg, N. (2017). *Far-right politics in Europe.* Belknap Press of Harvard University Press.
Collyer, M. (2014). Inside out? Directly elected 'special representation' of emigrants in national legislatures and the role of popular sovereignty. *Political Geography, 41*(1), 64–73. https://doi.org/10.1016/j.polgeo.2014.01.002
Dostal, V., Győri, L., Meseznikov, G., Przybylski, W., & Zgut, E. (2018). Illiberalism in the V4: Pressure points and bright spots. Political capital and FSE. Political capital and Friedrich Naumann Stiftung. Retrieved March 18, 2020, from www.politicalcapital.hu/pc-admin/source/documents/pc_fnf_v4illiberalism_pressurepoints_20180605.pdf
Dumbrava, C. (2019). The ethno-demographic impact of co-ethnic citizenship in Central and Eastern Europe. *Journal of Ethnic and Migration Studies, 45*(6), 958–974. https://doi.org/10.1080/1369183X.2018.1440490
European Commission. (2016). *Annual report on intra-EU labour mobility.*
Gamlen, A. (2006). *Diaspora engagement policies: What are they, and what kinds of states use them?* (COMPAS Working Paper No. 32). University of Oxford.
Gamlen, A., Cummings, M., Vaaler, P. M., & Rossouw, L. (2013). *Explaining the rise of diaspora institutions* (International Migration Institute Working Paper No. 78). University of Oxford.
Greenfeld, L. (1992). *Nationalism: Five roads to modernity.* Harvard University Press.
Grzymała-Kazłowska, A., & Grzymała-Moszczyńska, H. (2014). The anguish of repatriation: Immigration to Poland and integration of Polish descendants from Kazakhstan. *East European Politics and Societies and Cultures, 28*(3), 593–613. https://doi.org/10.1177/0888325414532494
Héjj, D. (2018). Węgierska diaspora i polityka narodowościowa jako element rywalizacji politycznej na Węgrzech [Policy towards diaspora and kin-minorities as an element of political rivalry in Hungary]. In H. Chałupczak,

M. Lesińska, E. Pogorzała, & T. Browarek (Eds.), *Polityka migracyjna w obliczu współczesnych wyzwań* [Migration policy in the face of contemporary challenges] (pp. 229–248). UKSW Press.

Hungarian Citizenship Act of 2010, No. XLIV, novelty of Law LV/1993.

Karta Polaka Act of 7 September 2007, No. 180, Item 1280.

King, C., & Melvin, N. J. (1999/2000). Diaspora politics: Ethnic linkages, foreign policy, and security in Eurasia. *International Security, 24*(3), 108–138. https://doi.org/10.1162/016228899560257

Kovács, E. (2017). Post-socialist diaspora policies: Is there a Central-European diaspora policy path? *Hungarian Journal of Minority Studies, 1*(1), 89–109.

Kovács, E. (2020). Direct and indirect political remittances of the transnational engagement of Hungarian kin-minorities and diaspora communities. *Journal of Ethnic and Migration Studies, 46*(6), 1146–1165. https://doi.org/10.1080/1369183X.2018.1554315

KSH. (2011). *10,4 millióan vallották magukat magyar nemzetiségűnek a térségben* [10.4 million have declared themselves to be of Hungarian nationality in the region]. Retrieved January 3, 2020, from https://hirado.hu/2013/05/09/ksh-104-millioan-vallottak-magukat-magyar-nemzetis/

KSH. (2017). *Új magyar állampolgárok:Változások az egyszerűsített honosítási eljárás bevezetése után* [New Hungarian citizens: Changes after the introduction of the preferential naturalization process]. Retrieved January 3, 2020, from http://www.ksh.hu/docs/hun/xftp/idoszaki/pdf/ujmagyarallampolgarok.pdf

Lesińska, M. (2019). *Niełatwe związki: relacje polityczne między państwem pochodzenia a diasporą. Polska i polska diaspora w okresie przełomu 1989 roku i później* [A difficult relationship: Political relations between the country of origin and the diaspora. Poland and Polish diaspora in the transition of 1989 and later]. University of Warsaw Press.

Ministry of Foreign Affairs. (2010–2017). *Annual consular reports of the Ministry of Foreign Affairs*. Retrieved January 4, 2020, from https://www.msz.gov.pl/pl/informacje_konsularne/raporty_konsularne/

Ministry of Foreign Affairs. (2015). *Rządowy program współpracy z Polonią i Polakami za granicą w latach 2015-2020* [Government programme of cooperation with the Polish community abroad]. Retrieved January 10, 2020, from https://www.msz.gov.pl/pl/p/msz_pl/polityka_zagraniczna/polonia/rzadowy_program_wspolpracy_z_polonia/

Ministry of Foreign Affairs. (2016). *Polskie dziedzictwo duchowe i kulturowe na Wschodzie w 1050. rocznicę Chrztu Polski* [Polish spiritual and cultural heritage in the East on the 1050th anniversary of the baptism of Poland]. Retrieved September 27, 2019, from ttps://www.msz.gov.pl/pl//polityka_zagraniczna/polonia/wydarzenia/europa/publikacja___polskie_dziedzictwo_duchowe_i_kulturowe_na_wschodzie_w_1050__rocznice_chrztu_polski__

National Election Office. (2018). *Országgyűlési képviselők választása, 8.04.2018, A levélben leadott listás szavazatok megszámlálása* [Election of Members of Parliament, 8.04.2018, counting of correspondence votes]. Retrieved October 10, 2019, from http://www.valasztas.hu

Nowosielski, M., & Stefańska, R. (2018). Repatriacja [Repatriation]. In M. Lesińska & M. Okólski (Eds.), *25 Wykładów o migracjach* [25 lectures on migration] (pp. 321–333). Scholar.

Office for Foreigners. (2018). *Karta Polaka: Rośnie liczba zezwoleń na pobyt stały* [Pole's Card: The number of permanent residence permits is increasing]. Retrieved January 5, 2020, from https://udsc.gov.pl/karta-polaka-rosnie-liczba-zezwolen-na-pobyt-staly/

Péti, M., Szabó, B., & Szabó, L. (2017). A Kárpát-medence országaiból Magyarországra áttelepült népesség területi mintázata [Spatial pattern of the immigrant population from countries of the Carpathian Basin to Hungary]. *Területi Statisztika, 57*(3), 311–350.

PKW. (2019). The State Electoral Commission database. Retrieved October 21, 2019, from https://sejmsenat2019.pkw.gov.pl/sejmsenat2019/

Pogonyi, S. (2017). *Extra-territorial ethnic politics, discourses and identities in Hungary*. Palgrave Macmillan.

Polish Radio One. (2019, July 30). Interview with the Marshal of the Senate, Stanisław Karczewski. Retrieved January 6, 2020, from https://www.polskieradio.pl/7/129/Artykul/2348133,Stanislaw-Karczewski-Polacy-za-granica-to-oczko-w-glowie-senatu

Publicus Institute. (2018). *Határon túli magyarok egyes jogairól* [On certain rights of Hungarians living abroad]. Retrieved January 10, 2020, from http://www.publicus.hu/blog

Ragazzi, F. (2009). Governing diasporas. *International Political Sociology, 3*(4), 378–397. https://doi.org/10.1111/j.1749-5687.2009.00082.x

Róbert, L. (2018). *Nem hozott a külhon mandátumot a Fidesznek, a „győzteskompenzációval" együtt viszont 7-et is* [It did not bring a foreign mandate to Fidesz, but with 'victory compensation' it did 7]. Retrieved March 21, 2020, from http://www.valasztasirendszer.hu/?p=1943608

Rothschild, J. (1974). *East Central Europe between the Two World Wars*. University of Washington Press.

Sadecki, A., & Iwański, T. (2018). Ukraine–Hungary: The intensifying dispute over the Hungarian minority's rights. OSW Commentary, 218. Retrieved March 29, 2020, from https://www.osw.waw.pl/en/publikacje/osw-commentary/2018-08-14/ukraine-hungary-intensifying-dispute-over-hungarian-0

Sata, R., & Karolewski, I.P. (2020). Caesarean politics in Hungary and Poland. *East European Politics*, *36*(2), 206–225. https://doi.org/10.1080/21599165.2019.1703694

Szijjártó, P. (2017a). *Hungary is not supporting Croatia's and Romania's bids for membership of the OECD*. Retrieved March 29, 2020, from https://www.kormany.hu/en/ministry-of-foreign-affairs-and-trade/news/hungary-is-not-supporting-croatia-s-and-romania-s-bids-for-membership-of-the-oecd

Szijjártó, P. (2017b). *Hungary is unable to support Ukraine's integration aspirations*. Retrieved March 29, 2020, from https://www.kormany.hu/en/ministry-of-foreign-affairs-and-trade/news/hungary-is-unable-to-support-ukraine-s-integration-aspirations

Waterbury, M. A. (2010). *Between state and the nation: Diaspora politics and kin-state nationalism in Hungary*. Palgrave Macmillan.

Waterbury, M. A. (2014). Making citizens beyond the borders. Non-resident ethnic citizenship in post-communist Europe. *Problems of Post-Communism*, *61*(4), 36–49. https://doi.org/10.2753/PPC1075-8216610403

Zespół do Spraw Migracji. (2019). *Polityka migracyjna Polski. Projekt z dnia 10 czerwca* 2019 [Poland's migration policy. Project of June 10, 2019].

Zgut, E. (2020, February 6). New and old enemies. *Visegrad/Insight*. Retrieved March 19, 2020, from https://visegradinsight.eu/new-and-old-enemies-hungary-poland-minorities-judiciary/

Minority Protection and Kin-State Engagement: *Karta Polaka* in Comparative Perspective

ANDREEA UDREA ⓘ AND DAVID SMITH ⓘ

ABSTRACT   In this article, the authors propose a new normative approach that recognises and responds more adequately to the quadratic political reality of kin-state—kin minorities relations. The authors' point of departure is the dual contention that home-states have the primary duty to achieve full and effective equality between their citizens, while accommodating fairly their internal cultural and linguistic diversity; and that kin-states have a legitimate interest in their co-ethnics abroad. Building on this foundation, the authors argue that kin-state engagement should complement home-states' domestic commitments to cultural justice, in order to foster more effective minority protection. The authors conclude by outlining a concept of shared responsibility for minority protection between kin-state and home-states.

Introduction

While ties between kin-states and their co-ethnics abroad must today be acknowledged as a political reality, the recent intensification of kin-state engagement across Central and Eastern Europe (CEE) has hardly been consonant with promoting and protecting at the very least those minority rights guaranteed under international instruments. As outlined elsewhere in this volume, the kin-state engagement of both Hungary and Poland is justified as a remedy to historical injustices against an ethnoculturally defined nation. However, the evolution of their kin-state policies towards facilitating access to citizenship has in fact shown the increasing prevalence of a neoliberal state rationality regarding their trans-sovereign identity politics (Mavelli, 2018) legitimised by the mainstreaming of ethnopopulism domestically (Jenne, 2018; Stroschein, 2019). Such policies have continued to be a source of tension between the two kin-states and the states in which their co-ethnics reside.

Despite this development, the sole authoritative evaluation to date of the legislation on kin-minorities in Europe remains the one conducted by the Council of Europe's Venice Commission in 2001. This defines a kin-state's role as one of minority protection (Council of Europe [CoE], 2001, Section D), and thus implicitly as a matter of justice. Yet, the European norms and standards of minority protection developed since the start of the 1990s provide little if any concrete guidance as to how and to what extent a kin-state's engagement could actually contribute to protecting non-dominant groups within their home-states, since the latter are still deemed to hold exclusive responsibility in this area. In this respect, we argue, the 'Quadratic Nexus' (Smith, 2002) of relationships that captures the reality of ethno-cultural diversity politics in CEE has not moved beyond the state-centric, securitised and nationalist logic inherent to Brubaker's original 'Triadic Nexus' (1996). Caught between competing state interests are kin-minority groups themselves: primarily focused on preserving their cultural authenticity and attaining equal citizenship for their members within their home states, these communities broadly welcome external kin-state support to promote their language and culture. As we demonstrate here, however, co-ethnics abroad are increasingly conscious of being strategically exploited by kin-states for purposes that are 'indifferent, indeed hostile' (Brubaker, 1996, pp. 131–132) to promoting specific minority group interests.

In this article, we propose a new normative approach that recognises and responds more adequately to the abovementioned quadratic political reality and could contribute to fostering more effective minority protection. Developing insights from our research on kin-state engagement and liberal multiculturalism (Udrea, 2011, 2014) and minority participation and autonomy (Smith, 2020a; Smith & Hiden, 2012) respectively, we advance a case for redefining the protection of kin minorities as a shared responsibility between home-state and kin-state. Our point of departure is the dual contention that: (a) home-states have the primary duty to uphold minority protection, namely to achieve full and effective equality between their citizens, while accommodating fairly their internal cultural and linguistic diversity; and (b) kin-states have a legitimate interest in their co-ethnics abroad. Building on this foundation, we argue that kin-state engagement—whether in the form of direct assistance or political advocacy on behalf of co-ethnics abroad—should complement home-states' domestic commitments to cultural justice. Consistent with O'Neill's view, cultural justice as a form of constitutional justice refers here to a normative framework that promotes the recognition of particular group identities, acknowledging the relationship between individual freedom, collective self-expression and equal citizenship (2000). The article proceeds as follows: in the first section we discuss existing conceptions of minority protection in international law, demonstrating that these have centred on individual rather than collective rights and strengthened the exclusive responsibility of home-states rather than encouraging shared responsibility. This fact—we then argue in the second section—has rendered the international norms and standards of minority protection unable to accommodate the growing trend towards kin-state engagement in CEE. In the third section, we then discuss the examples of Hungary and Poland, using new empirical data to shed light on the often-neglected perspective of kin-minorities themselves.[1] We then proceed in the final section to outline a concept of shared responsibility for minority protection between kin-state and home-states.

The International Protection of Minority Ethno-cultural Groups

The need for and extent of the protection of minority ethnocultural groups in Europe have always been thorny issues, since they continuously challenge forms of sovereignty that promote congruence between citizenship, common cultural belonging, rights and territory. The international norms and standards of minority protection adopted in the last two decades have contributed to a modest diffusion of liberal multiculturalism and strengthened home-states' primary responsibility for minority protection. However, the ongoing crisis of solidarity in Europe evident since the 2008 financial crisis has been steadily eroding the already fragile European inter-state co-operation regarding the protection of individual and group rights (Owen, 2018). Various statements at an event to mark the 10th Anniversary of the Bolzano/Bozen Recommendations on National Minorities in Inter-state Relations (2018) stressed that the most visible impact of the crisis has been the erosion of multilateralism and the weakening of reciprocity as the regulatory mechanism on which the European minority protection regime has been constructed after 1989. Overall, then, the protection of minorities has diminished, with recent political developments turning its effectiveness into a major point of contention between minority ethnocultural groups and home-states (Marko, 2018). In this context, the continuing expansion, diversification and institutionalisation of kin-state support has appeared to offer an alternative form of minority protection that is generally welcomed by kin-minority groups. As a first step towards understanding how this kin-state engagement might be conceived in terms of shared responsibility with a minority's home-state, this section examines current international norms and standards of minority protection and the implications they hold for the allocation and nature of responsibility in this area.

Minority protection in Europe has evolved from an approach defined by 'minority guarantees' following the post–First World War territorial settlements, to one centred on promoting individual rights after the Second World War. 'Minority guarantees' in the interwar period referred to obligations to accommodate minority ethnocultural groups assumed by states voluntarily or under the pressure of other states, generally kin-states which exercised their power directly or indirectly. *De facto* the main object of these arrangements was to secure inter-state peace and the territorial borders drawn by the post-war settlements (Jackson Preece, 2005, pp. 1–17). Voluntary in nature and easy to rescind, they contributed very little to sheltering minority ethnocultural groups from the discriminatory and assimilationist effects of their home-states' policies (Jackson Preece, 1998, pp. 67–94; Smith & Hiden, 2012, pp. 1–8).

The significant shift towards a novel conception of minority protection took place after the Second World War. While minority issues were relegated entirely to home-states, becoming a matter of domestic determination, the international institutions focused on developing universal norms and procedures to guarantee the rights enshrined in the Universal Declaration of Human Rights (1946). The common view has become that minority protection was ensured when states refrained from discrimination and from curtailing individual liberties (McGarry & O'Leary, 2013). A basic minority-related Article was only introduced in the UN International Covenant on Civil and Political Rights, stating that

> In those States in which ethnic, religious or linguistic minorities exist, persons belonging to such minorities shall not be denied the right, in community with the other members of their group, to enjoy their own culture, to profess and practise their own religion, or to use their own language. (UN General Assembly, 1966, Art 27)

Experience had shown that the principle of non-discrimination is but a minimal requirement, and in fact, if minority rights are to protect a group's ethno-cultural identity, ensure its integration and help achieve substantive equality, 'minority protection requires affirmative action to the extent that may not be covered by a non-discrimination provision' (Bloed & van Dijk, 1999, p. 3).

The escalation of ethnic tensions in CEE during the 1990s led to a concerted effort by international organisations to define explicit standards of minority protection and enforce home-states' duties vis-à-vis their minority ethnocultural groups. As early as 1992, the UN Declaration on the Rights of Persons Belonging to National or Ethnic, Religious and Linguistic Minorities advanced a set of rights that persons belonging to minority groups should enjoy and affirmed that home-states have a responsibility to fulfil them (UN General Assembly, 1992). Such rights include not only the protection of a group's existence and identity (Art 1), but also the promotion of its specific identity, participation in cultural, social, economic and public life, cultural autonomy and cross-border cooperation (Art 2) and they entail corresponding obligations on the part of the home-states (Art. 3-8).

In Europe, the UN Declaration was followed by the adoption of various instruments defining the standards of minority protection. The Framework Convention for the Protection of National Minorities (CoE, 1995)[2] asserts that the protection of national minorities is inseparable from that of human rights and as such makes it the object of international cooperation (Art 1). Furthermore, it assigns home-states the primary responsibility to promote full and effective equality between people belonging to minority groups and those belonging to the majority (Art 4) and asserts that states have a responsibility to promote the participation of the members of minority groups in public affairs, as well as that in the social, cultural and economic life (Art 15). An important step towards making non-discrimination effective was the EU Racial Equality Directive (Council of the European Union, 2000). This puts forth a European principle of equal treatment irrespective of ethnic and racial origin which applies to all EU citizens regardless of their residence and citizenship. Most importantly, minority protection has become one of the fundamental values of the European Union following the consolidation of the Article 2 of the Treaty of Lisbon (EU, 2012).

The consistent engagement of international intergovernmental organisations in CEE since the start of the 1990s has made them key actors in the domestic and international politics of the region, ensuring that minority claims have become enmeshed in a *quadratic* rather than simply triadic nexus (Smith, 2002). These organisations have not only played an important role in persuading states to better accommodate their ethnocultural minority groups, but have also assisted and monitored such changes. As such, there was extensive discussion during the late 1990s and early 2000s as to whether this engagement would serve to moderate and transcend competing forms of nationalism in the region (Budryte, 2005; Jackson Preece, 2005; Kymlicka & Opalski, 2001). European minority rights standards were adopted in the 2000s by many countries eyeing a smooth accession to EU membership. This was hailed as a clear sign of democratisation and an indication of the successful, if modest, diffusion of liberal multiculturalism in the post-communist states (Kymlicka, 2007, pp. 3–25).

Nonetheless, the potential to promote new forms of sovereignty-sharing on the one hand, and to ensure a comprehensive protection of minorities on the other (Carrera et al., 2017) has been challenged by the absence of a normative framework, as well as by political developments preceding the Covid crisis. Bellamy and Kröger persuasively argue that the European Union has met the minimal conditions for discussing international cooperation as a matter of social and political justice (2019).[3] However, many forms of cross-border and inter-state cooperation, as well as the expansion of the EU citizenship regime, have been frustrated in recent years by the decreasing porosity of borders in the aftermath of the European financial crisis in 2008, compounded by the rise of virulent nationalism. Moreover, despite the EU's commitment to a principle of equality understood as equal opportunity to pursue one's life choices in a way that is consistent with one's cultural norms, the accommodation of cultural and linguistic diversity continues to be the exclusive duty of home-states. In effect, many scholars note that European integration has had only a minimal impact on the allocation and scope of a responsibility to protect ethnocultural minority groups. While it has facilitated inter-state cooperation, in reality it has only contributed to promoting an integrationist form of minority protection, albeit rooted in human rights and consistent with the liberal defence of individual freedom (Mabry, 2013), and to encouraging novel forms of cross-border cooperation (McGarry & O'Leary, 2013).

Defining the Limits of Kin-State Engagement

Measured in terms of its scope and institutional extent, the minority protection regime in post-Cold War Europe has arguably been a success. As already noted, however, in recent years it has been challenged by resurgent nationalism, leading to a multiplication of cases on all four areas of concern identified by the UNHR Office of the High Commissioner for minority groups (n.d.): (a) protecting a group's existence and survival (*e.g.* Aromanians in Romania*)*; (b) protecting and promoting the social and cultural identity of minority groups (*e.g.* ethnic Russians in Latvia*)*; (c) ensuring effective non-discrimination and equality (*e.g.* Roma in Romania and Hungary); and (d) safeguarding the effective participation of minority ethnocultural groups in public life (*e.g.* ethnic Serbs in Kosovo or ethnic Albanians in Macedonia).

Over the last three decades, the exclusive responsibility of home-states in relation to the protection of their minority groups has also been challenged by the multiplication in form and reach of kin-states' extra-territorial involvement, especially in CEE. Yet, it was only from 2001 that the relationship between kin-states and kin-minorities began to attract significant international attention. The catalyst for this was Hungary's Act LXII on Hungarians Living in the Neighbouring Countries (Hungarian Parliament, 2001). The terms of Act LXII were contested by governments in neighbouring Romania and Slovakia, which portrayed it as an infringement of their bilateral treaties with Hungary (Tomiuc, 2001). Specifically, the Official Position of the Romanian Government on the Act, submitted to the CoE's Venice Commission in 2001, claimed that Hungary's policy breached the principles of non-discrimination and subsidiarity in international law, as well as that of reciprocity enshrined in the bilateral treaties it had signed with the neighbouring countries. Most importantly, the main contention addressed the scope of the policy, which extended beyond the preservation of cultural and linguistic identity. Here, the report of the Romanian Government not only referred to those provisions which encourage labour migration and facilitate access to discounted or free transport, but also questioned the quasi-legal connection that the Certificate of Hungarian Ethnic Origin and Certificate for Dependents of Persons of Hungarian Nationality creates between Hungary and ethnic Hungarians who are both citizens and residents of neighbouring states (Romanian Government, 2001).

It was at the request of the Romanian Prime Minister Adrian Năstase and the Hungarian Minister of Foreign Affairs János Martonyi that the CoE's Venice Commission carried out its 2001 comparative evaluation of legislation and practices regarding states' preferential treatment towards their kin-minority groups (CoE, 2001). The report concludes that 'the emerging of new and original forms of minority protection, particularly by the kin-States, constitutes a positive trend insofar as they can contribute to the realisation of this goal' (Council of Europe [CoE], 2001, Section D). Rather than devising new standards and innovative mechanisms in this area, however, the report strengthened the principle of non-intervention in international relations, enforcing the relationship between citizenship, territory and rights. In this regard, a kin-state's engagement with its co-ethnics abroad has generally been accepted as legitimate in so far as: (a) it does not generate inter-state conflict; and (b) does not challenge the primary responsibility home-states bear in relation to their minority ethnocultural groups (Palermo, 2011). However, Palermo pointedly notes that in fact 'the legitimacy of kin-state policies largely depends on the context and on the practical effect in inter-state relations' (2011, p. 15). Even though the 2001 CoE report states that kin-state engagement should comply with the four principles of international relations—state territorial sovereignty; *pacta sunt servanda*; friendly relations amongst states; and the respect of human rights and fundamental freedoms (CoE, 2001)—it failed to harmonise the freedom to establish, maintain and develop ties within communities residing across different states—as defined in Article 17 of the Framework Convention for the Protection of National Minorities (CoE, 1995)—with the right of states to preserve their sovereignty (Palermo, 2011). Nevertheless, despite its shortcomings, the Report conferred normative significance to Hungary's Act LXII by placing it at the centre of the only comparative evaluation of the legitimacy of kin-state involvement carried out In Europe.

Since that time, other international organisations have become increasingly engaged in issues of minority—kin-state relations, most notably the Office of the OSCE High Commissioner on National Minorities (OSCE HCNM). which in 2008 issued its Bolzano/Bozen Recommendations on National Minorities in Inter-state Relations (OSCE HCNM, 2008). These Recommendations recognise that the well-being of national minority groups abroad may be an object of legitimate concern on the part of states to which such groups are linked by common ethnic, cultural, religious, or linguistic identity, or common cultural heritage (Rec 4). At the same time, the importance of inter-state cooperation is deemed essential, as these Recommendations are primarily an instrument of conflict prevention geared to preserving good neighbourly relations and peace (OSCE HCNM, 2008, pp. 1–2). However, the Recommendations not only enforce a home-state's exclusive responsibility for the protection of minority groups within their territories, but also attempt to define the limits of a kin-state's engagement: a kin-state's involvement can be limited if it undermines the integration of minority ethnocultural groups in their home-states.[4] In practice, the accommodation of national minority groups in inter-state relations is carried out by encouraging 'best practices' which remain highly contextualised and lack normative power (OSCE HCNM, n.d.).

Kin-states thus continue to operate in a very weak international legal environment, and consequently the capacity of international organisations to regulate a kin-state's engagement remains rather limited (Bloed & van Dijk, 1999; Huber & Mickey, 1999; Kemp et al., 2011; Kymlicka, 2007, pp. 3–25; Palermo, 2011; Tesser, 2015). The Bolzano/Bozen Recommendations may have made it at least somewhat 'more difficult for States to exploit and abuse legal and normative uncertainties surrounding the issue of kin-state activism and to justify their actions' (Sabanadze, 2009, p. 314). However, in so far as they do not impose legally binding obligations, they remain difficult to enforce if a state does not comply voluntarily. Moreover, while the Bolzano/Bozen Recommendations acknowledge common identity or heritage as minimal grounds for a legitimate interest on the part of an external state, they underestimate how this provides kin-state actors with scope to instrumentalise co-ethnics abroad in pursuit of domestic political legitimacy, a resolution of internal economic problems, or other external state policy objectives. In this respect, minorities' continued disenchantment with their home-states' policies of accommodation only increases space for manipulation by the kin-state.

Overall, then, the European minority rights regime has had only limited effectiveness when it comes to addressing issues of minority-kin state relations. Having failed to respond adequately and effectively to a new political reality defined by the existence of dual and often overlapping obligations assumed by home—and kin-states, it is now threatened by the increasing re-institutionalisation of virulent monocultural nationalism. Already prior to the 2008 financial crisis, various scholars argued convincingly that a kin-state's nationalism has a much stronger impact on the nature and extent of its engagement with its kin-minorities than do considerations of regional security or international norms (Jenne, 2004; Saideman, 2002; Waterbury, 2008). With the subsequent rise of ethnopopulism as a significant factor, kin-state policies have evolved in ways that further challenge any attempt to justify them as forms of minority protection.

Divergent Understandings of Engagement: Instrumentalisation vs. Kin-Minority Aspirations

As various examples testify, different forms of kin-state assistance are today instrumentalised for achieving goals which are at odds with the understanding and standards of minority protection.[5] *Karta Polaka* offers a case in point, as it is geared to strengthening Poland's ties with its co-ethnics abroad, and providing assistance largely within Poland's state borders (Polish Sejm, 2007). *Karta Polaka* has, moreover, been accompanied by legislation facilitating access to citizenship for ethnic Poles abroad, again within the borders of Poland. Increasingly conceived as a way of tackling a growing demographic crisis within the kin-state itself, this policy has encouraged long-term migration of ethnic Poles to Poland, rather than protecting their minority rights and supporting the promotion of Polish language and culture within their home states.[6]

Similar instrumentalist trends have been evident in Hungary since 2010, not least in the decision to extend full citizenship to Hungarians abroad. While this form of citizenship is extra-territorial rather than linked to residence in Hungary, securing a Hungarian passport has made it easier for ethnic Hungarians from neighbouring states (especially those in Ukraine and Serbia) to depart and seek work in Hungary or another EU state (Tátrai et al., 2017). In the Hungarian case, however, instrumentalisation has occurred against the background of a pre-existing system conferring extensive support to Hungarian minorities *in situ*, of which Act LXII of 2001 constitutes the cornerstone. Consequently, the post-2010 shift towards *passportisation* and efforts to recruit Hungarians abroad as a source of labour has led to a struggle within Hungary itself to re-define the aims and direction of its kin-state engagement (Tátrai et al., 2017).

The nature and extent of the two states' engagement also impacts on their institutional capacity to assume responsibility for minority protection. In the case of Poland, access to citizenship only offers its bearers, outside the territory of Poland, a right to diplomatic protection, a right to return and voting rights. By contrast, Hungary has developed and implemented long-term programmes to support its co-ethnics abroad in addition to the recently safeguarded rights of external citizenship, such as generous funding of culture and education offered to its co-ethnics abroad in their home countries, as well as economic development schemes targeting ethnic Hungarian entrepreneurs in the neighbouring countries (Kántor, 2014, 2019). Its trans-sovereign institutionalisation remains the most complex in Europe.

While Hungarian minority ethnocultural groups have generally welcomed the more active involvement of their kin-state, they have nevertheless continued to direct demands for political and/or social justice primarily towards their home-states. From interviews with Hungarian minority elites in Romania during 2015–2016, for instance, it was clear that most respondents saw responsibility for improving the accommodation of ethnocultural minority groups as lying exclusively or at least primarily with the home-state. At the same time, respondents saw cultural support from Hungary as highly beneficial in terms of supporting the well-being of Romania's Hungarian minority and consolidating and sustaining its distinct identity. For many, the award of extra-territorial citizenship by Hungary could be seen—at least potentially—as consistent with this agenda. As one elected Hungarian official in Romania observed:

> Hungarian citizenship is beneficial for Transylvanian Hungarians only if this is accompanied by programmes supporting remaining in the homeland. If this isn't there, then basically I think it does more harm than good. [...] [T]hat a Hungarian person can't live the same full life as a Romanian person. This is how I approach the question. ... [A] full life includes the ability to use our symbols, and the ability to use my language in administration and governance, and about having the same chance of getting a well-paid job as the other.[7]

Other recent studies of minority-kin state relations also testify to the complexities of identity and multiple belonging within Central and Eastern Europe, showing that a minority's identification with a culturally defined transnational community should not automatically be taken to imply a threat to the home state (Cheskin, 2015; Cheskin & Kachuyevski, 2019; Kallas, 2016; Waterbury and Lodzinski in this volume). Ethnic Hungarian respondents in Romania also pointed out that ties to an external kin state are already an established and non-controversial feature of various minority settings, citing examples ranging from South Tyrol to Quebec.[8] Another maintained that dual citizenship does not 'go against either Romanian laws or EU practice, because there are a lot of states that acknowledge [this] and encourage it'.[9]

Yet, whereas longer-standing EU member states have historically addressed kin-minority issues within a framework of meaningful inter-state cooperation, such an approach has been noticeably absent in contemporary CEE. Here, the sustained engagement by international organisations in the region since the 1990s has yet to dilute the logic of competition between states still structured according to the Westphalian logic of 'groups competing for the ownership of a territory' (Palermo, 2015, p. 29). The political manipulation of minority-kin-state links can be seen, for instance, in Romania's recent attempt to frame Hungary's kin-state support not as a complement to domestic policies of minority accommodation, but as a pretext for the home state to abdicate its own responsibilities in this area (Government of Romania, 2018, p. 16, fn 4). A further interview respondent in Romania conveyed the current state of affairs well by declaring that:

as long as the Transylvanian Hungarian community has been living as a minority, it has never before been in such a legally and politically consolidated position. ... The problem is that this consolidation is built on institutions that were created to a large extent with the support of Hungary. ... [and their] foundations ... are in sharp conflict with the Romanian concept of the nation-state.[10]

In seeking to redraw this political project along more pluralistic lines, respondents expressed little faith in the continued capacity of international organisations to influence the situation following Romania's entry to the EU in 2007.[11] Against this background, one referred to the 'confrontational' politics now pursued by the Hungarian government at the European level and its unwillingness to 'open new fronts with the Romanians', claiming that no meeting of the intergovernmental commission had been called for a number of years.[12] There were further allusions to the lack of extra-territorial support actually provided by the kin-state, including the limited practical value of obtaining Hungarian citizenship. Here, one respondent observed that 'Hungarian national politics went for quantity, how many citizenships it can boast,' rather than paying attention to the actual quality of support provided in situ for the kin minority.[13] The Hungarian government was thus called upon to: 'fill citizenship with substance, so that there are advantages too. Advantages that can be enjoyed here in the homeland without going to Budapest.'[14]

Overall, while respondents clearly welcomed direct support from the kin-state in different areas, many were conscious of a growing instrumentalization of kin minority issues by a Hungarian government which 'regards [the entire transborder Hungarian population] as a diaspora, so a multitude of Hungarian individuals who live beyond the borders, and not as a community that lives in its historical homeland and is supported in this'.[15] Within this context, the Hungarian citizenship extended after 2011 was not understood as a complement to a (primary) Romanian citizenship embracing Hungarians within a pluralistic political community: in so far as it was ascribed anything other than symbolic value, it was seen as something that might help to consolidate Hungarian identity in the face of a nationalising home state and mobilise the local community behind claims for autonomy.[16] Given the many different views within the community on the desirability and utility of obtaining Hungarian citizenship, one academic respondent argued for a fuller and more open public debate regarding the extent and scope of Hungary's trans-sovereign engagement, yet noted that the dominant political discourse allowed little space for this.[17]

Conclusion: Moving Beyond the *Status Quo*

In parallel to and aided by European integration, we have witnessed an expansion in the cross-border political and social institutionalisation of the ties between kin-states and their co-ethnics abroad in the last decade, which has strengthened their mutual interdependence. The existence of dual and overlapping obligations vis-à-vis members of ethnocultural minority groups, reinforced by the strengthening of the ties between a kin-state and its co-ethnics abroad, raises the following question: Can the responsibility for minority protection be shared fairly between a home-state and a kin-state?

According to Nollkaemper, sharing responsibility is a novel practice in international law which has been welcome in the global governance of peace-keeping, climate change, migration and conservation of natural resources. Generally, it is intended to address responsibility gaps in situations in which inter-state cooperation has already been agreed

(Nollkaemper, 2018). In political theory, conceptions of shared responsibility have been widely discussed in relation to German collective guilt for the atrocities perpetrated during the Second World War (Arendt, 1963) and, more recently, regarding the allocation of responsibility for global poverty (O'Neill, 2016; Young, 2011). Young argues that the responsibility for structural processes that have unjust outcomes extends beyond a state's borders and it is collective as well as personal in that we all participate in those processes that produce and perpetuate harm (Young, 2011, pp. 95–122). More specifically, O'Neill argues that the (home-)statist approach that dominates discussions on the allocation of responsibility for justice fails to value the potential of other agents to contribute to justice and to define their involvement in terms of *justiciable rights* (O'Neill, 2016, pp. 151–192). Owen highlights the ground-breaking normative importance of the commitment already assumed by the international community to share the responsibility for capacity-building and disposition-building in relation to human rights (Owen, 2018). Yet, despite the persuasiveness of such accounts and the highlighted benefits of sharing responsibility, international law continues to affirm the centrality of the principle of independent responsibility of states and international organisations (Nollkaemper, 2018).

In our view, the potential of sharing responsibility between a kin-state and home-state merits serious consideration, as a means of limiting the instrumentalisation of a kin-state's engagement and strengthening its commitment to protecting co-ethnics abroad as members of indigenous minority groups. We endorse the principle of sovereignty and, in line with the European commitment to full and effective equality, assert that home-states have the primary duty to achieve equality of citizenship, as well as one to fairly accommodate their internal cultural and linguistic diversity. However, consistent with the Bolzano/Bozen Recommendations, we also acknowledge and build upon the assertion that kin-states have a legitimate interest in their co-ethnics abroad which is often found articulated in their domestic legislation as a duty of care.[18] Building on these, we propose a re-articulation of the relationship between a kin-state and its co-ethnics abroad in the following way:

> a. A kin-state's engagement with its co-ethnics abroad is legitimate, as long as it contributes to their protection as members of minority ethno-cultural groups in their home-states.

As shown in the first section of this paper, the norms and practices of minority protection in Europe have been made consistent with liberalism's central view that membership in a state generates legitimate demands for political, social and cultural justice. *Prima facie* the nature and extent of a kin-state's engagement with its co-ethnics abroad suggests that its duty of care, if viewed as responsibility for justice, is generally stronger than its human rights duties, but weaker than that owed by a state to its (resident) citizens. Even though the trans-sovereign scope of a kin-state's responsibility suggests some empirical similarity to cosmopolitan models of justice, the nature of its obligations and the importance conferred to common belonging as national membership brings it closer to liberal nationalism. The obligations tied to citizenship remain special: they only extend to those who are members (and residents), and their nature and scope are determined by the social and political arrangements in a specific country, which often differ from one to another (Dworkin, 2005; Sangiovanni, 2007). For liberal nationalists the sense of common belonging defined by membership in a nation-state is necessary for realising political and social justice (Miller, 2007; Tamir, 1993). Distinctively, however, a kin-state's obligations are generated by common ethno-cultural membership, they are different in nature and scope than those of kin-state citizenship, but overlap with those of home-state citizenship.

Consequently, we suggest that in order to be consistent with the allocation and extent of a liberal state's commitment to social and political justice and to accommodate its linguistic and cultural diversity, and at the same time, to enhance home-states' cultural duties, shared responsibility for minority protection needs to be tied to an idea of complementarity between a kin-state's engagement and home-states' multiculturalism. However, this would require, as a minimum, cooperation rather than competition between the states involved, as well as converging notions of fairness in relation to the accommodation of ethnocultural minority groups. Complementarity may strengthen a home-state's responsibility towards its non-dominant ethnocultural groups, but it would also allow kin-states to intervene when home-states fail to meet their commitments and/or lack the financial capacity to fulfil them, such as in the case of ethnic Hungarians in Romania and Ukraine.[19] Therefore, we suggest the following:

b. Home-states have the primary duty to achieve full and effective equality between their citizens, as well as one to accommodate fairly their internal cultural and linguistic diversity. A kin-state's engagement whether in the form of direct assistance or political pressure on behalf of its co-ethnics abroad should complement home-states' domestic commitments to cultural justice.

The main obstacles to articulating an understanding of shared responsibility for minority protection between a kin-state and home-state consistent with the liberal egalitarianism advocated by the EU and the norms governing inter-state relations in Europe are: the existence of competing notions of fairness in relation to minority protection[20] and the securitisation of certain minority groups in inter-state relations, such as the Hungarian minority in Romania in the early 1990s or the Russian minorities in Ukraine and the Baltic states. Different institutional designs alter the relations between a citizen and state, and hence they generate different notions of fairness (Bellamy & Kröger, 2019; Sangiovanni, 2007). For example, the social and political institutions in CEE and beyond remain strongly embedded in the history of minority-majority relations, the history of the relations between kin-state and kin-minority groups, different institutionalisation of multiculturalism, and most importantly, a political context in which nationalism was (re-) institutionalised and, in many cases, is being diffused beyond the kin-states' borders.

This securitisation of the relations between states and kin-minority groups has strongly shaped the accommodation of minority ethnocultural groups in CEE following the collapse of communism. Scholarship in this area highlights the fact that minority political mobilisation has been seen as a 'subversive tendency challenging the dominant architecture of the [nation-] state system', rather than something associated with 'positive conceptions of what justice and democracy require' (Bauböck, 2000, pp. 12–13). Furthermore, it has been stressed that the existence of a kin-state which actively engages with its kin-minority groups often leads to the internationalisation of domestic disputes (Roter, 2011). As a result, the existence of minority groups in Europe whose accommodation remains securitised impedes not only inter-state cooperation, but, as Kymlicka convincingly shows, also weakens any attempts at internationalising minority rights as a matter of justice: 'security fears have driven out considerations of justice, distorting decisions about both categories and conditions, with results that are detrimental not only to justice, but also, paradoxically, for security' (Kymlicka, 2007, p. 9).

A norm of complementarity which is not only consistent with the norms and standards of minority protection and strengthens the liberal commitments of home-states towards their citizens, but also aims to allocate fairly the responsibility for minority protection should at the very least mark the limits of a kin-state's engagement also by strengthening the voice of minority ethnocultural groups and ensuring their participation in inter-state decision-making. Minorities' own perspectives on their relations with kin-states and how the latter might potentially support their accommodation within the home state are all too often overlooked.

Acknowledgements

Earlier versions of this paper were presented at the conference 'Poland's Kin-state Policies: Opportunities and Challenges' (University of Warsaw, May 2019), and the workshops 'Polish Studies: Today and Tomorrow' (UCL SSEES, September 2019) and 'Integration in a Transnational World: Poland, Scotland and Polish Communities Abroad' (House for An Art Lover, Glasgow, November 2019). The authors would like to thank the participants for their comments which benefited our research. The authors' special gratitude is reserved to Zsuzsa Csergő, Sherrill Stroschein, Karl Cordell and the anonymous reviewer for their insightful comments and advice.

Funding

The work for this article was mainly supported by the project 'Poland's kin-state policies: Opportunities and Challenges' (pomp.com.pl/en/programy-2017/polands-kin-state-policies-opportunities-and-challenges/ - administered under University of Glasgow project code 300460-01), but partly also by the project 'National Minority Rights and Democratic Political Community' (ES/L007126/1).

Notes

1. The research for this article was partly supported by the Economic and Social Research Council (ESRC) under grant number ES/L007126/1. All references to interviews found below are taken from the dataset from this ESRC project (Smith, 2020b).
2. Henrard stresses that in contrast to the UN Declaration, the framework 'is a Convention and hence legally binding on the contracting states, but it cannot be denied that the wording of the Convention leaves considerable discretion to the states' (2008, p. 94).
3. Bellamy and Kröger substantiate this point by showing that the acceptance of the idea of differentiated integration has substantially changed the nature of inter-state cooperation between the EU member-states. The empirical conditions that allow to apply principles of social and political justice to different forms of cooperation in the EU are: the existence of political community created by the EU citizenship policy, the increased inter-state cooperation in all sectors, and the deepening of cross-border cooperation which created the possibility to accommodate capacity and sovereignty concerns and might lead, or has already led, to institutional harmonisation (Bellamy & Kröger, 2019).
4. The Bolzano/Bozen Recommendations only offer a sociological understanding of integration rather than a normative one. Integration appears to be synonymous with social cohesion. An attempt to put forth a definition of integration can be found in the Ljubljana Guidelines on Integration of Diverse Societies (OSCE HCNM, 2012, Introduction):

Integration is a dynamic, multi-actor process of mutual engagement that facilitates effective participation by all members of a diverse society in the economic, political, social and cultural life, and fosters a shared and inclusive sense of belonging at national and local levels.

5. The most marked instance of this can be seen in efforts by states (*e.g.* Russia, Romania, or Serbia) to strengthen their regional power by using their ties with co-ethnics abroad to engage in overt or hybrid intervention.
6. See Pudzianowska in this volume.
7. Interview with Mayor of Sfântu Gheorghe/ Szentgyörgy, 25 April 2016. ROM-1.1.1 in Smith (2020).
8. Interview with member of Hungarian People's Party of Transylvania, Sfântu Gheorghe/ Szentgyörgy, 25 April 2016. ROM-1.1.3 in Smith (2020b).
9. Interview with member of Democratic Union of Hungarians in Romania, Cluj-Napoca/ Kolozsvár/ Klausenburg, 14 October 2015. ROM-1.3.2 in Smith (2020b).
10. Interview with member of Political Science Department, Babeş-Bolyai University, Cluj-Napoca/ Kolozsvár/ Klausenburg, 12 October 2015. ROM-2.2.3 in Smith (2020b).
11. Interview with Mayor of Sfântu Gheorghe/ Szentgyörgy, 25 April 2016. ROM-1.1.1 in Smith (2020); Interview with member of Democratic Union of Hungarians in Romania, Cluj-Napoca/ Kolozsvár/ Klausenburg, 13 October 2015. ROM-1.3.3 in Smith (2020b).
12. Interview with member of Hungarian National Council of Transylvania and Hungarian People's Party of Transylvania, Miercurea Ciuc (Csíkszereda), 27 April 2016. ROM-1.2.3 in Smith (2020b).
13. Interview with President of Hungarian People's Party of Transylvania, Cluj-Napoca/ Kolozsvár/ Klausenburg, 12 October 2015. ROM-1.3.5 in Smith (2020b).
14. Interview with President of Hungarian People's Party of Transylvania, Cluj-Napoca/ Kolozsvár/ Klausenburg, 12 October 2015. ROM-1.3.5 in Smith (2020b).
15. Interview with Associate Professor, Babeş-Bolyai University, Cluj-Napoca/ Kolozsvár/ Klausenburg, 16 October 2015. ROM-2.2.1 in Smith (2020b).
16. Interview with researcher at the Romanian Institute for Research on National Minorities, Cluj-Napoca/ Kolozsvár/ Klausenburg, 14 October 2015. ROM-2.2.2 in Smith (2020b).The implication here was that autonomy could only be achieved by local community leaders themselves, with another respondent observing that Hungary supported autonomy only 'declaratively' (Interview with Associate Professor, Babeş-Bolyai University, Cluj-Napoca/ Kolozsvár/ Klausenburg), 16 October 2015. ROM-2.2.1 in Smith (2020b).
17. Interview with member of Department of Social Sciences, Sapientia University, Miercurea Ciuc/ Csíkszereda, 27 April 2016. ROM-2.1.1 in Smith (2020b).
18. For example, Article 6.2 of the Constitution of the Republic of Poland (1997) states that '[t]he Republic of Poland shall provide assistance to Poles living abroad to maintain their links with the national cultural heritage' (Polish Sejm, 1997). Article D of the Fundamental Law of Hungary defines its kin-state duty of care in the following way: '[the constitution is] motivated by the ideal of a unified Hungarian nation, Hungary shall bear a sense of responsibility for the destiny of Hungarians living outside her borders' (National Assembly, 2011).
19. For example, the most recent report of the Advisory Committee on the Framework Convention for the Protection of National Minorities [FCNM] highlights that financial support of the Romanian state allocated for the preservation and promotion of the cultures of national minorities remains limited (Advisory Committee on FCNM, 2017, Art. 5). However, this report fails to acknowledge that education and culture remain chronically underfunded in Romania, and to discuss this issue in the broader context, for example of the overall quality of primary and secondary education in Romania (see World Bank, 2007).
20. Observe, for instance, the differing interpretations of minority rights put forward by Hungary and Romania during the signing of the 1996 bilateral treaty between the two states, specifically in relation to the CoE Parliamentary Assembly Recommendation (1201/1993) for an Additional Protocol to the European Convention on Human Rights (Salat, 2014, p. 133).

ORCID

Andreea Udrea ⓘ http://orcid.org/0000-0002-3763-5216
David Smith ⓘ http://orcid.org/0000-0002-3346-3824

References

Advisory Committee on the Framework Convention for the Protection of National Minorities. (2017, June 22). *Fourth opinion on Romania.* https://www.coe.int/en/web/minorities/romania

Arendt, H. (1963). *Eichmann in Jerusalem. A report on the banality of evil.* Penguin Books.

Bauböck, R. (2000, May). *Political community beyond the sovereign state. Supranational federalism and transnational minorities* (ICE Working Paper No. 7). Vienna: Austrian Academy of Sciences.

Bellamy, R., & Kröger, S. (2019). *Differentiated integration as a fair scheme of cooperation.* Robert Schuman Centre for Advanced Studies Research Paper, 2019/27. https://ssrn.com/abstract=3373593

Bloed, A., & van Dijk, P. (1999). Bilateral treaties: A new landmark in minority protection; an introduction. In A. Bloed & P. van Dijk (Eds.), *Protection of minority rights through bilateral treaties. The case of Central and Eastern Europe* (pp. 1–15). Kluwer Law International.

Brubaker, R. (1996). *Nationalism reframed: Nationhood and the national question in the New Europe.* Cambridge University Press.

Budryte, D. (2005). *Taming nationalism?: Political community building in the Post-Soviet Baltic states.* Ashgate.

Carrera, S., Vosyliūtė, L., Guild, E., & Bard, P. (2017). *Towards a comprehensive EU protection system for minorities.* https://www.ceps.eu/ceps-publications/towards-comprehensive-eu-protection-system-minorities/

Cheskin, A. (2015). Identity and integration of Russian speakers in the Baltic States: A framework for analysis. *Ethnopolitics, 14*(1), 72–93. https://doi.org/10.1080/17449057.2014.933051

Cheskin, A., & Kachuyevski, A. (2019). The Russian-speaking populations in the post-Soviet space: Language, politics and identity. *Europe-Asia Studies, 71*(1), 1–23. https://doi.org/10.1080/09668136.2018.1529467

Council of Europe. (1995, February). *Framework convention for the protection of national minorities and explanatory note.* https://rm.coe.int/16800c10cf

Council of Europe. (2001, October 22). *Report on the preferential treatment of national minorities by their kin-states.* https://www.venice.coe.int/webforms/documents/?pdf=CDL-INF(2001)019-e

Council of the European Union. (2000, June 29). *Council Directive 2000/43/EC of 29 June 2000 implementing the principle of equal treatment between persons irrespective of racial or ethnic origin.* https://eur-lex.europa.eu/legal-content/en/TXT/?uri=CELEX%3A32000L0043

Dworkin, R. (2005). *Taking rights seriously* (first published 1977). Duckworth.

European Union. (2012, October 26). Consolidated version of the treaty on European Union. *Official Journal of the European Union, 326/13.* https://eur-lex.europa.eu/resource.html?uri=cellar:2bf140bf-a3f8-4ab2-b506-fd71826e6da6.0023.02/DOC_1&format=PDF

Government of Romania. (2001, August 21). *The official position of the Romanian Government on the Law on Hungarians living in the neighbouring countries.* https://www.venice.coe.int/webforms/documents/?pdf=CDL(2001)081-e

Government of Romania. (2018, February 16). *Comments of the Government of Romania on the fourth opinion of the advisory committee on the implementation of the framework convention for the protection of national minorities by Romania.* https://www.coe.int/en/web/minorities/news/-/asset_publisher/d4ZbHbFMMxCR/content/romania-publication-of-the-4th-advisory-committee-opinion

Henrard, K. A. M. (2008). The added value of the framework convention for the protection of national minorities; the two pillars of an adequate system of minority protection revisited. In A. Verstichel, A. Allen, B. De Witte, & P. Lemmens (Eds.), *The framework convention for the protection of national minorities: A useful pan-European instrument?* (pp. 91–118). Intersentia.

Huber, K., & Mickey, R. W. (1999). Defining the kin-state: An analysis of its role and prescriptions for moderating its impact. In A. Bloed & P. van Dijk (Eds.), *Protection of minority rights through bilateral treaties. The case of Central and Eastern Europe* (pp. 17–51). Kluwer Law International.

Hungarian Parliament. (2001, June 19). *Act LXII on Hungarians living in the neighbouring countries.* https://www.refworld.org/docid/3f460e764.html

Jackson Preece, J. (1998). *National minorities and the European nation-states system.* Clarendon Press.

Jackson Preece, J. (2005). *Minority rights. Between diversity and community.* Polity.

Jenne, E. (2004). A bargaining theory of minority demands: Explaining the dog that did not bite in 1990s Yugoslavia. *International Studies Quarterly, 48*(4), 729–754. https://doi.org/10.1111/j.0020-8833.2004.00323.x

Jenne, E. (2018). Is nationalism or ethnopopulism on the rise today? *Ethnopolitics, 17*(5), 546–552. https://doi.org/10.1080/17449057.2018.1532635

Kallas, K. (2016). Claiming the diaspora: Russia's compatriot policy and its reception by Estonian-Russian population." *Journal of Ethnopolitics and Minority Issues in Europe, 15*(3), 1–25.

Kántor, Z. (2014). Hungary's kin-state policies, 2010–2014. *Minority Research, 17*, 23–32. https://www.ceeol.com/search/article-detail?id=516058

Kántor, Z. (2019, May 23–24). *What is between the goals and the outcome of diaspora policy?* Presentation at the conference 'Poland's Kin-state Policies: Opportunities and Challenges', University of Warsaw.

Kemp, W., Popovski, V., & Thakur, R. (Eds.). (2011). *Blood and borders. The responsibility to protect and the problem of the kin-state.* United Nations UP.

Kymlicka, W. (2007). *Multicultural Odysseys. Navigating the new international politics of diversity.* Oxford UP.

Kymlicka, W., & Opalski, M. (Eds.). (2001). *Can liberal pluralism be exported? Western political theory and ethnic relations in Eastern Europe.* Oxford UP.

Mabry, T. J. (2013). Forked tongues: The language politics of divided nations. In T. J. Mabry, J. McGarry, M. Moore, & B. O'Leary (Eds.), *Divided nations and European integration* (pp. 55–88). University of Pennsylvania Press.

Marko, J. (2018). Introduction. In J. Marko & S. Constantin (Eds.), *Human and minority rights protection by multiple diversity governance* (pp. 1–11). Routledge.

Mavelli, L. (2018). Citizenship for sale and the neoliberal political economy of belonging. *International Studies Quarterly.* https://doi.org/10.1093/isq/sqy004

McGarry, J., & O'Leary, B. (2013). Conclusion: The exaggerated impact of European integration on the politics of divided nations. In T. J. Mabry, J. McGarry, M. Moore, & B. O'Leary (Eds.), *Divided nations and European integration* (pp. 341–391). University of Pennsylvania Press.

Miller, D. (2007). *National responsibility and global justice.* Oxford University Press.

National Assembly. (2011, April 25). *The fundamental law of Hungary.* https://www.kormany.hu/download/e/02/00000/The%20New%20Fundamental%20Law%20of%20Hungary.pdf

Nollkaemper, A. (2018). The duality of shared responsibility. *Contemporary Politics, 24*(5), 524–544. https://doi.org/10.1080/13569775.2018.1452107

O'Neill, O. (2016). *Justice across boundaries. Whose obligations?* Cambridge University Press.

O'Neill, S. (2000). Cultural justice and the demands of equal citizenship: The parading dispute in Northern Ireland. *Theoria: A Journal of Social and Political Theory, 96*(December), 27–51. https://doi.org/10.3167/004058100782485684

OSCE High Commissioner on National Minorities. (2008, June). *The Bolzano/Bozen recommendations on national minorities in inter-state relations and explanatory note.* https://www.osce.org/hcnm/bolzano-bozen-recommendations

OSCE High Commissioner on National Minorities. (2012, November). *The Ljubljana guidelines on integration of diverse societies.* https://www.osce.org/hcnm/ljubljana-guidelines

OSCE High Commissioner on National Minorities. (n.d.). *What we do.* https://www.osce.org/hcnm/107875

Owen, D. (2018). Refugees and responsibilities of justice. *Global Justice: Theory Practice Rhetoric, 11*(1), 23–44. https://doi.org/10.21248/gjn.11.1.141

Palermo, F. (2011). National minorities in inter-state relations: Filling the legal vacuum? In F. Palermo & N. Sabanadze (Eds.), *National minorities in inter-state relations* (pp. 3–27). Martinus Nijhoff Publishers.

Palermo, F. (2015). Owned or shared? Territorial autonomy in the minority discourse. In T. Malloy & F. Palermo (Eds.), *Minority accommodation through territorial and non-territorial autonomy* (pp. 13–32). Oxford UP.

Polish Sejm. (1997, April 2). *The constitution of the Republic of Poland.* https://www.sejm.gov.pl/prawo/konst/angielski/kon1.htm

Polish Sejm. (2007, September 7). *Ustawa z dnia 7 września 2007 r. o Karcie Polaka.* http://prawo.sejm.gov.pl/isap.nsf/DocDetails.xsp?id=WDU20180001272

Roter, P. (2011). Minorities, states and international security: The contribution of the Bolzano/Bozen recommendations to managing the 'minority problem'. In F. Palermo & N. Sabanadze (Eds.), *National minorities in inter-state relations* (pp. 45–61). Martinus Nijhoff Publishers.

Sabanadze, N. (2009). The Bolzano recommendations on national minorities in inter-state relations: Reconciling justice and security. *Security and Human Rights, 20*(4), 307–317. https://doi.org/10.1163/187502309789894820

Saideman, S. M. (2002). Discrimination in international relations: Analysing external support for ethnic groups. *Journal of Peace Research, 39*(1), 27–50. https://doi.org/10.1177/0022343302039001002

Salat, L. (2014). The chances of ethnic autonomy in Romania – between theory and practice. In Z. Kántor (Ed.), *Autonomies in Europe: Solutions and challenges* (pp. 123–140). L'Harmattan.

Sangiovanni, A. (2007). Justice and the priority of politics to morality. *The Journal of Political Philosophy, 16*(2), 1–28. https://doi.org/10.1111/j.1467-9760.2007.00291.x

Smith, D. J. (2002). Framing the national question in Central and Eastern Europe: A quadratic nexus? *Global Review of Ethnopolitics*, *2*(1), 3–16. https://doi.org/10.1080/14718800208405119

Smith, D. J. (2020a). The "Quadratic Nexus" revisited: Nation-building in estonia through the prism of national cultural autonomy. *Nationalities Papers*, *48*(2), 235–250. https://doi.org/10.1017/nps.2018.38

Smith, D. J. (2020b). *Elite and expert interviews on non-territorial autonomy practices in Central and Eastern Europe 2014–2017* [Data Collection]. Colchester, Essex: UK Data Archive. 10.5255/UKDA-SN-852375.

Smith, D. J., & Hiden, J. (2012). *Ethnic diversity and the nation state: National cultural autonomy revisited.* Routledge.

Stroschein, S. (2019). Populism, nationalism, and party politics. *Nationalities Papers*, *47*(6), 923–935. https://doi.org/10.1017/nps.2019.91

Tamir, Y. (1993). *Liberal nationalism.* Princeton University Press.

Tátrai, P., Erőss Á., & Kovály, K. (2017). Kin-state politics stirred by a geopolitical conflict: Hungary's growing activity in post-Euromaidan Transcarpathia, Ukraine. *Hungarian Geographical Bulletin*, *66*(3), 203–218. https://doi.org/10.15201/hungeobull.66.3.2

Tesser, L. M. (2015). Europe's pivotal peace projects: Ethnic separation and European integration. *European Policy Analysis*, *2015*(6), 1–23. http://www.sieps.se/en/publications/2015/europes-pivotal-peace-projects-ethnic-separation-and-european-integration-20156epa/

Tomiuc, E. (2001, October 4). Hungary: Status law causing dispute with neighbours. *Radio Free Europe/ Radio Liberty.* https://www.rferl.org/a/1097612.html

Udrea, A. (2011). *Culture, history, and a kin-state's obligations: A liberal evaluation of the Hungarian status law* (Doctoral dissertation). University College London.

Udrea, A. (2014). A kin-state's responsibility: Cultural identity, recognition, and the Hungarian status law. *Ethnicities*, *14*(2), 324–346. https://doi.org/10.1177/1468796812472145

UN General Assembly. (1966, December 16). *International covenant on civil and political rights.* https://www.ohchr.org/en/professionalinterest/pages/ccpr.aspx

UN General Assembly. (1992, December 18). *Declaration on the rights of persons belonging to national or ethnic, religious and linguistic minorities.* https://www.ohchr.org/en/professionalinterest/pages/minorities.aspx

UNHR Office of the High Commissioner for Minority Groups. (n.d.). *International standards.* https://www.ohchr.org/EN/Issues/Minorities/SRMinorities/Pages/standards.aspx

Waterbury, M. A. (2008). Uncertain norms, unintended consequences: The effects of European Union integration on kin-state politics in Eastern Europe. *Ethnopolitics*, *7*(2), 217–238. https://doi.org/10.1080/17449050701413427

World Bank. (2007). *Romania. Education policy note.* http://siteresources.worldbank.org/INTROMANIA/Resources/EducationPolicyNote.pdf

Young, I. M. (2011). *Responsibility for justice.* Oxford UP.

The Polish Minority in Germany: Marginal or Marginalised?

KARL CORDELL

ABSTRACT This paper commences with some general observations on Poland's kin-state policy followed by an analysis of that element of kin-state policy concerned with the Polish minority in Germany. The paper argues that the recent invigoration of kin-state politics cannot be viewed in isolation from wider global political trends. Rather it contends that this increased concern with the fate of claimed ethnic kin is part of a wider trend towards the privileging of identity politics. It is further argued that in turn this impulse is located within the growth of populism, the celebration of parochialism, anti-globalisation sentiment and Euroscepticism, all of which have been fuelled by the financial crash of 2007/2008. The paper concludes by pointing to a paradox between the pursuit of policies that seek to prioritise ethnic identification with a kin-state and the commitment of member-states of the European Union to ever-closer union among the peoples of Europe.

Introduction

Since Poland commenced its transition from communism in the late 1980s, successive administrations have played an active role in cultivating links between Poland and the Polish diaspora. In terms of its geographic spread, this diaspora is global in character, with particular concentrations in the USA, the UK and Germany. Overwhelmingly, taking into account a caveat with regard to Germany (see below) and given the passing of the wartime generation, the majority of the diaspora consists of economic migrants and their descendants, together with the children and grandchildren of refugees. Within this latter context, a particularly emotive issue is that of the Polish diaspora that lives on the territory of the former Soviet Union and as such is formed of two overlapping sub-groups. A handful of (willing) migrants to one side, this element of the diaspora is comprised of a tiny number of survivors of the mass deportations to the Soviet Union that occurred between 1939 and 1953.[1] More numerous are their descendants and the descendants of ethnic Poles deported in successive waves to the Russian/Soviet hinterland by the imperial regime and its communist successors from territory ruled by Moscow at various dates prior to 1939. They reside primarily in northern Russia, Siberia, Kazakhstan and Uzbekistan: in other words, the areas to which they or their ancestors were deported. In addition, ethnic Poles continue to reside within the territory of the second Polish Republic annexed by the Soviet Union in 1939, and which now forms part of the state territory of Lithuania, Belarus and Ukraine. After years of neglect and denial on the part of the communist regimes in Warsaw and Moscow, relations between this small and ageing group of people and the Polish state are governed by the *Karta Polaka* of 2007 and its subsequent iterations. The *Karta* affords them access to services provided by the Polish state, for example in the fields of health and education, which would normally be denied to non-citizens/residents. In other words, post-communist Polish governments have sought to ease the situation of a section of Polish society whose lives were blighted by the Molotov-Ribbentrop Pact of 1939 and its myriad consequences.

As stated above, and by way of contrast, the Polish diaspora in the USA and the UK, which unlike Polish communities in the former Soviet Union forms part of the wider *Polonia*,[2] is overwhelmingly comprised of economic migrants and their descendants. The Polish minority in the UK also has a different demographic structure to that of its US counterpart. Indeed, concerns among the 'indigenous population' over the rapid growth of the Polish minority in the UK since 2004 together with the arrival of other economic migrants from European Union (EU)-member-states was crucial in securing victory for British populists in the 2016 referendum on the UK's continued membership of the EU. With regard to the Polish minority/community in Germany, the situation is more opaque, and for many Poles, it is of particular concern and (historic) grievance. To be sure, there are large numbers of clearly self-defined ethnically Polish migrants who in recent years, like their counterparts in the UK, have taken advantage of freedom of movement among EU member-states in order to improve their life chances and those of their children. However, by way of complication, there also exist the descendants of other Polish citizens, whose identification with and relationship to the Polish state is not particularly clear-cut. For example, in and around Berlin and the Ruhr, in particular, live people who are clearly partly of Polish extraction. They are descended from migrants who arrived in Germany at various times during the nineteenth century, as Germany began its transition from political fragmentation and economic backwardness to political unification and economic might. The extent to which the descendants of such migrants see themselves as being Polish is open to question and interpretation.

To return to the main narrative, an even thornier issue surrounds the circumstances under which following the partitions of Poland during the late eighteenth century and the coincidental but simultaneous dissemination of the doctrine of nationalism, some Poles came to assume a German identity or even a dual Polish-German identity. In the wake of the partitions of 1772, 1793 and 1795, territory that had previously been part of the Polish-Lithuanian Commonwealth was annexed by Prussia. This change of sovereignty did not necessarily imply any loss of status or indeed the change of identity upon the part of the aristocracy. However, Prussian annexation of Polish state territory occurred during a period of particularly turbulent socio-economic change and the beginnings of the creation of a new type of state, the nation-state. For successive Prussian monarchs, who may be best described as enlightened rulers with despotic tendencies from 1813 the ultimate prize was to create a modern, united and prosperous Prussian-led German nation-state (Cyran, 1993). Prussian nation and state-building elites were never able to reconcile their imperial pretentions with their desire to create a German nation-state. However, they did attempt in a typically blunt manner to endow the peasantry and the embryonic working class with a single, namely German national consciousness. With regard to this objective, they did not differentiate between their German-speaking subjects and their newly acquired Polish-speaking/

West Slavic subjects.[3] This of course brought both Prussia and Germany into conflict with the nascent Polish national movement and its adherents, with the net result becoming a contest for hearts and minds that resulted in an indeterminate number of Polish-speaking Prussian subjects/German citizens undergoing a consciousness shift. This was particularly true with regard to the (descendants of) the huge numbers of Poles who migrated to the Ruhr and Berlin as the pace of modernisation and industrialisation increased in Germany.

During the period of partition (1772–1918), explicitly anti-Polish assimilatory strategies were employed, particularly by successive Prussian regimes, often within the context of the wider *Kulturkampf* c1872–c1886.[4] Numerous examples of the policy's constituent elements abound. Prior to 1830, the situation was comparatively relaxed, given that the somewhat novel national principle had only recently come to form the ultimate *raison d'état*. However, within the context of a process of Prussian led, German nation-state building and in the wake of the 1830 uprising (in Russian ruled Poland), Polish lost its legal standing in the courts and public sphere. In the late nineteenth century, legislation was passed in Prussia and later Germany as a whole that for example, banned Polish as a language of pedagogic instruction. Such legislation was complemented by a process of forced migration that occurred between 1885 and 1890, when around 30,000 Polish subjects of the Austrian and Russian empires were expelled from imperial Germany, presumably on grounds of what would now be called 'state security' (Struve, 2000, pp. 50–65). In addition, in an echo of the Plantation strategy applied to Ireland in the sixteenth and seventeenth centuries by Elizabeth I of England and James I of England and VI of Scotland, between 1886 and 1918, the Prussian Settlement Commission sought to Germanize eastern Germany. It did so by encouraging the migration of ethnic Germans from other parts of Germany, with grants of land and start-up loans.[5] Unsurprisingly, given the overall lack of industrial and commercial development in the areas concerned, this policy was something of a failure. Few migrants were attracted to this economically backward area and many such migrants re-migrated to Germany alongside Poles who sought work above all in the booming Ruhr and greater Berlin regions. Ironically and unsurprisingly, the aforementioned anti-Polish measures had the effect of promoting Polish national consciousness among the poorest sections of society for whom national identification had previously been solely within the remit of the aristocracy (Zamoyski, 2009, pp. 189–217).

Many Poles who migrated to Germany did therefore identify with the nugatory Polish nation. They began to organise themselves in a number of ways. For example, the League of Poles in Germany (LPN) was founded in Bochum in 1894. Banks such as the [Polish] Workers' Bank and assorted sports clubs also sprang into existence. By 1922 when the all-embracing, Union of Poles in Germany (ZPN) was founded, it was claimed that around 1.5 million Poles were resident in Germany. A year later, the ZPN had a claimed membership of around 35,000 (Berghahn, 2004). The year 1922 is doubly significant for our purposes as it also marks the entering into force of the Statute of Autonomy for those parts of Upper Silesia that continued to be ruled from Berlin following the partition of the overall territory in 1921. As the next section shows, the failure of the Federal Republic to revive this statute is a major cause of friction between Berlin and Warsaw. Returning to the question of overall numbers, it is difficult to discern from the perspective of 2019 just how accurate the aforementioned figures are and the extent to which Polish migrants had affinity with the newly-emergent Polish nation-state. In the inter-war German censuses, only around 200,000 respondents gave Polish as their mother tongue. Further, in inter-war elections, Polish parties received no more than 100,260 votes or 0.3% of the total vote (Nohlen & Stöver, 2010, pp. 790–795). For a variety of reasons, for example, assimilatory pressures and the proclivities of the census-takers, the census returns almost certainly understate the number of Polish respondents. Also, it is reasonable to assume that at election time many Poles would have voted for the *Zentrum* (Centre Party) that sought to represent Roman Catholics irrespective of ethnic provenance. As for the Statute of Autonomy, it was rescinded by the Nazis in 1940 and as noted much to the chagrin of wide sections of Polish society has never been reinstated. By the same token, today the whole of Upper Silesia lies wholly within Poland, thus negating the need for the original statute to be reinstated verbatim. With regard to the Nazis, discussion of their wider actions is beyond the scope of this essay. As history shows, the Nazi regime employed genocidal measures against nationally conscious Poles, and actively sought the deracination and enslavement of the survivors.

The Contemporary Situation

Returning to the present day, at bottom, the main issue for some politically active Poles is the fact that having migrated to Germany; second-generation and third-generation migrants, if people can indeed be so classified, are easily assimilated into German society with all that entails. In other words, Poles become Germans. For partisans of the view that identity is in essence a social construct and that civic identities trump narrowly defined ethnic markers, then there is no problem with such a state of affairs. However, this perspective is by no means universally held. For some, civically based nation-states are neither politically desirable nor inherently stable. For partisans of the idea that the ethnically constructed nation is both natural and logical, culturally defined markers such as language and custom are paramount and immutable, except through policies of deracination. For those who adhere to this latter concept of the nation, strategies of integration, let alone assimilation are both morally and politically problematic. When it comes to German–Polish relations, there is a poisonous legacy that often colours contemporary debates, coupled with accusations from the Polish side, that the Polish minority in Germany is not accorded the same rights as the German minority in Poland (see below), and similarly is denied the same status the indigenous Sorb, Frisian and Roma minorities. Therefore, from the Polish perspective, successive post-unification German governments have not acted in good faith and in the spirit of the bilateral 1991 Treaty on Good Neighbourly Relations (Polish Ministry of Foreign Affairs, 2016).

The aforementioned treaty is important for a number of reasons. First, together with the treaty of 1990 in which Germany recognised Poland's western border in international law, it marked a new era in German–Polish relations.[6] Secondly, it signalled recognition on the part of Warsaw that Poland hosted a German minority and that said minority would be accorded the right to organise as a minority in order to preserve collective German identity (*Verträge*, 1991). With this end in mind, in the late 1980s various German minority organisations were established: the overwhelming majority of which are now consolidated into the Association of German Social-Cultural Societies in Poland (VdG, 2019). This step was by no means uncontroversial in Poland and constituted a major change in official Polish attitudes with regard the vexed question of whether or not Poland hosted anything more than a few thousand aged Germans who had decided to die where they had been born. Crucially, Poland's German minority gained certain political privileges, such as exemption from electoral thresholds at national elections, which it initially used to surprisingly good effect at national, regional and local level (Cordell & Born, 2001, pp. 41–61). However, to the chagrin of significant elements of Polish society, successive German governments have refused to re-activate the Statute of Autonomy that governed the pre-1933 Polish minority in Germany. The German government argues that the European post-war minority rights regime as governed by the norms established by the Council of Europe applies to indigenous minorities and that the Polish minority is not indigenous to Germany but is rather made up of migrants and their descendants (Warchol-Schlottmann, 2001). Further the German government continues to argue that the former German/Polish ethno-cultural borderlands are now firmly located within Poland and that contemporary German state territory is clearly of German heritage. Therefore, there is no case for re-establishing the 1922 statute, which above all sought to cater for the needs of the Polish minority in German-ruled Upper Silesia, all of which is today firmly in Polish hands and whose sovereignty is not contested by all responsible political forces in Germany.

Today, the ZPN, which was reconstituted in 1945, continues to perform its co-ordinating function. In addition, there exist numerous other Polish oriented organisations whose activities cover a huge number of fields. These include religious pastoral organisations, socio-cultural organisations, publishing houses, and artistic ensembles. Their objective is dual. On the one hand, it is to reach out to the Polonia and nurture Polish identity and customs. On the other, they seek to present Poland in a positive light to a wider audience (Statistics Poland, 2018). Yet, the extent to which either the descendants of the nineteenth-century migrants or the children and grandchildren of the twentieth-century migrants to Germany have a special bond with Poland is open to question.[7] In terms of the overall number of Poles domiciled in Germany, figures as high as 3,000,000 are cited for the total ethnically Polish element of the wider German population. The official (estimated) figure from 2017 is 2,100,000 or 2.5% of the total population. Of this figure, only 783,085 do not hold German passports (Destatis.de, 2018). Put another way, over half of the estimated population from 2017 do not possess Polish citizenship. However, the statistics mask a number of elements to the equation, consideration of which reveals the situation to be more tangled and volatile than it appears at first sight. Since 1945, Germany has been the destination of huge numbers of migrants from Poland. In the early years in particular, arrivals from Poland were primarily clearly identifiable as ethnic Germans who had either fled or been deported from Poland. Even then, the case of the Mazurs, who were primarily Polish speaking but as Protestants overwhelmingly identified with Germany, illustrates that the situation was as ever not as clear-cut as some would like to believe (Blanke, 2001). Although marked by peaks and troughs, throughout the years of communist rule, migration to Poland did not cease. Over the next 40 years or so, a small number of political refugees to one side, migrants from Poland to Germany consisted of people who to varying degrees had kinship ties with Germany and more often or not dual if not multiple identities, precisely because they came from historical cultural borderlands, such as Upper Silesia. Of course, many of these migrants accentuated their previously inconvenient German roots in order to escape poverty. As such, the situation is opaque (Kamusella, 2000, pp. 92–112). However, rather than becoming involved in futile debates about the nature of identity in Upper Silesia or elsewhere in Poland, for our purposes, it is best to regard (ethnic) identity in this particular instance as existing by means of a continuum. In this example, at one end, there are people of an evidently German background and at the other, there are people of a clearly Polish background, with the majority of migrants existing at various point of the continuum, where the marker-points on the continuum are themselves contingent, situational and fluid. Whatever the case, there is no evidence, despite claims to the contrary from certain sections of Polish society, that shows that ethnic Poles resident in Germany constitute an overtly marginalised section of contemporary German society.

From the national-conservative Polish perspective, this refusal testifies to a continued ambivalence towards Poles that permeates huge sections of German society and results in the continued discrimination against ethnic Poles, who unlike the Danish and other minorities indigenous to Germany, are as a consequence unable to form their own political party. One of the more curious arguments that this author has encountered is that if the Roma and Sinti, (whose ancestors came from the Indian sub-continent), can be recognised as indigenous to Germany, there is no reason to deny such recognition to Poles (Cyiński, n.d.). The implication of such a proposition is clear: if people of Asian ancestry, even if their migration to Europe occurred around 900 years ago, can be treated as an indigenous minority in Germany, there is no reason why such a status cannot be conferred on Poles, who like Danes and Sorbs are clearly European in origin. Presumably, those who hold such ideas also believe that Europe needs to maintain its ethnic singularity in the face of 'globalist' threats. For those who hold the view that ethnic/national identity is in some way innate and for whom 'globalism' constitutes a threat to ethnically defined nations, a vigorous kin-state policy, such as that currently pursued by the Hungarian and Polish governments, is both virtuous and necessary. The assumption underlying such strategies is that the diaspora (target group) itself is some kind of undifferentiated mass whose collective concerns mirror those of their advocates in the ancestral homeland. This is a somewhat grand assumption, given that perforce the needs and desires of a migrant community (if such a thing indeed actually exists), cannot be identical to those of its co-nationals who reside in the ancestral homeland (Baser, 2015, pp. 8–13).

Both sides were aware of the issue during the rapprochement that began in the late 1980s and gathered pace during the 1990s as Germany acted as Poland's mentor during the accession negotiations that secured Polish membership of NATO and the EU (Garton Ash, 2003, pp. 357–410). Yet during the last 10 years or so the relationship of the Polonia to wider German society has come to play a more prominent role in Polish politics. In Germany on the other hand, both the Polonia and the German minority in Poland still remain below the mainstream political radar, although burgeoning support for the Alliance for Germany (AfD) may eventually force a re-appraisal of the situation. The question we must now ask and answer is one of 'why has this changed situation come to pass'? A facile response would be to argue that the salience of this identity issue revolves around the nationalist agenda of the ruling Law and Justice (PiS) party. However, the strident nationalism espoused by PiS and wider sections of Polish society has not appeared in a vacuum. It is symbiotically linked to collective perceptions of Poland's past, in particular the Second World War and the partitions of the eighteenth century and attitudes towards contemporary problems that pervade the political landscape in Poland and elsewhere in Europe. It is to analysis of these factors that we must turn in order to better understand the situation in Poland and therefore comprehend why PiS is so concerned with the fate of the Polonia in Germany. Having examined such dynamics, we will then be better placed to make some observations with regard to potential future scenarios for Germany's Polish minority.

Populism and its Discontents

The nativist, parochial attitudes evinced by PiS and its supporters since the party's foundation in 2001 are not unique to Poland and are in fact on the rise in the developed world and elsewhere. In short, such attitudes can be described as being populist and as such they possess key shared ingredients including belief in the virtuosity of the ethnically defined nation-state, hostility to globalisation, disapproval of multiculturalism, and in the European context Euroscepticism. In addition, liberalism, the liberal capitalist model of economics, 'elites' and in particular those with a liberal stamp are targets of populist ire (*Ethnopolitics*, 2018). Such views taken either collectively or in isolation are hardly new, but they have gained currency in recent years for a number of reasons.

In terms of its ideology, populism presents us with several paradoxes. Superficially, it may be regarded as leftist in its orientation, given the attitudes of its adherents towards ruling elites, liberalism and unfettered capitalism. However, it is most commonly associated with the political right, which self-evidently has a corporatist anti-liberal wing and in geopolitical terms, has a long political pedigree in North America (Magliocca, 2014). Here, as elsewhere, a majority rails against migration, globalisation and supranationalism. A minority, as apparently epitomised by the British Labour Party under the erstwhile leadership of Jeremy Corbyn and *SYRIZA* in Greece, rails against the dominance of both unfettered capitalism and established elites, whilst embracing multiculturalism. In today's Europe, populists of all stripes are above all united by two things: their disdain for liberalism and the cultural elites who created and sustain it. A second factor is distrust of the EU and ambivalence with regard to its future longevity (see below).

Two wide-ranging developments have been of particular importance with regard to the renewed popularity of populism. Firstly, there has been a general backlash towards the process of globalisation, which its opponents see as being rapacious, amoral and as a threat to traditional mores and belief systems. Secondly, there are the continued ramifications of the global economic meltdown that commenced in the autumn of 2007 and of the failure of the established political class to alleviate the consequences of this meltdown in an even-handed manner (Mudde & Kaltwasser, 2017). In the case of Poland, it is important to acknowledge that in part, PiS maintains its popularity precisely because it managed to insulate Poland from the crash and because it is generally perceived to be more efficient than its liberal/leftist predecessors. Expressed differently, given the success of PiS in managing the economy, small wonder that large numbers of Poles admire both its success and its message that Poland needs to be insulated from the negative aspects of globalisation and maintain its truly Polish characteristics.

As stated, prior to the onset of the economic crisis, populism was marginal to the political process in Europe and regarded as something of an anachronism of interest primarily to scholars of obscure political movements. The situation in 2020 is markedly different. In post-communist Europe, Poland and Hungary are governed by regimes that may be regarded as populist and populist parties are in the ascendancy throughout the continent. In Italy, their ideological kin also holds sway. Voters in the UK, spurred on by the United Kingdom Independence Party (UKIP), voted in the summer of 2016 to leave the EU and slam the door shut to above all migrants from post-Communist Europe. Elsewhere, most vividly in the USA, which alongside Canada, may be regarded as the spiritual home of populism; the creed has gained renewed support and credence through the prism of Donald Trump. In Europe until the recent past, populism found little political purchase. In the

1950s, France witnessed the rise and fall of the Poujadiste movement, but other examples of populism, particularly in the post-world war two era are difficult to find. No doubt, examples of populist movements from the pre-1939 period could also be identified, but given the way in which political parties sometimes mutate the extent to which such movements could be distinguished from more overtly fascist movements is moot.

Back to the Future

If we return to the main case in hand, namely Poland, we are faced with a regime that exhibits obvious populist characteristics. Further, it is a regime whose value system is congruent with that of wide sections of Polish society, regardless of party political affiliation. PiS and its supporters are clearly unhappy with the fundamentals of contemporary European liberalism. In no order of priority, abortion rights are limited: gay marriage is opposed; adherence to a particular form of Christianity is promoted in opposition to secular values and a close relationship between the (Roman Catholic) Church, state and society is favoured (Szczerbiak, 2017). In addition as has been made clear since at least 2015, PiS sees the preservation of the Polish state and nation from external threat as paramount. In general, large-scale inward migration is frowned upon, although an exception is made for Ukrainian economic migrants, who are sometimes presented by PiS and its adherents as political refugees and whose presence in Poland, therefore, gives the lie to accusation that Poland is hostile to asylum-seekers. On the other hand, the inward migration of Muslims and non-white people in general is opposed on the grounds of irreconcilable civilizational difference and threat. Stereotypes of the non-European, non-Polish other are easy to manipulate. With regard to Islam, Polish history books are replete with accounts of the centuries-long conflict between the Polish-Lithuanian Commonwealth and the Ottoman Empire and similar struggles with the Golden Horde and successive waves of Tartar and Ottoman interlopers (Zamoyski, 2009). To deny that these struggles occurred and that they were at times existential would be as churlish as it is untrue. The point is that today a policy of restricting asylum is in part legitimised by reference to an undeniable struggle that took place over a period of over 500 years and all but ceased with the crushing of Ottoman forces by Polish-led forces at Vienna in 1683. Contemporary Polishness, or rather a particular conservative, traditionalist version of it is celebrated as being the modern manifestation of a number of ancestral uniquely Polish traits, best summed-up by the slogan: 'God, Honour, Fatherland'. Moreover, the positive values of a virtuous Polish culture and the Roman Catholic values that underpin it are contrasted with the value systems those of its others including near neighbours, particularly Russia and Germany.

In a general sense, this negative attitude of PiS towards Germany further illustrates some of populism's salient elements, namely continued wariness towards historic enemies, even those to whom you are now allied. On the one hand, Germany is an important source of investment to Poland, a crucial trading partner, a fellow-member of NATO and the EU and a next-door neighbour. However, for PiS it is also an object of suspicion. As with potential Muslim migrants, the manipulation of historical memory plays a role here. Poles are reminded of Prussia's role in the partitions of the eighteenth century and above all of German aggression and criminality between 1939 and 1945. With a fascination that to an outsider sometimes borders on obsession, PiS insinuates that the associations that cater for the needs of post-war expellees from Poland and elsewhere, gathered together within the Federation of Expellees (BdV) are something more than the political irrelevance that they actually are (Cordell, 2014, pp. 102–120).[8] In so doing, it promotes continued insecurity within Poland about the viability of Poland's western border. By implication it also throws into doubt the loyalty to the Polish state on the part of the small German minority that still resides in Poland. Ultimately, it calls into question the foreign policy goals of Germany by implicitly posing the question: 'a European Germany or a German Europe'?

Similarly, as mentioned earlier in the text, PiS argues that the refusal of Berlin to reinstate the pre-war statue on autonomy that governed the Polish minority in Germany bears testimony to Germany's real as opposed to overt attitudes towards Poles and Poland. In sum, for PiS, Germany is everything that Poland is not. Germany is overbearing, lacks a democratic tradition, is percolated with anti-foreigner sentiment, and is obsessed by Poland. This worrying picture is (in effect) contrasted with an idealised picture of Poland, which is portrayed as being pacific in nature and open to other cultures (presumably as long as strict criteria are met). Further, Poland is presented as being possessed of the oldest established liberal democratic tradition in Europe (the May 1791constitution) whilst attempting to be both a good role model to all and sundry after having precipitated the liberation of the entire continent from the communist yoke in the 1980s (Garton Ash, 1991). Another result of this encounter with an unwelcome and (apparently) hostile reality is to shrink away from the alien other and hew ever closer to those of apparent common ancestry and ethnicity both at home and abroad, for example, the Polonia in Germany and elsewhere.

Welcome to Wonderland

The problem with such whimsical thinking is dual. The first is that it relies upon imagery so sharply drawn that the historically based realities upon which it is based become viewed as being 'fake news'. In other words, doubt is cast upon historically verifiable truth and repeated denial comes to substitute for fact. Secondly, it contributes to the creation of a dangerous political vortex within Europe as the rise of the AfD in Germany shows. The attitudes of the AfD also highlight the fact that such populist parochial misconceptions and misrepresentations are by no means confined to Poland. Having brought the AfD into our narrative, brief consideration of the wider circumstances that fostered the growth in popularity of this party will afford us the opportunity of fulfilling three objectives. The first is to further our understanding of why populism has gained such traction (in Poland) and with such speed. The second is to assess the impact these trends may have upon the Polish minority in Germany and finally its impact upon the broader ambit of Polish-German relations.

As we have noted, prior to the economic crash of 2007/2008, populism was marginal to the wider political process in Europe. Parties such as the Flemish Bloc (FB) in the Belgium, National Front/National Rally (FN/FR) in France and the Party for Freedom (PVV) in the Netherlands seemed forever to be destined as little more than niche parties. Irritants to the status quo, and of interest to small communities of scholars and voters perhaps but not more than that. The uneven and unequal nature of the post-2008 recovery is and was presented by populists as being the inevitable consequence of globalisation and its ideological handmaiden, namely neo-liberalism. Put another way, the political space in which the populists have thrived, was in part created by the very response on the part of the established parties to the crash and their self-evident complicity in creating the edifice came tumbling down in 2007/2008. For both convinced populists and less committed disillusioned and dispossessed sections of the electorate, the situation was made even worse by the 'asylum crisis' of 2015. For populists in Europe in general, and Germany in particular, the way in which established parties sought to deal with this crisis further exposed the poverty of globalisation and more importantly the folly of ceding power to supranational institutions, especially the EU. In turn, the EU is increasingly perceived as being remote, self-absorbed, and determined to dilute the character if not indeed instigate the destruction of traditional European values and the nation-state itself (europenow, 2018). It would be as well at this point to further explore the reasons for the growth of Euroscepticism with regard to post-communist Europe. It is not unreasonable to assume that in part, this outpouring of hostility towards the EU, illustrates the fact that in the 1980s huge sections of society in Europe, including Poland had no real understanding of the operation and goals of said entity. Rather, EU membership was symbolically equated with nebulous ideas of extensive welfare provision, a hazy and unformulated view of freedom and material prosperity as opposed to a given set of policy options and aspirations. In the wake of EU-wide freedom of movement migrants from post-Communist Europe arrived in Western Europe possessed of ill-defined and romanticised vision of Western Europe. Unused to the polyethnic diversity of major conurbations in Western Europe whilst being treated in an undifferentiated manner by a host population that itself lacked both knowledge of and curiosity in Post-Communist Europe, the (later) realisation that migrants from the EU received no special privileges vis-à-vis migrants from elsewhere, has by way of response produced atavism. As the reality of the European project, namely the 'creation of an ever-closer union', based upon civically as opposed to ethnically defined principles became apparent, so Euroscepticism grew fuelled by the crisis of 2007/2008, the 'migrant crisis' of 2015 and more general fears of globalisation. In sum, today populism finds fertile ground among those sections of the electorate who have concluded that the values of the European project are incompatible with their own traditionally based belief systems and who have not profited as much as they feel they should from the wider process of globalisation, or indeed feel that they have advanced and not because of it (Mudde & Kaltwasser, 2017).

With regard to inward migration, although in public at least, the language is usually coded and nuanced, the message is clear. In order to preserve the fundamentals of nation and state mass inward migration is an evil that must be halted, particularly if it involves the mass migration of people who do not ascribe to 'traditional European values' and who are therefore incapable of being socialised into societies marked by such value systems. Those who oppose such 'common-sense' values must be combatted at every turn. The enemies of 'traditional' values include international capital, the EU, globalists, the supporters of multiculturalism and the adherents of Islam, a religion that is portrayed as being a hostile undifferentiated mass in terms of its attitude towards Europe. The obvious contradiction in a country such as Poland in restricting inward migration whilst utilising outward migration as a means of alleviating social tensions was probably lost on large sections of Polish society, regardless of domicile, until the results of the UK's June 2016 referendum on EU membership came through (ipsos, 2016). As noted earlier, migration also played a role here, although it had as much to do with migration from post-communist Europe in general and Poland in particular as it did to 'hordes' of 'potential terrorists' arriving from countries such as Syria.

As yet, none of these developments directly affects Germany's Polish minority. The position of this minority certainly is not an issue of which most Germans particularly care about or are even aware. Anymore, incidentally, than they care about the residual *Volksdeutsch* communities scattered throughout post-communist Europe. Given the number of AfD activists with surnames of Polish origin, most prominently Georg Pazderski, neither is the fate nor ancestral provenance of Germany's Polish minority of at present of any great import to them as individuals or indeed to the AfD as a whole. However, the AfD is a party that exhibits populist, national conservative and quite possibly fascist characteristics. Just as supporters of PiS and those to their right in Poland have a view with regard to Nazi Germany's behaviour towards Poles and Poland, so do AfD members and supporters. It goes without saying these competing narratives of the past are precisely that, and as such they cannot be reconciled with one another. In the absence of reconciliation concerning such fundamental aspects of the past, the danger to the collective security of Europe is obvious.

Conclusion

Unpalatable as it may be to some, the fate of the Polish minority in Germany is symbiotically linked to that of the EU. In broad terms, three potential scenarios await the EU and its member-states. If a reconfigured version of the peace project that characterised West European politics from the late 1940s to the mid-1990s can be saved, then the position of Germany's Polish minority can be secured, with or without the legislation demanded by some sections of the Polish polity. Similarly, if the EU project is diluted and the goal of further integration is abandoned, there is no reason to assume that the rights of the Polish minority in Germany will be circumscribed. A neo-Gaullist 'Europe of the Fatherlands' does not necessarily presume the assimilation of ethno-national minorities. There is however a third scenario that needs to be taken seriously. Populist parties are on the rise throughout Europe and as of the time of writing, there is little to indicate that their support has plateaued, any more than there is reason to believe that (the prospect of) power moderates their objectives. Neither Poland nor Germany is immune from this trend. As alluded to at the end of the previous section, if the AfD were to come to power in Germany, as part of an overall upsurge in the populist wave, and the European peace project were to collapse, no-one should be under any illusions with regard to the consequences of such an eventuality. A parochial, nationalist, nativist, populist government in Berlin cannot enter into fruitful and sustained cooperation with its moral and intellectual counterpart in Warsaw. In the event of such an event coming to pass, both Germany and Poland would be faced with history repeating itself as a particularly tragic farce. At that point, the future of Germany's Polish minority would become as bleak as that of its German counterpart in Poland.

Acknowledgements

The author would like to thank David Smith, Andreea Udrea and Stefan Wolff for their comments on earlier drafts of this paper.

Notes

1. It is estimated that in 1940 and 1941 alone approximately 1.2 million Polish citizens were deported to the Soviet hinterland. There are no exact figures confirming the death toll, but minimum estimates begin at 150,000.
2. Poles living in the former Soviet Union are by convention excluded from the Polonia on the grounds that they are not the (descendants) of voluntary migrants.

3. Whether the ancestors of the contemporary remnant Kashubes and Mazurs were nationally conscious Poles is a matter of debate.
4. The *Kulturkampf* was a conflict between the German imperial government and the Roman Catholic Church, predominantly over the control of educational and ecclesiastical appointments. Given the allegiance of the overwhelming majority of Poles to the Roman Catholic Church, its wider ramifications are obvious.
5. The Plantation of English and Scots dissenters into Ireland was aimed at diluting the power of the Roman Catholic Church over the native Irish and securing the island of Ireland for the English Crown.
6. Germany in effect became a powerful lobbyist on behalf of post-Communist Poland in its efforts to 'return to Europe'.
7. Ain addition, as the author can testify, it is by no means easy for a person of Polish descent to obtain Polish citizenship. The process is time-consuming and expensive.
8. The political power of the BdV began to wane in the mid-1960s, first within the SPD and FDP and then within the CDU/CSU, as Ostpolitik became established in cross-party terms.

References

The Act of. 7 September 2007 (*Karta Polaka*), *Journal of Laws of the Republic of Poland* from 2007, No. 180, Item 1280, 2007. Retrieved November 4, 2018.
Baser, B. (2015). *Diasporas and homeland conflicts*. Ashgate.
Berghahn, V. (2004). *Imperial Germany 1871–1918*. Berghahn Books.
Blanke, R. (2001). *Polish-speaking Germans, language and identity among the Masurians since 1871*. Böhlau Verlag.
Cordell, K. (2014). The *Bund der Vertriebene* and Poland: A potential partner or a perpetual adversary? *German Political Studies, 31*(4), 102–120. https://doi.org/10.3167/gps.2013.310406
Cordell, K., & Born, K. (2001). The German Minority in Upper Silesia: Electoral successes and organizational patterns. *Nationalism and Ethnic Politics, 7*(1), 41–61. https://doi.org/10.1080/13537110108428620
Cyiński, P. (n.d). Why does the government in Berlin not want to return the Minority Status of German Poles that was illegally taken away from them'. Retrieved November 8, 2018, from https://polska.pl/politics/foreign-affairs/asymmetry-polish-german-relations
Cyran, E. (1993). *Preußisches Rokoko, Arani-Verlag*. Passim.
Destatis.de. (2018). Bevölkerung mit Migrationshintergrund – Ergebnisse des Mikrozensus 2017, pdf. Retrieved November 8, 2018.
Die deutsch-polnischen Verträge vom 14.11.1990 und 17.6.1991. (1991). Auswärtiges Amt und Bundesministerium des Innern in Zusammenarbeit mit der Botschaft der Republik Polen, Bonn/Köln.
Ethnopolitics. (2018). Symposium: Is nationalism on the rise? Assessing global trends. *Ethnopolitics 17*(5), 519–562. https://doi.org/10.1080/17449057.2018.1532635
Garton Ash, T. (1991). *The Polish Revolution*. Granta Books.
Garton Ash, T. (2003). *In Europe's name: Germany and the divided continent*. Jonathan Cape. (pp. 357–410).
https://www.europenowjournal.org/2018/01/31/nationalism-nativism-and-therevolt-against-globalization/, retrieved November 6, 2018.
https://www.ipsos.com/ipsos-mori/en-uk/how-britain-voted-2016-eu-referendum, retrieved November 4, 2018.
Kamusella, T. (2000). Silesia and the Dawning of the Modern Era. In K. Cordell (Ed.), *The politics of ethnicity in Central Europe* (pp. 92–112). Macmillan.
Magliocca, G. (2014). *The Tragedy of William Jennings Bryan: Constitutional Law and the politics of backlash*. Yale University Press.
Ministry of Foreign Affairs. (2016). The Asymmetry of Polish-German relations. https://polska.pl/politics/foreign-affairs/asymmetry-polish-german-relations/
Mudde, C., & Kaltwasser, C. R. (2017). *Populism a very short introduction*. Oxford University Press.
Nohlen, D., & Stöver, P. (2010). *Elections in Europe: A data handbook*. Nomos Verlag. (pp. 790–795).
Statistics Poland. (2018). The Polish Organisations and Institutions Abroad and Diaspora Organisations Institutions Database (pdf). Retrieved November 6, 2018.
Struve, K. (2000). The Germans and Central Europe in the pre-modern era. In K. Cordell (Ed.), *The politics of ethnicity in Central Europe* (pp. 50–65). Macmillan.
Szczerbiak, A. (2017). How is the European migration crisis affecting Polish politics? LSE European Politics and Policy (EUROPP).

Verband der deutschen sozial kulturellen Gesellschaften in Polen. (2019). Retrieved November 19, 2019, from http://www.vdg.pl/de/

Warchol-Schlottmann, M. (2001). Polonia in Germany. *Sarmatian Review*. Retrieved November 18, 2019, from http://www.ruf.rice.edu/~sarmatia/401/212schlott.html

Zamoyski, A. (2009). *Poland: A history*. Harper Press. (pp. 189–217).

Between Two Kin-States: The Round Table Meetings on the German Minority in Poland and the Poles in Germany 2010–2019

SŁAWOMIR ŁODZINSKI ⓘ

ABSTRACT This paper analyses the series of Polish-German Round Table meetings on supporting members of the German minority in Poland and the Poles in Germany which took place during 2010–2019. The course and results of these talks can be interpreted as a clash of kin-state policies that treat these groups as a 'foreign' extension of the nation and emphasise the need to care for them. They carry interesting conclusions regarding: the role of minority groups themselves as non-state entities influencing and shaping kin-state policies; and the tension surrounding the use of the terms 'national minority' and 'immigrant community'.

Introduction

This paper analyses the meetings of the Polish-German Round Table held between 2010 and 2019 on supporting persons belonging to the German minority in Poland and Poles in Germany. As well as including administrative and diplomatic representatives of both states, these meetings were also attended by representatives of the aforementioned minority groups and experts. So far, nine (official and working) meetings of this series have been held alternately in Berlin and Warsaw. The most important meetings took place during 2010–2011, when the first agreement was reached. The meetings continued until 2015, to be resumed in June 2019.

The German and Polish states organised these meetings to improve the implementation of articles 20–22 of the Treaty between the Republic of Poland and the Federal Republic of Germany on Good Neighbourliness and Friendly Cooperation (hereafter 'the Treaty'), signed in Bonn in June 1991 (art. 20–22). These articles guarantee members of the two minority groups the right to maintain their ethnic identity and develop obligations of the states in this field. At the same time, the Treaty clarifies the legal status of the protected groups. It refers to

Members of the German minority in the Republic of Poland, i.e. persons who have Polish citizenship, who are of German descent or who claim attachment to the German language, culture or traditions, as well as persons in the Federal Republic of Germany who have German citizenship and are of Polish descent or claim attachment to the Polish language, culture or traditions. (Treaty, 1992, Art. 20.1)

The recognition of the German minority in Poland was neither simple in legal terms nor easy in the court of public opinion (Cordell & Wolff, 2005, pp. 14–18). The acceptance of minority status began with the registration of the Socio-Cultural Association of the German Minority in Opole Silesia in February 1990 and ended with the signing of the Treaty in 1991. The Treaty was preceded by agreements on the inviolability of the western border of Poland (Treaty '2 + 4' of 9 December 1990) and a bilateral treaty between Poland and Germany confirming the existing border between them (14 November 1990), which were treated by Poland as the foundation for further treaty negotiations (Sułek, 2017, pp. 121–123).

Issues surrounding the protection of rights of persons belonging to the two minority groups proved the most difficult aspect of the negotiations on the Treaty. The methods for solving these contentions continue to cause controversy to this day, especially on the Polish side (Góralski & Sułek, 2016, p. 21, 60–61). The main object of this paper is to examine the Polish-German talks of 2010–2019 from the perspective of both countries as 'kin-states' and assess the participation of representatives of both minority groups. I show the importance of these talks as an example of a consultative mechanism regarding the situation of minorities in bilateral relations following the adoption of European documents on the protection of minorities by the two countries and their joint membership in the EU (Lantschner, 2018, pp. 308–309).

The structure of the paper is as follows: first, I introduce a theoretical context for these meetings. Second, I describe the meetings and their results. And third, I discuss the chief contentions surrounding the results of these meetings. The paper is based on the available materials from the meetings, including documents published by the German minority organisations in Poland and the Polish Ministry of Internal Affairs, as well as media articles and the scholarly literature. I also conducted two group interviews in the summer and fall of 2019 on the Round Table talks, one with representatives of the Polish administration and the other with representatives of the Poles in Germany.[1]

Before commencing the analysis proper, I must draw attention to two issues related to the demography and history of the two minority groups. The first concerns their current population size and socio-demographic nature. In the case of the Poles in Germany, the size of the group is difficult to estimate due to its heterogeneity. It is estimated that in 2018, approximately 2,253,000 Poles or people of Polish migratory origin lived in Germany, of which 1,668,000 were first-generation migrants (*Migrationshintergrund*). This category includes 232,000 Poles naturalised in Germany and 860,000 Polish citizens. Nowosielski describes the remaining population as individuals claiming German ancestry ((*Spät*)*Aussiedler*), who have migrated to Germany since the 1960s (2019, p. 86). In the case of the German minority in Poland, the data is more precise and comes from the 2011 population census: 144,238 Polish citizens declared German ethnic affiliation, compared to 147,094 in 2002 (*Fourth Report submitted by Poland ...* , 2019, p. 17). This means that Germans currently constitute the largest national minority in Poland.

The histories of these two groups remain particularly important for the Round Table talks. During the interwar period, both Poles in Germany and Germans in Poland had the status of national minorities. In the case of the Polish group, the German state abolished their status in 1940 and seized the property of Polish organisations. In turn, following the changes to Poland's borders and the displacement of most of its German population after World War II, the Polish government no longer recognised German national identification, with the exception of a small group living in the western and northern parts of Poland (Cordell & Wolff, 2005, pp. 9–14).

The establishment of two German states with different political systems in 1949 also gave rise to differences in bilateral relations with Poland regarding the recognition of the German minority. In the case of the German Democratic Republic (GDR), after the Zgorzelec Treaty of 1950, both parties agreed to suppress minority issues, including the issues raised by Germans in Poland. The GDR did not officially recognise the Polish population as a separate national group (Ruchniewicz, 2009, pp. 312–322).

This lack of recognition of the German minority burdened relations between Poland and the Federal Republic of Germany (FRG) until 1989. The FRG consistently sought official acknowledgement that people of German ethnicity live in Poland and demanded that they should have the right to learn the German language, develop German culture and create their own organisations (Cordell & Wolff, 2005, pp. 12–14). This situation changed in the 1980s as a result of the mobilisation of ethnic Germans living in Poland and was facilitated by the democratic changes after 1989 which enabled the recognition of ethnic Germans as a national minority. In the FRG, clusters of Poles originating from earlier waves of economic migration and those remaining after the end of World War II in the western occupation zones were more visible and larger than in the GDR. However, despite their presence, the FRG did not restore the status of national minority to the Poles, and the Polish authorities did not raise these matters. The Poles were considered to be well-integrated into German society and were described as an 'invisible minority' (Loew, 2017, pp. 225–236).

Theoretical Context of the Polish-German of the Round Table Meetings

The idea of 'round table' talks is well known from the contemporary political history of many countries in the world. It also often appears as a negotiating format in cases where the situation of a minority is rendered difficult due to political reasons or inadequate administrative mechanisms. From this point of view, the Polish-German Round Table meetings constitute an interesting example of kin-state engagement to improve the situation of kin minority groups in Central Europe (Waterbury, 2017) for several reasons. First, these meetings showcase the policy needs of minority groups necessary for the survival of their ethnic identity and culture. At this point, it is useful to refer to Gamlen's typology of a state's policy regarding its diaspora abroad (2015, pp. 166–171). Gamlen distinguishes between three groups of policies: tapping, embracing and governing. The tapping perspective is based on the state's perception of its diaspora as a valuable resource that can be used to meet the needs of its development, both economic and political. The embracing perspective focuses primarily on the issues of maintaining the national identity of the diaspora, treating it as a foreign extension of the nation. The governing perspective refers to the importance of international organisations and the diffusion of the legal solutions created within their framework. Also useful in capturing policies towards kin minorities is Zolberg's distinction

(1983) between policies of 'shaping the diaspora' (i.e. maintaining close relations with migrants' group) and those of 'generating the diaspora' (i.e. creating from migrants a recognised group in a new country). One aim of this paper is to offer a comparative analysis of Poland's and Germany's kin-minority policies in the context of the Round Table meetings.

Second, the Polish-German Round Table meetings exemplify attempts to resolve minority issues between two kin-states involving direct participation by representatives of the respective kin minority groups. They thus go beyond both the 'triadic nexus' framework described by Brubaker (involving a given national minority and both states) (Brubaker, 1996, pp. 70–98) as well as that of the 'quadratic nexus' that additionally includes involvement by European institutions in these relations (Smith, 2002). Rather, the meetings were an attempt to adopt a more democratic approach to state-minority relations in inter-state relations, based on the expectation that including representatives of minorities could help to counter the political 'securitization' (Csergő & Regelmann, 2017, pp. 215–218) of minority issues and encourage a pragmatic approach to their resolution of their problems. A further aim of this article is thus to examine the nature and effects of the participation of minority representatives in these meetings.

Third, for almost one decade a constant focus of these talks has been the need to recognise the Poles in Germany as a national minority. Both countries are parties to the most important European documents dealing with the protection of the rights of national minorities, *inter alia* the European Charter for Regional or Minority Languages of 1992 and the Council of Europe Framework Convention for the Protection of National Minorities of 1995. Focusing on these talks, this paper also considers why there has been a delay in recognising Poles in Germany as a national minority.

The Polish-German Round Table Meetings in 2010–2019

Following the geopolitical changes in Central Europe and the democratic transformation in Poland that started in 1989, a need to establish new political relations with Germany as it began its unification process emerged. In November 1989, the two countries signed the 'Joint Declaration' regarding mutual relations, which included a point (No. 45) about the need to recognise Germans as a national minority in Poland and also to regulate the legal status of the Polish group in Germany (Sułek, 2011, p. 4).

The 1991 Treaty constituted a breakthrough in the Polish-German political relations in the new geopolitical situation in Europe (Barcz, 2016, pp. 7–8). This agreement proposed a method of protecting the rights of persons belonging to minority ethnocultural groups and became a model for other bilateral treaties in Europe (Alfredsson, 1999). It was the beginning of a series of bilateral agreements concluded by Poland with all of its neighbours as well as other countries of Central-Eastern Europe in the 1990s. These agreements included provisions regarding the protection of national minorities in Poland and Polish minorities or Poles in the signatory countries. According to these agreements, the home-states sought to protect the identity of persons belonging to an ethnocultural minority, create conditions for the development of their culture and forbid any assimilation against individual wishes. According to this principle, states were obliged to jointly consider problems that could arise in the area of minority protection (Barcz, 1995, p. 41).

After signing and ratifying the treaty, the Polish government did not immediately raise the issue of recognition and protection of the rights of the Poles in Germany. This issue only gained importance after Poland became a member of NATO (1999) and the European

Union (EU) (2004). In 2005, the Polish parliament adopted a special Act on national and ethnic minorities and regional languages. This law introduced, *inter alia*, the possibility of introducing additional place-names in minority languages (which has been an important demand of the German minority in Poland since the 1990s).

During the opening of the Round Table in August 2009, Polish organisations in Germany sent a special letter to the German Chancellor Angela Merkel, which contained demands aimed at improving their situation. Three demands figured most prominently. The first was the need for financial support from the German government for teaching the Polish language as a national minority language in Germany. The second was the restoration of the legal status of national minority, which the Poles had had during the interwar period. The third was compensation for the persecution and death of about 2,000 Polish activists in Germany during World War II. The Polish government endorsed these demands in December 2009, in a special diplomatic note. The existence of a unified Polish association in Germany, a joint structure representing the interests of this group to the German government, played an important role in advancing these demands (Sandorski, 2010, p. 105).

As a result of these actions, the German government (at the request of representatives of the German minority in Poland) proposed the idea of organising talks as part of the Round Table. During these talks, not only ministries responsible for minority affairs in both countries, but also the representatives of the German minority in Poland and of the Poles in Germany were invited to participate. The first two meetings took place in February and November 2010. It was decided that the talks would be conducted in three working groups. Each working group included ten people, three delegated by each government, two by the German minority in Poland and two by the Poles in Germany (their representatives were independently selected within their own groups). During the first session, one working group addressed historical issues and memory policy. Among other topics, they focused on historicity in museum representation and the protection of historical documents of the German minority in Poland and of Poles in Germany The second working group analysed education problems raised by the German minority in Poland and the Poles in Germany, with emphasis on state aid for the establishment of educational institutions that deliver teaching in the respective minority languages. The third working group dealt with current affairs, including the organisation and financing of joint cultural projects.

During these first meetings, a working document was prepared outlining the intended support for both minority groups and using the 1991 Treaty as a framework. It was presented at the next meeting in March 2011 but encountered resistance from representatives of the Polish organisations in Germany because they deemed the German obligations to be too general (JAR, 2011). At that time, the needs of Polish organisations were supported by representatives of the German minority in Poland, who believed that German citizens of Polish origin should have the same rights and opportunities as the German group in Poland (PAP, 2012). In mid-June 2011, a compromise was reached in the form of a Joint Statement of the Round Table, which supported German citizens of Polish origin and Poles in Germany as well as the German minority in Poland, with reference to the German-Polish Treaty on Good Neighbourliness and Friendly Cooperation (Wspólne Oświadczenie ... 2011, hereafter Statement). This Statement remains the main reference document for further talks.

The Statement consists of a short preamble followed by two parts that highlight the home-states' obligations vis-a-vis the recognised ethnocultural groups in their own countries. The Polish side announced a revised strategy for the development of education in German as a minority language, as well as financial support for museum representation of the contemporary history of the German minority in Poland. In turn, the German side announced the establishment of a special documentation centre on the history of Poles in Germany, an office representing all Polish organisations in this country, as well as the preparation of a strategy for teaching Polish as a minority language and the principles for providing financial support to Polish cultural projects in this country.

All parties participating in the Round Table talks declared their willingness to continue, as they were aware that a large number of issues remained unresolved as far as the two communities were concerned. The German minority in Poland wanted to introduce the study of German history and geography in schools and develop Polish-German bilingual education. The Polish side was interested in creating a stable structure for financing Polish education and the Polish organisations in Germany, enacting a legal status of German citizens of Polish origin who are descendants of members of the Polish minority before 1940 and clarifying the legal status of the property of the Polish minority confiscated by the authorities of the Third Reich.

The next meetings of the Round Table were held in July and November 2012 and focused on problems related to the delay in the implementation of the adopted demands. Further meetings were held in 2013 and then 2015, but they did not bring the expected breakthrough. During the 2015 meeting, representatives of both governments and minority groups summarised the implementation status of the commitments taken in 2011 and concluded that the 25th anniversary of the signing of the Polish-German Treaty to take place in 2016 would be 'the good reference point for summarising activities as part of the Round Table' (Oświadczenie o stanie realizacji ... 2015). However, such a meeting never took place as a consequence of the tense political relations between Poland and Germany after the change of government in Poland in 2015. It was only in mid-December 2018, at the initiative of the Polish Minister of Foreign Affairs, that the idea of these talks was restored and the dormant Round Table was reactivated. Preparatory talks took place in Warsaw and Berlin in March and June 2019 respectively. The next meeting was planned in autumn 2019, and by that time the German authorities were to discuss the disputed matters with Polish organisations in Germany, and the Polish authorities were to carry out similar consultations with the representatives of the German minority. However, by the time of the completion of this paper (May 2020) no such meeting has taken place.

To sum up, the talks of the Round Table failed to bring the breakthrough regarding the two minority groups that had been expected in the period 2010–2011. These meetings have become, somewhat contrary to earlier assumptions, an inefficient diplomatic mechanism of consultations between the two countries.[2] But despite their criticism, these talks and the reciprocal pressure have benefited both minority groups, particularly through the establishment of special institutions documenting their activities and the funding made available for their cultural activities.

German Minority in Poland and Poles in Germany Between the Two Kin-States

Equality or Reciprocity?

The Polish-German Round Table meetings arose as a consequence of the dissatisfaction with the implementation of the provisions of the 1991 Treaty, expressed by the Polish government and Poles in Germany (Barcz, 1995, p. 374). The Treaty guarantees identical rights for the members of both minority groups, i.e. persons belonging to the German minority in Poland and Poles in Germany. However, the Treaty's implementation delivered uneven results. According to the Polish side, ethnic Germans are recognised as a national minority in Poland and its presence no longer raises political controversy. The German minority holds a seat in the Sejm (the lower house of the parliament) and is well represented at the level of regional and local authorities. Its cultural and educational activities are generously financed—in the 2016/2017 school year, 52,914 students studied at 809 schools in German as a minority language (Fourth Report submitted by Poland ... 2019, p. 17; see also Fourth Opinion on Poland ... 2019, pp. 38–39, par. 152).

According to the Polish side, such positive changes have yet to take place in relation to Poles in Germany (Trzcielińska-Polus, 2016). Representatives of the Polish organisations emphasise the insufficient funding from the federal and regional authorities for their activities and cultural projects and problems related to teaching Polish as a minority language. In the school year 2015–2016, over 11,000 students were studying Polish, half of them in North Rhine-Westphalia (Nowosad & Malik, 2018, p. 245). One of the main problems is that German regional authorities treat Poles as a migrant community, not as a national minority. This group status reinforces the German administrative authorities' negative responses to requests for financial assistance from Polish organisations (Sandorski, 2010, p. 103). From the Polish perspective, the question often raised is whether the political recognition of the rights of the Polish people in Germany as they are codified in the Treaty of 1991 is sufficient to protect their rights. Lack of recognition as a national minority raises problems when introducing Polish language education at the regional level in Germany. My interlocutors from the Polish association in Germany point out that the Polish-German relations are good, though the implementation of the 1991 Treaty with respect to rights of Poles in Germany remains a 'minor feature'. They add that one of 'the errors in the Treaty negotiations' was the failure to adopt specific procedures to complete the implementation of the Treaty in Germany (especially in relation to the provision about teaching in Polish language). In their opinion, the Polish side does not use European institutions to improve the situation of the Poles who emigrated, which is 'why we are beggars here for the German government'.[3]

In Poland, some argue that there is a need to negotiate an additional agreement on teaching Polish as a minority language, suggesting the creation of special federal funds for this purpose on the German side (Sułek, 2017). These same voices also talk about returning to the principle of reciprocity in minority protection. One of the high officials of the Polish Ministry of Foreign Affairs recently expressed this view in September 2019, saying that

the German side has its expectations, but the first step must be its progress in [guaranteeing] the rights and benefits to the Polish minority. We expect to overcome this great imbalance, then we can think about how it will be possible to meet these expectations. (Usz, 2019)

The German minority and other national minorities in Poland, fearing reciprocity, responded to this statement with fierce protest. This statement was also criticised by the Advisory Committee (Fourth Opinion on Poland ... 2019, p. 22, par. 82). However, the statement received no other reaction from the Polish authorities, which suggests that the expectations of the Polish authorities for the implementation of the rights of Poles in Germany have tightened and become one of the conditions for further the Round Table talks. Confirmation of this position can be found in the Polish government's commentary to the Fourth Opinion on Poland, in which the accusation of 'the "mutuality" principle' is rejected and an example of greater involvement of the Polish authorities in protecting the German minority in Poland is shown (Comments of the Government of Poland on the Fourth Opinion ... 2020, p. 7).

Participation of Representatives of Minority Groups

From the perspective of the participation of both minority groups, meetings of the Round Table gave them the opportunity to speak 'in their own voice' about their situations and needs, as well as to advance proposals for improvement. During these meetings, according to my interlocutors, they were independent partners for the representatives of the governments of both countries, actively influencing the course of the discussion and the content of the commitments made.[4] From the beginning, the assumption of these talks was that the representatives of Polish and German organisations participated on an equal footing with those of the two governments. They were to play an active role in them, contributing to the arrangements made. They were consulted on the working documents discussed during the talks, which, however, they often rejected or supplemented. This was evident in 2011 when the representatives of Polish organisations rejected the negotiated agreement, and in 2015, when the representatives of the German minority, in turn, prepared a critical assessment of the talks held so far (a similar opinion was prepared in spring 2019 before the start of the next round of talks). The positive aspects of their participation in these meetings were the specificity of their demands and the conditions for their implementation (they avoided vague diplomatic language). The weak one was that, above all, they had no real impact on the pace of implementation of these commitments.[5]

One of the problems that emerged during the Round Table meetings and influenced the negotiations was the representation and degree of organisation of the two minority groups. This primarily concerned the divisions and variability of the participation of the representatives of Polish organisations in Germany in these talks. The main factor was the heterogeneity of this group—different migration waves not only differ from each other, but have maintained limited contacts between themselves and tended to create their own institutions and organisations. Thus, despite the existence of a developed network of Polish organisations (numbering about 180 in total), the Polish community in Germany is still dispersed, poorly organised and internally conflicted. Poles are not very active in German public life, and they do not have representatives in the Bundestag and the parliaments of the *Länder* (Nowosielski, 2016). Despite attempts by the Polish government, it has not been possible to create a stable platform for all Polish organisations in Germany, and the selection of their representatives for these talks has always aroused divisions among them. For Polish diplomats, discussing the representation of Polish organisations and adopting a common negotiating position have always been a 'major challenge' ahead of each round of talks.[6] However, according to Poles in Germany, the Polish authorities did not strive to ensure a uniform representation for them.[7]

In the case of the German minority in Poland, the situation was in stark contrast: their representation was stable during the talks and the representatives had obtained democratically a negotiating mandate. This group is well organised, remains active in Poland at the regional level and knows how to use the opportunities to support the German minority provided under Polish law. This was particularly evident in May 2019 during the preparations for the new round of Round Table talks. At the annual congress of the Association of German Associations in Poland (the umbrella organisation of the German minority in Poland), a joint programme for the forthcoming talks was developed highlighting the three areas in which progress was expected: education, presentation of minority history and research on German heritage in Poland (*Rezolucja Zgromadzenia ZNSSK w Polsce … 2019*).

Dispute About the Legal Status of the Poles in Germany

When it came to organising the Round Table meetings, the issue of recognising Poles as a national minority in Germany was constantly there in the background. It was already present during negotiations on the Treaty of 1991, but the Polish side was not able to restore the pre-war status of a national minority to Poles in Germany at that time.

Poles in Germany are viewed by successive Polish governments in the same way as the Poles from the former Soviet Union, as lost compatriots to whom the Polish state has special historical and moral obligations (Nowosielski & Nowak, 2017, p. 155). Although the Poles in Germany are not victims of territorial changes and historical population movements, but they are perceived as hostages of international politics after 1989, following Poland's efforts to integrate with Western structures. According to the Polish negotiator of the Treaty:

> The Germans issued an ultimatum: either we will give up the fight for granting the status of national minority to Poles … or the Treaty shall not be reached. We have assumed that we are acting in the name of higher interests and have agreed to a compromise. We gave up on raising the issue of the status of the Poles in the name of overriding interest: facilitating talks about Poland's accession to NATO and the European Union. (Sułek, 2017)

According to representatives of the Polish authorities, there would be no problem in recognising Poles in Germany as a national minority if the provisions of the Treaty from 1991 were fully implemented.[8] While this did become an issue in the Round Table talks and remains on the agenda of the Polish side, it was not especially prominent in the talks and remains subject to divergent opinions. Policy documents dealing with the Polish diaspora and Poles abroad speak about the Polish group in Germany using the phrase 'national minority', which is applied to Polish communities living in the neighbouring countries to Poland's east, especially Lithuania, Belarus and Ukraine (*Strategy of Polish Foreign Policy…* 2017, p. 24). However, this status would only arguably apply to a small group of Poles from Germany, primarily to descendants of the so-called 'old immigration' from before World War II. These policy documents also encompass those who have migrated from Poland to Germany in recent years for work, and created a new Polish diaspora in this country.

These diverging opinions can be found within the Polish organisations in Germany.[9] There are two different strategies to recognise Poles in Germany as a national minority. The first (more pragmatic) focuses on the structural fulfilment of the Treaty provisions regarding the rights of Poles in Germany, which—it is argued—will naturally lead to their political or legal recognition. The second (more political) consists in seeking, as soon as possible, an official recognition of Poles as a national minority. The most notable activity in this regard took place in 2014, when the Union of Poles in Germany (one of the Polish umbrella organisations existing in Germany before World War II) applied to the German Ministry of Interior Affairs to enter the Polish group in the registry of national minorities. The German government refused this registration, justifying its decision by stating that Poles living in Germany do not meet the recognition criteria for a national minority. They are not natives and traditionally settled in Germany (i.e. they are not so-called recognised minorities) (IAR, 2014).

The German authorities have consistently maintained their position of not recognising more ethnic groups as national minorities than those included during the ratification of the FCNM in 1997, i.e. Sorbian, Danish, Sinti and Roma and Frisian minorities (*First Report submitted by Germany*... 2000, p. 4). The official stance is that to qualify for the status of national minority, a groups is required to fulfil the following conditions: the possession of German citizenship by its members; clear distinction from the majority group defined by their own language, culture and history (and other cultural elements); the will to maintain their identity and traditional residence within the territory of Germany and to function within the territory of traditional settlement (*Fourth Report submitted by Germany* ..., 2014, pp. 33–34). The official German position is that Poles living in Germany do not meet these conditions. The latest German government report on the implementation of the FCNM put forth similar arguments. It emphasised that citizens of Polish origin in Germany do not meet the criteria for recognition as a national minority in Germany (*Fifth Report of the Federal Republic of Germany* ... 2019, p. 131). Information on the efforts of Polish organisations in Germany to obtain such recognition was included in the opinions of the Council of Europe Advisory Committee on the subsequent reports of the German government on the implementation of the provisions of the FCNM (*Fourth Opinion on Germany* ..., 2015, pp. 7–8).

The preceding discussion raises a number of broader questions central to current debates of minority issues. The first concerns the possibility of using the legal phrase 'national minority' in cases where the demographic composition of a group changes due to migration. The second is the extent to which historical arguments regarding a past status in a given country can be deemed valid. The third would be how important are the opinions of a minority group's members about the need to guarantee their status and to officially recognise them as a national minority? And fourth, by extension, the question relating to the division between the legal and political recognition of a given group as a recognised minority. The 1991 Treaty preceded the official enumeration of recognised minorities carried out by the German authorities made when ratifying the FCNM in 1997, in which the Polish group was not included. However, official recognition of Poles as a national minority could open similar demands from immigration communities in Germany, especially the Turkish one.

Conclusion

The 10-year experience of the Polish-German Round Table meetings analysed in this paper is interesting for several reasons. First, the talks and outcomes to date have been defined by Germany and Poland's position as 'kin-states' as well as a continued cognisance in both countries of post-war territorial changes and population movements (Cordell & Wolff, 2007, pp. 6–10). In the administration of both states (in Poland only after 1989) the need for a policy of assistance towards their 'compatriots' living outside their national borders remains deeply rooted, regardless of the political orientation and changes in subsequent governments.

Second, from the perspective of the typology of policies towards 'kin-minorities', we can interpret the Round Table meetings as a clash of the policies of states treating their groups as a 'foreign' extension of nations and emphasising the need to keep in touch with them. Referring to the above-mentioned distinction between two types of policies towards diaspora advanced by Zolberg, in the case of German state policy towards the German minority in Poland we are dealing with an approach aimed at 'shaping the national minority', while in the case of the Polish state policy towards the Poles in Germany one can talk of attempts to create a national minority from a Polish diaspora.

Third, these talks were an example of a negotiating quadrangle, including on equal terms diplomatic representatives of both countries and minority groups. At the same time, they constitute an attempt to exclude minority issues from the broader, sometimes conflictual, political relations between Poland and Germany. However, the composition and support of both minority groups played a large role in maintaining these specific issues on the agenda. The analysis also offers regarding how the long-standing categorical differentiation between protected 'national minority' and 'migratory community' affects minorities' ability to participate as non-state actors shaping the policies of their kin-states.

Acknowledgements

I would like to thank Andreea Udrea, David Smith, Karl Cordell, Dorota Pudzianowska and Michał Nowosielski for all their helpful comments. I am also grateful to the anonymous reviewers for their constructive feedback during the peer-review process.

Notes

1. Author interviews were conducted with two employees of the Department of Religious Denominations and National and Ethnic Minorities (Ministry of the Internal Affairs and Administration) who participated in the preparation to the Round Table talks in 2018–2019 (July 2019)—interview No. 1—[GI1] and with representatives of Polish organisations in Germany who participated in the conference entitled 'The situation of Polish minorities and organisations in neighbouring countries—three looks' organised by the Warsaw University (November 2019)—the interview No. 2 [GI2].
2. This view was expressed by the interlocutors from both sides (i.e. government and Polish organisations)—[GI1] and [GI2].
3. According to author interview with representative of Związek Polaków Niemczech—[GI2].
4. Opinion expressed by interlocutors from Polish organisations in Germany —[GI2].
5. Opinion from interlocutors from Polish organisations in Germany—[GI2].
6. Opinion from the one employee from the Department of Religious Denominations ... —[GI1].
7. Opinion expressed by interlocutors from Polish organisations in Germany —[GI2].
8. Opinion from the employees from the Department of Religious Denominations ... —[GI1].
9. Opinions expressed by interlocutors from Polish organisations in Germany [GI2].

ORCID

Sławomir Łodzinski http://orcid.org/0000-0002-7484-8659

References

Alfredsson, G. (1999). Identifying possible disadvantages of bilateral agreements and advancing the most favored minority clause. In A. Bloed & P. van Dijk (Eds.), *Protection of minority rights through bilateral treaties: The case of Central and Eastern Europe* (pp. 165–175). Kluwer Law International.

Barcz, J. (1995). Sytuacja prawna Polaków w Niemczech w świetle Traktatu z 17 czerwca 1991 r. i prawa krajowego RFN. *Państwo i Prawo, 5*, 36–51.

Barcz, J. (2016). W XXX-lecie Traktatu polsko-niemieckiego kilka refleksji. *Przegląd Zachodni, 3*, 7–17.

Brubaker, R. (1996). *Nationalism reframed: Nationhood and the national question in the New Europe.* Cambridge University Press.

Comments of the Government of Poland on the Fourth Opinion of the Advisory Committee on the implementation of the Framework Convention for the Protection of National Minorities by Poland – received on 6 April (2020). Ministry of Interior and Administration, April.

Cordell, K., & Wolff, S. (2005). Ethnic Germans in Poland and the Czech Republic: A comparative evaluation. *Nationalities Papers, 33*(2), 255–276. https://doi.org/10.1080/00905990500088610

Cordell, K., & Wolff, S. (2007). Germany as a Kin-State: The development and implementation of a norm-consistent external minority policy towards Central and Eastern Europe. *Nationalities Papers: The Journal of Nationalism and Ethnicity, 35*(2), 289–315. https://doi.org/10.1080/00905990701254367

Csergö, Z., & Regelmann, A.-C. (2017). Introduction to special issue Europeanization and minority political action in central and Eastern Europe. *Problems of Post-Communism, 64*(5), 215–218. https://doi.org/10.1080/10758216.2017.1364113

Fifth Report of the Federal Republic of Germany in accordance with Article 25 (2) of the Council of Europe Framework Convention for the Protection of National Minorities. (2019). Federal Ministry of Interior, Building and Community.

First Report submitted by the Federal Republic of Germany under Article 25, paragraph 1, of the Council of Europe's Framework Convention for the Protection of National Minorities 1999. (2000). Council of Europe.

Fourth Opinion on Poland - adopted on 6 November. (2019). Advisory Committee on the FCNM, Strasbourg: Council of Europe.

Fourth Report submitted by Poland pursuant to Article 25, paragraph 2 of the Framework Convention for the Protection of National Minorities – received on 9 April. (2019). Ministry of Internal Affairs and Administration.

Gamlen, A. (2015). The rise of diaspora institutions. In N. Sigona, A. Gamlen, G. Liberatore, & H. N. Kringelbach (Eds.), *Diasporas re-imagined: Spaces, practices and belonging* (pp. 166–171). Oxford University.

Góralski, W. M., & Sułek, J. (2016). 25 lat traktatu dobrosąsiedzkiego RP-RFN. Polska i Niemcy w Europie XXI wieku. Razem czy osobno?, Warszawa; Instytut Obywatelski.

IAR. (2014). Polacy w nie będą mniejszością narodową. Niemieckie MSW odrzuca wniosek, dziennik.pl, 8.11.

JAR. (2011). *Nie chcemy dokumentu kłamstwa. Nie będzie polsko-niemieckiej deklaracji.* Gazeta Wyborcza, 6.05.

Lantschner, E. (2018). Commentary of articles 17 and 18 of the framework convention for the protection of national minorities. In R. Hoffmann, T. H. Malloy, & D. Rein (Eds.), *The framework convention for the protection of national minorities. A commentary* (pp. 298–309). Brill Nijhoff.

Loew, P. O. (2017). My niewidzialni. Historia Polaków w Niemczech, Warszawa; Wydawnictwo Uniwersytetu Warszawskiego (in German – Wir Unsichtbaren. Geschichte der Polen in Deutschland, München 2014).

Nowosad, I., & Malik, H. (2018). Organizacja nauki języka polskiego w szkolnictwie publicznym Niemiec. Stan aktualny, problemy i perspektywy. *Studia z Teorii Wychowania, 3*(24), 235–251.

Nowosielski, M. (2016). Polskie organizacje w Niemczech. Stan i uwarunkowania. Instytut Zachodni.

Nowosielski, M. (2019). Dynamika migracji z Polski do Niemiec i charakterystyka polskiej zbiorowości. *Studia BAS, 4*(60), 75–100. https://doi.org/10.31268/StudiaBAS.2019.31

Nowosielski, M., & Nowak, W. (2017). Między Wschodem a Zachodem – geograficzne ukierunkowanie polityki polonijnej i jego przemiany w latach 1989-2017. *Rocznik Instytutu Europy Środkowo-Wschodnie, 15*, 139–158.

Oświadczenie o stanie realizacji postanowień Wspólnego Oświadczenia Okrągłego Stołu w sprawie wspierania obywateli niemieckich polskiego pochodzenia i Polaków w Niemczech oraz mniejszości niemieckiej w Polsce, zgodnie z polsko-niemieckim Traktatem o dobrym sąsiedztwie i przyjaznej współpracy (2015). Retrieved May 4, 2019 from http://mniejszosci.narodowe.mswia.gov.pl/mne/mniejszosci/okragly-stol-w-sprawie/8793

PAP. (2012). *Mniejszość niemiecka w Polsce popiera postulaty Polonii w RFN*, www.gazetaprawna.pl [access, 16.01.2012]

Rezolucja Zgromadzenia ZNSSK w Polsce w związku z planowanym wznowieniem rozmów polsko-niemieckiego Okrągłego Stołu, Góra św. Anny. (2019). Retrieved May 4, 2020 http://www.vdg.pl/pl/portal/aktualnosci/polityka/item/4941-rezolucja-ws-okraglego-stolu

Ruchniewicz, K. (2009). Polacy w NRD. In B. Kerski, A. Kotula, K. Ruchniewicz, & K. Wóycicki (Eds.), *Przyjaźń nakazana? Stosunki między NRD i Polską w latach 1949–1990* (pp. 311–325). Oficyna Wydawnicza ATUT.

Sandorski, J. (2010). Polska mniejszość narodowa w Niemczech w świetle prawa międzynarodowego, *Ruch Prawniczy. Ekonomiczny i Socjologiczny, 2*(72), 89–111.

Smith, D. J. (2002). Framing the national question in Central and Eastern Europe: A quadratic nexus? *Global Review of Ethnopolitics, 2*(1), 3–16. https://doi.org/10.1080/14718800208405119

Strategy of Polish Foreign Policy 2017–2019 [Strategia Polskiej Polityki Zagranicznej 2017-2021]. (2017). Ministerstwo Spraw Zagranicznych.

Sułek, J. (2011). Historia powstania Traktatu Dobrosąsiedzkiego RP–RFN z 17 czerwca 1991 r. (ze wspomnień głównego negocjatora). *Przegląd Zachodni, 2*, 4–45.

Sułek, J. (2017). Traktat Graniczny RP-RFN z 14 listopada 1990 roku jako ostateczne zamknięcie polsko-niemieckiego sporu o granice po II wojnie światowej (ze wspomnień głównego negocjatora po 25 latach). *Niepodległość i Pamięć, 57*, 3–127.

Treaty between the Republic of Poland and the Federal Republic of Germany on Good Neighbourliness and Friendly Cooperation, signed in Bonn on 17 June 1991 (Journal of Laws of 1992, No 14, item 56).

Trzcielińska-Polus, A. (2016). Ewolucja roli mniejszości niemieckiej w Polsce oraz Polonii w Niemczech w stosunkach polsko-niemieckich pod koniec XX i na początku XXI wieku, Krakowskie Studia Międzynarodowe, XIII, 23-41.

Usz. (2019). *Wybory parlamentarne 2019. Kowalski i Szynkowski o prawach Polaków w Niemczech*. Retrieved December 28, 2019, from https://opole.wyborcza.pl/opole/7,35086,25252982,wybory-parlamentarne-2019-kowalski-i-szynkowski-o-prawach-polakow.html

Waterbury, A. M. (2017). National minorities in an era of externalization. Kin-state citizenship, European integration, and ethnic Hungarian minority politics. *Problems of Post-Communism, 64*(5), 228–241. https://doi.org/10.1080/10758216.2016.1251825

Wspólne Oświadczenie Okrągłego Stołu w sprawie wspierania obywateli niemieckich polskiego pochodzenia i Polaków Niemczech oraz niemieckiej mniejszości w Polsce, zgodnie z polsko niemieckim Traktatem o dobrym sąsiedztwie i przyjaznej współpracy. (2011). Retrieved May 4, 2019, from http://www.vdg.pl/pl/article/2341-wspolne-oswiadczenie

Zolberg, A. (1983). The formation of new states as a refugee-generating process. *The ANNALS of the American Academy of Political and Social Science, 467*(1), 24–38. https://doi.org/10.1177/0002716283467001003

Relations Between Polish Immigrant Organisations in Germany and Institutions of the Polish and German States

MICHAŁ NOWOSIELSKI ⓘ

ABSTRACT   This paper assesses relations between Polish immigrant organisations and institutions of the Polish and German states as well as the impact of these relations on how such organisations function. According to empirical research, Polish immigrant organisations have limited contact or co-operation with the institutions of the German state and have far greater relations with Polish diplomatic missions. The reasons for that may lie within specific attitudes held by all three parties. Polish immigrant organisations seem to be passive in relation to the rather reactive institutions of the German state while, at the same time, the institutions of the Polish state actively support the Polish diaspora organisations. Such a state of affairs can exert a negative impact on the organisations, especially with regard to their financial situation.

Introduction

The reasons for interest in the issue of relations between Polish immigrant organisations in Germany and the institutions of the country of origin and the state of residence are twofold. First, Polish migrants in Germany constitute a significant (though often scarcely noticeable) group. It is estimated that in 2018 there were 2,253,000 people of Polish migration background (*Migrationshintergrund*) living in the Federal Republic of Germany (FRG), 1,668,000 of whom were first-generation migrants. That category includes 232,000 Poles naturalised in the Federal Republic of Germany and 860,000 Polish citizens (Destatis, 2019).[1] Following migrants from Turkey, Poles constitute the second largest immigrant community in Germany, amounting to nearly 11% of all those with a migration background (Destatis, 2019). The nature of migrants from Poland is also very heterogeneous—mostly because of diverse ethnic identity which is a result of the migration of *Aussiedler* (resettlers) and *Spätaussiedler* (late resettlers) that took place in the years 1950–1990.[2] This diversity is reflected *inter alia* in the fact that German is the main language in 958,000 out of 1,346,000 households in which at least one member comes from Poland, and Polish only in 387,000 (Destatis, 2019).[3]

Due to the large number of people of Polish extraction as well as the long tradition of migration to Germany, there is an extensive network of Polish immigrant organisations (PIOs)[4] numbering over 100 associations. Although the history of some of the PIOs is almost a century old, most of them were established in the 1990s. There is also a significant new group of European Union (EU) post-accession organisations. The social background of the PIOs seems to be highly diverse, which reflects the heterogeneity of Polish immigrant community in Germany. Previous research (Nowosielski, 2016, 2020) shows that the biggest group among their members are immigrants who came to Germany in the 1980s and later. In many cases *Spätaussiedler* are also members and leaders of those organisations. The same applies to the PIOs' clientele, which is also very diverse and consists of people with different backgrounds. The main groups of recipients are 1980s (including those *Spätaussiedler* who maintain strong bonds with the Polish culture and language) and 1990s migrants as well as post-accession migrants.

Current research indicates that the situation of the PIOs is rather precarious (Nagel, 2009; Nowosielski, 2012, 2016, 2018, 2020). The most characteristic features of Polish immigrant organisations are: a lack of institutional completeness, a state which exists when the immigrant community created its own institutions parallel to those of the country of residence meeting all or at least most of the immigrants' needs (Breton, 1964) (the main focus is placed on cultural issues, especially those related to cultural affirmation), insufficient human resources resulting from weak social engagement of immigrants from Poland (only about 7% of the Polish immigrant population declares participation in the PIOs), conflicts and problems with the creation of joint representation in the form of an umbrella organisation, as well as a parlous financial situation negatively affecting the PIOs' activities.

Secondly, Polish immigrant organisations usefully illustrate the tensions caused by being subjected to diaspora policies of the country of origin and the integration policies of the country of residence. Such an entanglement, earlier defined as 'the trap of transnationalism' (Nowosielski, 2011), strongly influences the situation of immigrant organisations which in interaction with institutions of both states are often expected to adapt either to diaspora or to integration policy. In addition, the issues related to the situation of the Polish community in Germany and the condition of the PIOs are also part of the complicated domain of Polish-German relations. It can even be argued that the PIOs are to some extent implicated or entangled in Polish-German bilateral relations. A good illustration of the problem is the Polish–German Treaty of Good Neighbourly and Friendly Relations (1991) and its implementation on the issues related to the Polish community in Germany. Although the provisions of the Treaty provide for special treatment of the Polish community in the areas of culture and education, including support for cultural activities and studying Polish as a native language (Barcz & Góralski, 2011), in practice this type of support on the part of the German state is either insignificant or non-existent (Czachur, 2010; Grupa Kopernika, 2013; Łodziński, 2016).

Immigrant organisations—defined here as associations established by and for immigrants to provide social, economic and cultural services or those which represent and seek to advance the broadly understood interests of communities (Rodriguez-Fraticelli et al., 1991)—serve as an important enabler of social involvement by migrants ('Introduction', 1985). They have been of interest to migration researchers primarily due to the functions they perform towards immigrants (Owusu, 2000), the country of origin (Elwert, 1982; Schoeneberg, 1985), and the country of residence (Pries & Sezgin, 2012a). Although research appears to have progressed considerably (Moya, 2005; Portes & Fernández-Kelly, 2016; Pries & Sezgin, 2012b; Sardinha, 2009; Schrover & Vermeulen, 2005), immigrant organisations are often overlooked in the scholarly literature (Pries & Sezgin, 2012a). This especially applies to the issue of the complicated relations that exist between immigrant organisations and states—both of origin and residence.

This paper focuses on the relations between the PIOs and Polish and German state institutions, seeking to reconstruct them based on the statements of external experts as well as those of PIO and state representatives. I seek to establish how these relationships are described and evaluated from the perspective of the parties involved. In turn, the analysis of the respondents' statements determines how the relations between the PIOs and Polish and German public administration affect the condition of the former.

Immigrant Organisations and Their Relations with the Home and Country of Residence

As a theoretical framework, I use the model explaining the situation of immigrant organisations proposed by Nowak and Nowosielski (2016), who emphasise the importance of four factors: (a) the characteristics of the migration process and immigrant community; (b) the characteristics of the country and society of origin; (c) the characteristics of the country and society of residence; and (d) the bilateral relations between the country of origin and the country of residence (see Table 1).

Here, I only focus on certain elements of the model, namely the factors related to the country of origin and the country of residence, which most adequately illustrate 'the trap of transnationalism'. These factors will be operationalised in the paper as the impact of

Table 1. The factors influencing the situation of immigrant organisations

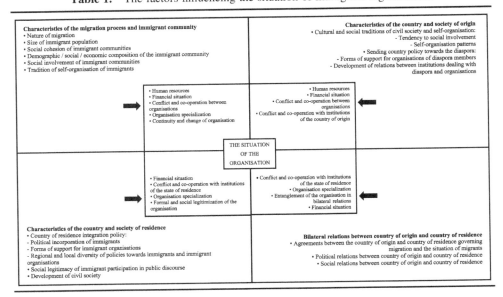

Source: Nowak and Nowosielski (2016).

diaspora and integration policies, as well as the relations between the public administration institutions of both countries and the immigrant organisations. The institutions of the Polish state referred to in the article are Polish diplomatic missions; as regards the German state, I examine institutions responsible for immigrants' integration at different levels of administration (federal, regional and local).

Relations Between Immigrant Organisations and Institutions of the Country of Residence

When analysing the political conditions of the country of residence that may influence the situation of immigrant organisations, the analytical scheme of the political opportunity structure, originally used in research on social movements, is particularly useful (Koopmans, 2004). Hooghe (2005) adapted this model to study immigrant (ethnic) organisations in Flanders in Belgium and analysed how formal rules and institutions, informal rules of interaction with challengers, power configuration within political elites and the response of political elites to the claims of pretenders tend to influence these organisations.

I focus here on the impact of integration policies, as well as the formal and informal patterns of interaction between the institutions of the German state and PIOs. In the case of integration policies the crucial issue concerns the nature of state support for immigrant organisations, such as available public funds and technical support and access to knowledge about other groups or entities that can provide resources (Bloemraad, 2005). Grants made available to immigrant communities as a mechanism of integration policy are of particular importance for the development of such organisations because they can affect their financial situation and, in some cases, influence the profile of organisations (by funding only specific types of organisations, such as those dealing with culture or welfare) (Moya, 2005).

There are several negative aspects of the German integration system from the point of view of immigrant organisations. First, social assistance for immigrants available from the German state is primarily provided through German institutions, with limited support for migrant institutions and organisations (Heckmann, 2003). Secondly, for many years organisations representing 'foreigners' (*Ausländer*) were outside the public domain, as well as beyond the scope of the integration policy. Only recently has the significance of immigrant organisations for integration in Germany begun to be recognised. This, however, has not always had positive consequences for the organisations themselves, which are sometimes viewed as a kind of 'fire brigade' for issues of integration in Germany and accordingly face an excessive increase in demand for their services. The German state has opened opportunities to finance immigrant organisations at the level of the federation, the *Bundesländer*, and local authorities. However, the support system, mostly based on financing projects, is not very well developed, which entails frequent shortages of resources, mostly financial (Weiss, 2013). Thirdly, a specific turn towards mainstreaming has also been observed in recent years, meaning that institutions dealing with integration target society as a whole rather than specific migrant groups (Scholten et al., 2017). Consequently, German state institutions more willingly support those activities of immigrant organisations that are not focused on the needs of just one ethnic group (e. g. Poles, Turks) but rather are aimed at the broader society.

Previous research on the PIOs in Germany suggests that their relations with the institutions of the country of residence are important in determining the situation of these organisations, especially their access to funding (Nowosielski, 2016). Firstly, the PIOs are not commonly recognised in Germany as instruments for building relationships with the Polish community or as entities that may support its integration. In consequence, they are rarely financially subsidised under the integration policy Secondly, PIOs themselves do not seem to take advantage of the opportunities offered by the German state. Even if migrants from Poland are not a priority group, PIOs still could apply for such support which, as shown here, they rarely do. Thirdly, most of the PIOs are primarily focused on the affirmation of Polish culture, which is at odds with the mainstreaming focus of Germany's integration policy.

Relations Between Immigrant Organisations and the Institutions of the Country of Origin

While analysing the relations between the immigrant organisations and the institutions of the country of origin, it is certainly necessary to pay attention to the policies of the state towards the diaspora scattered around the world (Bonacich, 1972) and, related to this point, the relationship between the organisations and the public administration of the country of origin (Schiller et al., 1995). Diaspora policy can be defined as 'institutions and practices of the state that relate to members of society who live outside the state' (Gamlen, 2008). It often includes actions towards immigrant organisations bringing together and representing diaspora members that can condition their accommodation. The state of origin often makes attempts to influence emigrant organisations, often by supporting those whose goals are in line with its policy and goals but also by limiting organisations' freedom or even seeking their liquidation (Sardinha, 2009).

Although Poland's diaspora policy (*polityka polonijna*) has undergone multiple transformations over last 30 years[5] there are a few important features which have remained unchanged or have changed only temporarily. The first is a focus on cultural affirmation translated into an effort to sustain the links with Polish identity, culture and language aimed at building a centrally oriented transnational Polish society (Gamlen, 2008). This emphasis on identity issues has been visibly stronger since Law and Justice (*Prawo i Sprawiedliwość*) came to power in Poland in 2015. The second feature is connected with a differentiated approach to Poles in the East and those in the West (Hut, 2014; Nowosielski & Nowak, 2017a): the obligations of the Polish state towards the former group are perceived to be more important. However, the Polish state has also developed a system of diaspora support in which non-governmental organisations, including Polish immigrant organisations play a vital role. Polish institutions can directly or indirectly finance some of the PIOs' activities as long as they comply with the priorities set by Poland's diaspora policy. The PIOs' projects are financed either directly by the Polish diplomatic missions or by Non-Governmental Organisations (NGOs) which distribute money through the system of diaspora support. This support for PIOs can be interpreted firstly as an effect of policy which instrumentally grants diaspora members specific rights and, in consequence, aims at enforcing their obligations (Gamlen, 2008); and secondly, as a consequence of the specific rationale of Poland's diaspora policy which has often been perceived as 'taking care' of the diaspora (Nowak & Nowosielski, 2018).

Recent analysis of the influence of Poland's diaspora policy on the situation of PIOs shows that, for several reasons, it has never significantly contributed to supporting the growth of such organisations (Nowosielski, 2016, 2020). First, Poland's diaspora policy prioritises Poles in the East and supports financially PIOs elsewhere only to a small extent. This reflected a belief that organisations operating in western European states—such as Germany—would 'fend for themselves'. Secondly, although PIOs are viewed as a useful medium for achieving certain objectives of the diaspora policy and facilitating contact with Poles living abroad, they are at the same time perceived as weak and powerless. Thirdly, the effectiveness of diaspora policy is impeded by its limited budget. The amounts spent on promoting the policy are paltry considering the size of the Polish community abroad. For many years, the funding made available to projects pursued by the PIOs in Germany was merely a trickle. Fourthly, support from the institutions of the Polish state, despite the generally good climate, can be unstable and changeable, depending for instance on the political situation or the changing priorities of Poland's diaspora policy. This means that PIOs with a distinct political profile are more or less intensively supported depending upon their ideological proximity to the major party in Poland. Also, PIOs which deal with issues not directly connected to the protection and affirmation of Polish identity and focus on social problems and social help are less prioritised (Nowosielski, 2016, 2020).

Polish Immigrant Organisations in a Transnational Constellation—Empirical Analysis

Data

The article uses data from a larger research project, with the following sources selected for analysis: a survey among the PIOs in Germany ($N = 24$), conducted using an institutional survey technique,[6] in-depth interviews with representatives of German state institutions, namely people involved in planning and implementing the integration strategy ($N = 7$), in-depth interviews with the experts on PIOs in Germany ($N = 7$), such as Polonia journalists, activists, representatives of the Polish diplomatic missions, and in-depth interviews with the representatives of the selected PIOs in Germany ($N = 5$). The research was conducted between 2016 and 2019.

Relations Between Polish Immigrant Organisations and German State Institutions

Quantitative research conducted among the Polish organisations in Germany indicates that most of them enter into rather limited contacts or co-operation with the institutions of the German state. In the case of the institutions at the federal level, as many as 12 out of the 19 PIOs declared that they do not undertake such co-operation. Sporadic co-operation was declared by four and regular co-operation by only three organisations. The organisations declared a slightly better level of co-operation in the case of institutions of the German state at the regional level—the federal states (*Bundesländer*). Although the number of regularly co-operating PIOs still remained low and amounted to three out of 20 which answered the question, the number of sporadically co-operating organisations was slightly higher and amounted to eight. As many as nine organisations stated that they did not conduct such co-operation. At the local level, one organisation declared regular co-operation and 10 only sporadic, while nine organisations stated that such co-operation was not conducted at all. It can therefore be concluded that co-operation between PIOs and the institutions of the German state is developed to an insignificant extent.

While examining the qualitative descriptions of the relations between the PIOs and German public administration institutions, it is noteworthy that the respondents (both experts and representatives of the PIOs and institutions of the German state) noted the different understandings and expectations held by organisations on the one hand and state institutions on the other.

Those respondents who emphasise the role of organisations in relations with state institutions often point out that PIOs themselves are not active in these relations. In this regard, they observed that organisations either do not want to or cannot effectively influence the German administration and are thus unable to achieve their goals.

> This is not a bureaucratic problem; it is a more technocratic one. That means we can't expect the bureaucrat to read our thoughts or take the first step. No, the essence of such a system is that they need to be forced to act.[7]

According to some respondents, this passive attitude is reinforced by a relative lack of knowledge about how the institutions of the German state function, what they expect, what their goals are or what the possible scope of support offered to organisations is.

As an illustration of this passivity, experts and representatives of German state institutions cited instances in which PIOs were either unwilling or unable to apply for funds available to them under the German system of support for third sector institutions.

> In Germany there are hundreds, if not thousands of foundations that finance various things, and unfortunately Polish diaspora organisations do not know that they can submit a project [...]. They don't know that. They kind of function precariously.[8]

However, apart from these examples of passivity, the respondents also indicated that there are some PIOs that are more proactive and able to develop effective strategies for co-operation with the institutions of the German state. In some cases, the respondents indicated that it was easier to establish such co-operation with those organisations that have a more pronounced profile, e.g. professional organisations such as medical or engineers societies.[9] Interestingly, some PIOs very pragmatically approach the issue of co-operation, shaping their programme and their activities to adapt to the expectations of German state institutions or even specific persons responsible for their functioning.[10] In that context, one can speak of an instrumentalisation of co-operation.

The descriptions of how German state institutions approach co-operation with PIOs also vary. Some respondents emphasised the generally positive attitude held by these institutions. For instance, one representative of an organisation dealing with teaching the Polish language noted that:

> The German side with whom we co-operate only locally [...], this co-operation is very good. And here again I can say, there is the local Mayor Office for example.[11]

A positive approach on the part of state institutions, however, does not necessarily entail a proactive attitude. On the contrary, experts believe that the institutions are rather reactive and take action only when there is pressure from more active organisations.[12] Other respondents indicated that state institutions treat PIOs neutrally, like all other immigrant associations. PIOs are not therefore discriminated against, but at the same time there is no special treatment of the Polish community and its organisations.

Regular, same as any other organisation. They [PIOs—MN] neither enjoy privileges nor face [difficulties—MN]. So, practically speaking, when an organisation wants to register, it does, if it wants to submit a grant for its own purposes, it does. [...] Germany is a well-organised state, and, above all, they absolutely do not exclude Poles, I would not put that in those categories. They simply do not distinguish Poles as a special nation, which is why we do not have the status of a national minority.[13]

However, there were also statements indicating negative assessments of the attitude of state institutions towards Polish organisations. Experts' statements often show attempts to describe the relationship between the PIOs and the institutions of the German state in terms of a zero-sum game in which the latter has a stronger position. Some of the experts note that the institutions of the German state co-operate with the PIOs but only in areas connected with the priorities of the integration policy, such as teaching the German language to Polish and other migrants. Other potential co-operation areas—for example teaching Polish as a native language—are less prioritised, or even overlooked. Consequently, some of the goals important for the organisations, especially those related to the affirmation of Polish culture, cannot be implemented in co-operation with the institutions of the German state.

Germans often display a structural lack of trust in Polish organisations [...] that's why they also say—we have our structures like [...] Caritas or Diakonie,[14] that also have some kind of Polish-speaking people, but still do not advise Poles [...]. These are not places where Polishness can be maintained [...] or the Polish traditions can be transmitted in Germany.[15]

In turn, one of the respondents surveyed indicated that support for PIOs may simply be unprofitable for the German state. This would result firstly from the fact that people of Polish origin integrate into German society with ease. An additional argument could be that the PIOs have too little social coverage or cannot act as an effective intermediary between the Polish community and the German public administration.

Of course, they can participate in any other programme, even here in NRW [Nordrhein-Westphalen—MN]. But I don't think any Polish organisation will be financed. Perhaps from the point of view of this instrumental approach they do not think it necessary and only fund Turkish Arab organisations [...]. If the basis of the instrumental approach is the desire to reach certain parts of society, I do not think that Polish organisations can easily do it or reach these people.[16]

Relations Between Polish Immigrant Organisations and the Institutions of the Polish State

In the light of the quantitative data, co-operation between the PIOs and the institutions of the Polish state, in particular the Polish diplomatic missions, seems to be well developed. Out of the 23 organisations which responded to this question, 10 declared regular co-operation and 11 sporadic, with only two saying that they did not maintain such co-operation at all. It can therefore be concluded that the co-operation is better developed than it is with the German state institutions.

In many cases, the qualitative descriptions of the relations between the PIOs and the Polish state and its institutions mainly offered an assessment of the policy towards Poles in Germany and the organisations themselves. In addition, clear differences in the tone of expression could be seen among experts who were employees of Polish diplomatic missions. In their case, the statements were understandably usually more positive.

When it comes to how the Polonia policy is defined, in the documents one can discuss certain focal points, but in principle it is described properly. At least for the area of Germany, I think that in Western Europe it is working well.[17]

Some of the experts unrelated to Polish diplomatic circles, such as Polonia journalists, also expressed a similarly positive opinion. They drew attention, among other things, to the constant desire of the Polish diplomacy to unite the PIOs, i.e. to establish a strong umbrella organisation that could be treated as a representative of the Polish community in Germany.

I think there is [...] a policy and a specific strategy, it consists in supporting people of Polish descent, it is obvious that such is also the responsibility of the state. [...]. I am under the impression that Polish diplomacy undertook, all the time undertook such integration activities and aimed at those organisations co-operating, speaking in one voice.[18]

However, most experts took a more critical approach, often claiming either that no such coherent policy existed or that they did not know what it could basically consist of. Based on their own experience, they clearly found it difficult to determine the attitude of the Polish state to the PIOs in Germany or the nature of its strategy towards them.[19]

Importantly, the institutions of the Polish state most often support those activities that are focused on cultural affirmation and sustaining the Polish identity, language and the links with Polish culture. Recently, the Polish state has started to show an interest in historical policy and the politics of memory, seeking for instance to re-define the role of Poland during Second World War by objecting to the use of expressions such as 'Polish death camp' and 'Polish concentration camp' in the public discourse (primarily in Israel and the US but also sometimes in Germany). This tendency has been even more visible since 2015 when Law and Justice became the major party in Poland.

Consulates are showing more and more good will, but this is a little bit because the political situation has been changing, and organisations in Germany and these educational organisations have started to appear as if under a magnifying glass, for various reasons.[20]

So usually they promote: involvement in Polish affairs, sustaining identity, and now concentration camps—to fight for that.[21]

Alongside this type of general statement, there were also opinions referring to specific areas of co-operation with the institutions of the Polish state, primarily diplomatic missions, but also other institutions responsible for maintaining contact with Poles living abroad. Noteworthy here are statements of the representatives of the organisations surveyed which usually corroborate relatively good experiences:

> Yes, there are two wonderful consuls [...] who are really open. We co-operate, they co-finance us, for example [our events—MN]. And we are hence greatly supported.[22]

Co-operation is usually positively evaluated by the representatives of the PIOs that have received support from the institutions of the Polish state in one form or another. However, such experiences are not necessarily shared by all organisations.[23] It is also worth noting that in some situations the support provided by the Polish state institutions is not stable: it appears, disappears or changes. Access to funding often depends on fluctuations in the political priorities of the major party in Poland, and in many cases is only available to those organisations which maintain ideological proximity with it.

> However, if I already hear that Poland will be increasingly supporting 'Gazeta Polska' Clubs[24] around the world and inviting them. (...) And they meet somewhere in various nice hotels in order to build a new foothold. (...) Because they would also like to ... like in Poland, change from A to Z, replace all the staff, they can do anything in the Polish diaspora, because all they have to do is turn off the financial tap and (...) we have no chance.[25]

In addition, some of the statements indicated that in some cases the PIOs and their activities are treated instrumentally. The research pointed to cases of implicating some organisations in current political games.[26] Reactions of organisations towards this politicisation are differentiated. Some of them take advantage of the new trend and engage even more strongly in activities focused on cultural affirmation. Others, however, distance themselves from the institutions of the Polish state and the political issues they promote. Lastly, there are organisations which simply avoid engaging in any actions that might be negatively perceived by the representatives of the Polish state.

Conclusion

This paper demonstrates that there are differences in the relations between the PIOs in Germany with the institutions of the country of residence on the one hand, and those of the country of origin on the other. In the case of the relations between the PIOs and the German public administration, the picture is ambiguous. On the one hand, the respondents mostly pointed out that the German state institutions are either generally friendly or neutrally oriented towards PIOs and, at the same time, passive, awaiting the initiative of the organisations themselves. The reactivity of the institutions of the German state may result from the neutral approach which the German public administration adopts towards all immigrant organisations, but it may also result from the belief that more active support for PIOs is unnecessary because it would not impact any further on the integration of the Polish community.

On the other hand, the attitude of many organisations was also described as passive. The respondents described situations in which PIOs had not used the opportunities offered by the German system of migrant integration. The research shows that there may be several reasons for this specific passive attitude. Firstly, it may result from a lack of appropriate skills (linguistic or technical) necessary to prepare an effective application for funding. Secondly, it may also be connected to the unrealistic expectations—arising from the 1991 Treaty—that the institutions of the German state themselves will provide special measures to accommodate the Polish community. Thirdly, there are organisations which believe that the German public administration is engaged in a kind of zero-sum game, resulting from the fact that the goals important from the point of view of German state institutions are incongruent with those of the PIOs. The divergent goals of the PIOs and the German integration institutions may worsen the financial situation resulting from a lack of possibility or willingness to apply for funds available from the German state. In addition, this passivity contributes to the further marginalisation of the PIOs, which will gradually become invisible to the German administration and, therefore, irrelevant.

The relationship between the organisations and the Polish public administration, especially the diplomatic missions, is perceived differently. Although the implementation of Poland's diaspora policy is sometimes criticised, the co-operation between PIOs and the institution of the Polish state is generally viewed as positive. One might even venture to claim that that for a large part of the PIOs, it is more appealing to maintain relations with the Polish state than it is to create and sustain relations with German state institutions. Two reasons can be highlighted here. Firstly, the institutions of the Polish state are perceived to be more active partners of the PIOs than those of their German counterpart. Secondly, there are no language barriers resulting from the lack of the German language proficiency of some PIOs leaders. However, closer relations with the institutions of the Polish state also remain burdened by unpredictable risks associated with the increasingly explicit politicisation of the support offered to the Polish diaspora. In response to this, some of the organisations clearly adjust their profile of activity in order to access the funds allocated for cultural affirmation and the protection of Polish identity. Others limit the threats resulting from politicisation by trying to remain politically neutral.

Funding

This work was supported by the National Science Centre under Grant 'Polish immigrant organisations in Europe' [grant number 2014/14/E/HS6/00731]; and Deutsch-Polnische Wissenschaftsstiftung under Grant 'Migrants from Poland—cultural aspects' [grant number 2016-17].

Notes

1. When analysing the Microzensus data, it should be acknowledged that German researchers indicate that the number of people of the Polish migration background is in all likelihood underestimated (Halm et al., 2012, p. 38).
2. As of 2016, out of 1,868,000 people of Polish migration background in Germany as many as 500,000 were *Aussiedler* or *Spätaussiedler* (Destatis, 2017, pp. 82–100). Such migrants left Poland for Germany on the basis of having or claiming German nationality. Since being granted the status of a resettler was connected with being a German citizen (or an ancestor of a citizen) or having lived in the territories which belonged to the German Reich prior to 31 December 1937, this broad category grouped people with different identities: German, so-called 'autochthonic' people such as: Silesians, Kashubes, Mazurs, as well as people of Polish identity for whom *Aussiedler* status offered one of the very few possibilities to migrate from communist Poland (Stola, 2010). In consequence, many of the resettlers, especially late resettlers, maintained with the Polish culture and language (Schmidt, 2009). They are also important in terms of establishing and constituting the beneficiaries of the Polish immigrant

organisations (Nowosielski, 2016). For more on the migration of *Aussiedler* (see Bade and Oltmer, 1999; Dietz, 2006).

3. For more detailed information on the language behaviour and cultural participation of Polish migrants (see: Jeran et al., 2019).
4. Since most of the Polish or Polonia organisations in Germany, even those with longer tradition and referring to the heritage of the pre-war Polish minority, are currently run by first generation immigrants from Poland, we use the term Polish immigrant organisations.
5. Perhaps the most important change was the shift from 'old' to 'new' diaspora policy observed in years 2011–2015 (Nowosielski & Nowak, 2017b; Nowak & Nowosielski, 2019).
6. Institutional survey is a technique used in the research on institutions and organisations. The main issues that the institutional survey is intended to shed light on are: the structure of the organisation (e.g. age, geographical territory, or management structure), the organisation's areas and methods of activity, the number and characteristics of members, and, if applicable, employees; revenues and expenses; the social environment of the organisations; and/or the arising problems (Klandermans & Smith, 2002, p. 4).
7. Author's interview, 6 July 2016, Nordrhein-Westphalen, Germany.
8. Author's interview, interview 1, 21 February 2017, Berlin, Germany.
9. Author's interview, 7 July 2016, Nordrhein-Westphalen, Germany.
10. Author's interview, 18 November 2017, Bavaria, Germany.
11. Author's interview, interview 1, 5 July 2016, Nordrhein-Westphalen, Germany.
12. Author's interview, interview 1, 6 July 2016, Nordrhein-Westphalen, Germany.
13. Author's interview, interview 2, 6 July 2016, Nordrhein-Westphalen, Germany.
14. Caritas is the catholic social service organisation, while Diakonie is charitable organisation of Protestant churches in Germany.
15. Author's interview, interview 1, 21 February 2017, Berlin, Germany.
16. Author's interview, interview 2, 5 July 2016, Nordrhein-Westphalen, Germany.
17. Author's interview, 7 July 2016, Nordrhein-Westphalen, Germany.
18. Author's interview, interview 1, 5 July 2016, Nordrhein-Westphalen, Germany.
19. Author's interview, 22 February 2017, Berlin, Germany.
20. Author's interview, interview 1, 5 July 2016, Nordrhein-Westphalen, Germany.
21. Author's interview, 15 March 2017, Bavaria, Germany.
22. Author's interview, 23 February 2017, Berlin, Germany.
23. Author's interview, 18 February 2018, Mecklenburg-Western Pomerania, Germany.
24. Local discussion clubs created by readers of 'Gazeta Polska', a right-wing conservative Polish newspaper, also popular abroad.
25. Author's interview, 3 March 2018, Berlin, Germany.
26. Author's interview, interview 1, 6 July 2016, Nordrhein-Westphalen, Germany.

ORCID

Michał Nowosielski ⑫ http://orcid.org/0000-0001-7383-4872

References

Bade, K. J., & Oltmer, J. (Eds) (1999). *Aussiedler: deutsche Einwanderer aus Osteuropa*. Rasch.

Barcz, J., & Góralski, W. M. (2011). Traktat o dobrym sąsiedztwie i przyjaznej współpracy: Koncepcja, zasadnicze regulacje i porozumienia towarzyszące. In W. M. Góralski (Ed.), *Przełom i wyzwanie. XX lat polsko-niemieckiego Traktatu o dobrym sąsiedztwie i przyjaznej współpracy 1991–2011* (pp. 284–308). Dom Wydawniczy Elipsa.

Bloemraad, I. (2005). The limits of de Tocqueville: How government facilitates organisational capacity in newcomer communities. *Journal of Ethnic and Migration Studies*, *31*(5), 865–887. https://doi.org/10.1080/13691830500177578

Bonacich, E. (1972). A theory of ethnic antagonism: The split labor market. *American Sociological Review*, *37*(5), 547–559. https://doi.org/10.2307/2093450

Breton, R. (1964). Institutional completeness of ethnic communities and the personal relations of immigrants. *American Journal of Sociology, 70*(2), 193–205. https://doi.org/10.1086/223793

Czachur, W. (2010). Status i możliwości społeczności polskojęzycznej w Niemczech. *Sprawy Międzynarodowe, 1*, 85–92.

Destatis. (2017). *Bevölkerung und Erwerbstätigkeit—Bevölkerung mit Migrationshintergrund—Ergebnisse des Mikrozensus 2016*. Statistisches Bundesamt.

Destatis. (2018/2019). *Bevölkerung und Erwerbstätigkeit. Bevölkerung mit Migrationshintergrund—Ergebnisse des Mikrozensus 2018*. Retrieved September 1, 2019, from https://www.destatis.de/DE/Themen/Gesellschaft-Umwelt/Bevoelkerung/Migration-Integration/Publikationen/Downloads-Migration/migrationshintergrund-2010220187004.pdf?__blob=publicationFile

Dietz, B. (2006). Aussiedler in Germany: From smooth adaptation to tough integration. In L. Lucassen, D. Feldman, & J. Oltmer (Eds.), *Paths of integration: Migrants in Western Europe (1880–2004)* (pp. 116–136). Amsterdam University Press.

Elwert, G. (1982). Probleme der Auslanderintegration. Gesellschaftliche Interaktion durch Binnenintegration. *Kölner Zeitschrift fur Soziologie und Sozialpsychologie, 34*, 717–731.

Gamlen, A. (2008). *Why engage diasporas?* (COMPAS Working Paper, 63). Retrieved September 13, 2019, from https://www.compas.ox.ac.uk/wp-content/uploads/WP-2008-063-Gamlen_Why_Engage_Diasporas.pdf

Grupa Kopernika. (2013). Raport nr III Grupy Kopernika, Społeczność Polskojęzyczna w Niemczech, Wrzesień 2001. In D. Bingen & K. Wóycicki (Eds.), *Grupa Kopernika. Komunikaty i raporty z posiedzeń (2000–2012)* (pp. 34–39). Oficyna Wydawnicza ATUT—Wrocławskie Wydawnictwo Oświatowe.

Halm, D., Pielage, P., Pries, L., Sezgin, Z., & Tuncer-Zengingül, T. (2012). Polish and Turkish organisations in Germany. In L. Pries & Z. Sezgin (Eds.), *Cross border migrant organisations in comparative perspective* (pp. 37–98). Palgrave Macmillan.

Heckmann, F. (2003). From ethnic nation to universalistic immigrant integration: Germany. In F. Heckmann & D. Schnapper (Eds.), *The integration of immigrants in European societies: National differences and trends of convergence* (pp. 45–78). Lucius & Lucius.

Hooghe, M. (2005). Ethnic organisations and social movement theory: The political opportunity structure for ethnic mobilisation in Flanders. *Journal of Ethnic and Migration Studies, 31*(5), 975–990. https://doi.org/10.1080/13691830500177925

Hut, P. (2014). *Polska wobec Polaków w przestrzeni poradzieckiej. Od solidaryzmu etnicznego do obowiązku administracyjnego*. ASPRA JR.

Introduction: Political participation and civil rights of immigrants, a research agenda. (1985). *International Migration Review, 19*, 400–414. https://doi.org/10.2307/2545847

Jeran, A., Nowak, W., & Nowosielski, M. (2019). *Migranci z Polski w Niemczech—aspekty kulturowe. Raport z badań*. Ośrodek Badań nad Migracjami UW. http://www.migracje.uw.edu.pl/wp-content/uploads/2019/09/Raport_MPN_ko%C5%84cowy_PLx.pdf

Klandermans, B., & Smith, J. (2002). Survey research: A case for comparative designs. In B. Klandermans & S. Staggenborg (Eds.), *Methods of social movement research* (pp. 3–31). University of Minnesota Press.

Koopmans, R. (2004). Migrant mobilization and political opportunities: Variation among German cities and a comparison with the United Kingdom and the Netherlands. *Journal of Ethnic and Migration Studies, 30*(3), 449–470. https://doi.org/10.1080/13691830410001682034

Łodziński, S. (2016). Mniejszość niemiecka w Polsce a Polacy w Niemczech. Uwagi o ochronie mniejszości narodowych na marginesie cyklu spotkań polsko—niemieckiego Okrągłego Stołu w latach 2010-2015. In L. Nijakowski (Ed.), *Niemcy* (pp. 203–219). Wydawnictwo Sejmowe.

Moya, J. C. (2005). Immigrants and associations: A global and historical perspective. *Journal of Ethnic and Migration Studies, 31*(5), 833–864. https://doi.org/10.1080/13691830500178147

Nagel, S. (2009). *Zwischen zwei Welten. Kulturelle Strukturen der polnischsprachigen Bevölkerung in Deutschland*. IFA.

Nowak, W., & Nowosielski, M. (2016). Zarys uwarunkowań funkcjonowania organizacji imigranckich—propozycja modelu wyjaśniającego. *Studia Migracyjne—Przegląd Polonijny, 3*, 31–52.

Nowak, W., & Nowosielski, M. (2018). The state, diaspora policy and immigrant organisations—lessons from the polish case. *Yearbook of the Institute of East-Central Europe, 16*, 159–176.

Nowak, W., & Nowosielski, M. (2019). Leadership struggles and challenges for diaspora policies: A case study of the Polish institutional system. *Innovation: The European Journal of Social Science Research*. Published online 26 March 2019. https://doi.org/10.1080/13511610.2019.1594716

Nowosielski, M. (2011). The trap of transnationalism—Polish organisations in Germany. *Polish Sociological Review, 175*, 39–57.

Nowosielski, M. (2012). *Polish organisations in Germany—their present status and needs*. Peter Lang. Internationaler Verlag der Wissenschaften.

Nowosielski, M. (2016). *Polskie organizacje w Niemczech. Stan i uwarunkowania*. Instytut Zachodni.

Nowosielski, M. (2018). Poles in Germany engagement in immigrant organisations and its determinants. *Studi Emigrazione—Migration Studies*, *3*, 449–463.

Nowosielski, M. (2020). *Raport podsumowujący badania w Niemczech*. Ośrodek Badań nad Migracjami UW.

Nowosielski, M., & Nowak, W. (2017a). Między Wschodem a Zachodem—geograficzne ukierunkowanie polityki polonijnej i jego przemiany w latach 1989–2017. *Rocznik Instytutu Europy Środkowo-Wschodniej*, *15*, 139–158.

Nowosielski, M., & Nowak, W. (2017b). 'Nowa polityka polonijna'—obszar tworzenia wspólnoty czy przestrzeń gry interesów? *Problemy Polityki Społecznej. Studia i Dyskusje*, *37*, 73–89.

Owusu, T. Y. (2000). The role of Ghanaian immigrant associations in Toronto, Canada. *International Migration Review*, *34*(4), 1155–1181. https://doi.org/10.1177/019791830003400404

Portes, A., & Fernández-Kelly, P. (Eds). (2016). *The state and the grassroots: Immigrant transnational organisations in four continents*. Berghahn Books.

Pries, L., & Sezgin, Z. (2012a). Migration, organisations and transnational ties. In L. Pries & Z. Sezgin (Eds.), *Cross border migrant organisations in comparative perspective* (pp. 1–36). Palgrave Macmillan.

Pries, L., & Sezgin, Z. (Eds). (2012b). *Cross border migrant organisations in comparative perspective*. Palgrave Macmillan.

Rodriguez-Fraticelli, C., Sanabria, C., & Tirado, A. (1991). Puerto Rican non-profit organisations in New York City. In H. E. Gallegos & M. O'Neill (Eds.), *Hispanics in the non-profit sector* (pp. 33–48). The Foundation Center.

Sardinha, J. (2009). *Immigrant associations, integration and identity: Angolan, Brazilian and Eastern European communities in Portugal*. Amsterdam University Press.

Schiller, N. G., Basch, L., & Blanc, C. (1995). From immigrant to transmigrant: Theorizing transnational migration. *Anthropological Quarterly*, *68*(1), 48–63. https://doi.org/10.2307/3317464

Schmidt, J. (2009). *Nowe tożsamości w czasach transformacji europejskich. Imigranci z Polski w Niemczech*. Wydawnictwo NEWS.

Schoeneberg, U. (1985). Participation in ethnic associations: The case of immigrants in West Germany. *International Migration Review*, *19*(3), 416–437. https://doi.org/10.1177/019791838501900302

Scholten, P., Collett, E., & Petrovic, M. (2017). Mainstreaming migrant integration? A critical analysis of a new trend in integration governance. *International Review of Administrative Sciences*, *83*(2), 283–302. https://doi.org/10.1177/0020852315612902

Schrover, M., & Vermeulen, F. (2005). Immigrant organisations. *Journal of Ethnic and Migration Studies*, *31*(5), 823–832. https://doi.org/10.1080/13691830500177792

Stola, D. (2010). *Kraj bez wyjścia? Migracje z Polski 1949–1989*. Instytut Pamięci Narodowej—Komisja Ścigania Zbrodni przeciwko Narodowi Polskiemu, Instytut Studiów Politycznych PAN.

Weiss, K. (2013). Migrantenorganisationen und Staat. Anerkennung, Zusammenarbeit, Förderung. In D. Thränhardt & G. Schultze (Eds.), *Migrantenorganisationen: Engagement, Transnationalität und Integration* (pp. 21–31). WISO Diskurs.

Does Polish Origin Matter? The Integration Challenges of Polish Card Holders in Poland

MYROSLAVA KERYK ⓘ

ABSTRACT   This paper discusses the process of obtaining the Polish Card; the functions attributed to the Card both by politicians and by its holders; the problems of integration faced by Card holders in Poland and the controversies surrounding introduction of the Card in Poland and Ukraine. The principal argument is that *Karta Polaka* has been transformed from a policy instrument supporting Polish minorities in the Post-Soviet countries into one facilitating access to the Polish labour market. Ultimately, it will lead to the cultural assimilation of the Card holders, especially those from the younger generation which have settled in Poland. The article is based both on desk research and on informal interviews with experts and knowledge gathered during my work at a non-governmental organisation that deals with the integration of migrants in Poland.

Introduction

Introduced in 2007, *Karta Polaka* was initially directed at people of Polish descent who are citizens of the 15 post-Soviet states. Nowadays, it is open to citizens of all countries who have Polish origins. While over 200,000 people have received a Polish Card since 2007, the procedure through which the Cards are obtained poses ongoing challenges for the Polish state, as does the integration of Card holders. The Polish authorities justify *Karta Polaka* in terms of a need to support Poles abroad, but it can be argued that it has been transformed from an instrument supporting the Polish minorities in the Post-Soviet countries into one facilitating labour immigration to Poland from these countries, and especially from Ukraine and Belarus. Many Ukrainians and Belarusians apply for the Card primarily because it allows them unimpeded access to the Polish labour market, free-of-charge education and facilitated access to one-year residence visas. However, their proficiency in Polish is generally very low, which causes problems with integration into the labour market and wider society. Their long-term settlement and career advancement depend on language proficiency, as well as the recognition of their qualifications. Regardless of their Polish origin, they are still perceived as foreigners and non-Poles. Despite the low level of Polish language proficiency among Card holders, violations to the procedure for granting the Card and accusations that it brings non-Poles to Poland, *Karta Polaka* still functions as an instrument for the polonisation of Card holders, especially those of the younger generation which have settled in Poland.

The introduction of *Karta Polaka* in 2007 was an important event for the ruling Law and Justice party and was promoted as the main form of state support for the diaspora (Sawicz, 2018, p. 218). It also met with the approval of Polish minorities abroad, but from the beginning it was highly politicised in Poland and also caused much controversy in the neighbouring countries where Polish minority groups live. While some in Poland hailed the support given to Polish minorities abroad, others claimed that *Karta Polaka* would encourage Poles abroad to emigrate to Poland, leading to depopulation of minority communities (Kresy.pl, 2016, 2019). Other critics argued that the Polish government threatens the security of the neighbouring states and is creating new Poles among people living there who had not previously identified themselves as such. Some claimed that the Polish state was forcing people to betray their national identity (Sawicz, 2018, pp. 212–216).

While much research has already been carried out on migration to Poland from neighbouring countries, the beneficiaries of *Karta Polaka* have so far received comparatively little attention (Kowalski, 2015; Opiela et al., 2014). To date, specific research on *Karta Polaka* has focused primarily on its adoption, its legislative evolution and the start of its implementation (Sawicz, 2018; Pudzianowska, 2021). This gap could be explained by the problematic access to data on the Polish Card holders in Poland and abroad and the political objections to conducting such research. The findings could be unexpected and unplanned for the Polish authorities and could provide grounds for criticism of the current government. At the same time, the absence of research makes it difficult to diagnose the problems and obstacles that Card holders encounter in Poland and to devise policies for their integration. The discovery of violations in granting the cards could also lead to restrictions on access to them, which would be criticised by the Polish diaspora. Checks carried out by the Supreme Audit Office (NIK) in 2015–2017 revealed numerous violations of the procedure for issuing the Cards by Polish consulates and the Ministry of Foreign Affairs, including the use of intermediaries for faking documents (Najwyższa Izba Kontroli, 2018). That gave rise to criticism from nationalistic organisations and in the media.

This paper examines the functioning of the procedures for obtaining the Polish Card, the controversies around *Karta Polaka* in Poland and Ukraine and the integration challenges that Ukrainian citizens holding the Card face in Poland. It draws on desk research on these topics, as well as informal interviews with experts and consultants who support migrants in legalising their residence and work in Poland. In the article I have also included findings from my work at a non-governmental organisation dealing with the integration of migrants and from research defining the barriers to such integration.

A Brief History of Karta Polaka

Karta Polaka was introduced in 2007 following several years of discussions (Pudzianowska, 2021). According to its initiators, the Polish Card provides recognition of the holder's belonging to the Polish nation as well as conferring some benefits. Through subsequent amendments, eligibility to apply for the Polish Card has been widened from citizens of the 15 post-Soviet states to encompass those of all states. At the same time, however, it has been limited to people who can demonstrate Polish nationality (*narodowść*), thus excluding non-ethnic Poles who formerly held Polish citizenship and their descendants.[1]

In parallel to the discussions on *Karta Polaka*, the Polish authorities discussed and accepted the Repatriation Act, which was intended to provide a mechanism for the return of former Polish citizens and their ancestors to Poland.[2] The Act was approved in 2000 and amended in 2017. Contrary to the Repatriation Act, the main idea behind the introduction of *Karta Polaka* was to support the Polish minority communities in the East, which, according to the policy-makers, had suffered oppression at the hands of the Soviet regime. It was, therefore, seen as necessary to acknowledge their belonging to the Polish nation and develop their links with Poland (Polskie Radio 24, 2019).

Alongside this symbolic dimension, economic and demographic factors were cited as reasons for the introduction of *Karta Polaka*. Andrzej Stelmachowski, advisor to President Lech Kaczyński during 2007–2009, underlined that policy-makers also took account of the high level of emigration from Poland and the consequent lack of qualified specialists in the country. They saw the solution to this problem as lying in the employment of citizens from the former Soviet states: 'If we have to accept people from abroad who want to work in our country, than it is better to give priority to our compatriots from the East' (Sawicz, 2018, p. 220).

A further important motivating factor for the introduction of *Karta Polaka* was Poland's entry to the Schengen zone in 2007. The introduction of Schengen visas placed an obstacle in travelling to Poland for Poles from the Post-Soviet countries. Holders of the Polish Card were provided with the possibility to obtain a free-of-charge one-year Polish national visa (Sawicz, 2018, pp. 218–221).

Since 2019 *Karta Polaka* has become available to people of Polish origin from across the world. Michał Dworczyk, the Head of the Prime Minister's Office and one of initiators of *Karta Polaka* attributed this change in the law to the fact that the repatriation procedure was not working as expected:

> When the Law on Karta Polaka was designed in 2005, the main idea was to facilitate contacts with the homeland for our compatriots who wish to remain in their place of residence. The situation changed in 2016, when we noted that repatriation does not work; we then created the conditions for holders of the Polish Card to move to and settle in Poland. The concept has changed. (Kresy.pl, 2019)

Nowadays, the Polish Card is viewed both by its creators and its critics as a mean of encouraging settlement in Poland (Kresy.pl, 2019; Niezalezna.pl, 2019). Card holders can automatically receive a permanent residence permit and apply for citizenship after having lived in Poland for one year, with the possibility also to apply for the financial support to settle.

After the introduction of *Karta Polaka,* the Polish government expected to receive over 200,000 applications in the first year. The reality showed that these expectations were exaggerated, and only 26,000 persons applied for the Card during this period (Sawicz, 2018, p. 230). There are several probable explanations for this: many interested persons were still unfamiliar with the application procedure; the number of persons in the post-Soviet countries who identify themselves as Poles was exaggerated; providing the necessary documents was problematic; potential applicants came from multicultural families and identified themselves with the titular nation of the country of residence; potential applicants had insufficient resources to study Polish and to apply (consulates are often situated far from where potential applicants live) (Sawicz, 2018, pp. 227–234). To sum up, in the ten years after

Karta Polaka was implemented (2008–2018), Poland issued 255,325 Polish Cards (Demographic Yearbook of Poland, 2019, p. 450). Of these, most went to citizens of Belarus (125,828) and Ukraine (107,636). Given that there are currently more than a million citizens of Ukraine living in Poland, holders of the Polish Card thus constitute a minority among recent Ukrainian migrants to the country (especially since not all Card holders have actually taken up residence in Poland).[3]

The first wave of applicants were representatives of the Polish minority in Ukraine, for whom the Card had a symbolic meaning of linkage with Poland. Gradually, however, more instrumental considerations like access to the labour market and education have come into play for Ukrainians and Belarusians. Demand for the Polish Card in Ukraine was initially lower than expected, but it grew following the introduction of the new benefits and the economic decline in Ukraine due to the Russian-Ukrainian war and the occupation of Crimea. The number of applications from Ukrainian citizens increased after 2014.

The Polish Card 'Industry'

The introduction of *Karta Polaka* has given rise to what can only be described as an industry surrounding the distribution of Polish Cards. The Ministry of Foreign Affairs of Poland had to prepare the infrastructure of the Polish consulates in the post-Soviet countries, which meant increasing the number of employees and consuls dealing with the *Karta Polaka* procedure, training them in how to evaluate the authenticity of supporting documents and conduct interviews with applicants (Supreme Audit Office 2018, pp. 14–19). Under the terms of the Law, Polish minority organisations were given the right to recommend candidates for the Card and, in the case of applicants who lack the necessary documents proving their origins, to provide certificates testifying to their active civic participation in the organisation. These organisations adjusted their activity to meet the demands of applicants for courses in Polish language and culture and support in the application procedure.

A network of intermediaries has also developed in Ukraine to provide multiple services to applicants for the Polish Card. These advertise their services in Ukrainian cities and towns and in the Ukrainian segment of the internet. Language schools have opened courses in Polish and special Polish language schools dedicated to preparing applicants to pass the interview with the consul or the language exam for the residence permit have appeared. Other services offered by intermediaries include: support with collecting and filling in the necessary documentation for the Card, including archival research; training for the interview with the consul; certificates regarding activity in Polish minority organisations for those who cannot provide documents about their ancestors; and registration for the submission of documents.

In particular, the intermediaries offer help to those who do not actually have Polish origins. Many anonymous companies advertise on the online marketplace OLX.com or other social media platforms. In one such advert, a company offered 'help to obtain a Polish Card regardless of whether you have Polish roots, and without faking documents. We provide services via the Polish community'. Another provided the name of an organisation that would issue the certificate of active work for the Polish community, though since no address was provided it was not possible to verify whether or not this organisation actually exists. The applicant has to pay for the services provided and the advert did not state whether involvement in the community is actually a requirement.

Since there is no recent research on *Karta Polaka*, it is difficult to estimate how many people have received the Card via Polish organisations, which could also mean via the services of intermediaries. Research on *Karta Polaka* from 2014 shows that 91,4% of respondents applied for a Card on the basis of documents testifying to Polish origin, and only 8,6% on the basis of a certificate from an organisation. This research, however, was not representative and was based on a small sample of 35 persons (Opiela et al., 2014, p. 65).

Media in Poland and Ukraine often describe violations of the application procedure for a Polish Card, especially illegal practices by intermediaries. The media claimed that the price for such services ranged from 700 to 4000 euros (Korrespondent, 2013). In December 2019 journalists from the Lviv information portal 'Vholos' conducted an investigation into one intermediary company that offers the range of services described above. It charged a price of 1500 euros, with 300 euros payable in advance (kresy24.pl, 2020; Vholos, 2019). The persons behind the company (later arrested) had advertised themselves on social media as experts on *Karta Polaka* and claimed that they could provide certificates from a Polish organisation based in Lviv. The leader of the organisation, however, claimed that it had only ever issued two such certificates during the course of its existence (WZ, 2020b). This offers a clear example of how such agencies exploit the interest of Ukrainian citizens in obtaining a Polish Card, as well as their lack of confidence in their ability to apply themselves without external support. Many Ukrainian citizens perceive the procedures of applying for visas or the Polish Card as complicated; moreover, their Polish is not of a sufficient standard to fill in the written application form. Thus, they often seek the assistance of such intermediaries, even if they have Polish origins.

In 2018 the Supreme Audit Office of Poland (NIK) evaluated the systems for granting Polish Cards, assessing the practice of the Polish consulates in Ukraine, Belarus and Kazakhstan for the period 2015–2017. Despite the political importance attached to *Karta Polaka* by the Ministry of Foreign Affairs, NIK found that there is no unified digital system in place to deal with applications and that the procedure is time-consuming: on average, applicants have to wait 120 days for an interview with a consul. NIK indicated that the human resources are insufficient, pointing to formal and procedural mistakes in the decisions issued by the consulates, inadequate training for employees about the procedures and practicalities of issuing the Cards and a lack of equipment for verifying the authenticity of documents provided by applicants. NIK also discovered that consuls did not inform the authorities about cases of falsified documents: there were 151 such cases during 2015–2017, but in 134 of these (89%), the consular employees did not report this fact to Polish law enforcement (Supreme Audit Office 2018, p. 41–42). With regard to the consulates in Vinnytsia and Astana, NIK also discovered instances where certificates concerning civic activity in Polish minority organisations had been purchased (Supreme Audit Office 2018, p. 35–37).

The demand for information about *Karta Polaka* means that the Ukrainian internet is full of support materials for the applicants. There are blogs and numerous YouTube channels offering instructions on how to apply, who is eligible, the questions consuls ask at interviews, etc. In Belarus, a special app has been created to help applicants prepare for interview, listing collated questions asked by consuls (Szoszyn, 2020).

Controversies

The implementation of *Karta Polaka* demonstrates the difficulty of defining nationality in the borderland regions of Ukraine, Belarus, Lithuania and Poland. The national identity of persons living in this area developed during the second half of the nineteenth and first half of twentieth century and for many people living there it became a matter of choice between several different identities (Snyder, 2003). Many people from this region identified themselves primarily by religion, with nationality only coming later. If one takes the example of Ukraine, unification of the country under Soviet auspices and the policies of Russification pursued by the USSR have complicated matters further: many citizens either still profess multiple national identities or can cite diverse national origins despite professing belonging to the titular nation (Prawo.pl, 2018). For the inhabitants of the borderland regions the question is how to define Polish identity: on the basis of religion, language or the language of one's ancestors? What to do in the case of multicultural or inter-faith marriages, when choice of religion depended on the faith of the father or mother?[4] Research on the Polish Card holders shows that 10% declared a nationality other than Polish (Kowalski, 2015, p. 36).

The case of Ukrainian students in Przemyśl exemplifies the complexity of this situation. In October 2014, a group of Ukrainian students posed for a photograph in a local shopping centre with the red and black flag used by the Ukrainian Insurgent Army (UPA) during World War II. The flag is used by right-wing movements in present-day Ukraine but has also come to symbolise the current struggle against Russian aggression in the country's east. In Poland this flag is not formally prohibited, but is perceived negatively, due to UPA's involvement in the murder of Poles in Volynia in 1943 (Wyborcza.pl, 2014). The students took the photo to demonstrate support for Ukraine in its fight against Russia and claimed that they were unaware of how the flag is perceived in Poland (Wyborcza. pl, 2014). It appeared that six of the students have Polish origins and are holders of the Polish Card. Nationalist media and activists brought this case to attention at the national level and made it the focus for an anti-Ukrainian campaign, demanding that the students be expelled from Poland and their Polish Cards annulled (kresy.pl, 2014, 2016). Regardless of their origins, the students were branded Ukrainian nationalists and promoters of fascism, though they themselves issued a statement insisting:

> By this photo we did not promote fascism. We apologise to the Polish nation for the offence. Please accept our explanation that we are not *Banderowcy*. We all have Polish roots. We did not want to promote a nationalistic idea. We wanted to do something for our homeland. (Wyborcza.pl, 2014)

This case shows the complexity of the identity of Polish Card holders. On the one hand, they identify themselves with the country of their citizenship, but their Polish origins mean that they also identify with the Polish nation. Their identity is, therefore, not exclusive, but inclusive.

The criteria for obtaining a Polish Card require citizens of Post-Soviet states to fit into a canon of Polishness, which also means professing the Catholic faith. Multi-ethnic origins are accepted, providing that some of the ancestors were Poles, but not multiple identity. The questions that consuls ask during the interviews for the Polish Card refer to Polish culture and traditions based on the Catholic religion, without taking into account the local cultural context of the Poles living in the borderlands (Sawicz, 2018, pp. 210–211).

Polish minority organisations in the neighbouring countries criticised the criteria and procedure for granting the Card. For them, one of the main problems lay in the elimination of former Polish citizenship as a criterion for proving belonging to the Polish nation. Here they insisted that, due to the loss of documents during Soviet times, it is often difficult to prove one's Polish origins (Sawicz, 2018, p. 210).

Karta Polaka is also criticised for stimulating the migration of Poles to Poland, which diminishes the membership of Polish minority organisations. Nationalistic media and organisations in Poland refer to this as the 'depolonisation of the borderlands' (Kresy.pl, 2016, 2019). They insist that the goal of *Karta Polaka* is to support the national minorities in the places where they live, and not to motivate them to migrate to Poland. Migration means that the minority loses its young and active generation and remains weak:

> It cannot be like this that the Polish Card becomes an encouragement for young 'singles' to settle in Poland. This document should be such as it was planned from the beginning—that is, as a replacement for [Polish] citizenship in a country, where they [the minority] cannot have it (this was the original idea), but also as instrument to support and unify the minorities in their places. (Kresy.pl, 2019)

They also criticise the authorities for granting Polish Cards to non-Poles. Sociologist Robert Wyszyński, who often comments on *Karta Polaka* for the far-right portal kresy.pl, has even claimed that the Polish Card could be called the Card of the Former Citizen of the Second Polish Republic (Kresy.pl, 2019).

Karta Polaka also found its critics in Ukraine, especially after 2014, when migration to Poland increased due to the economic crisis. The Ukrainian authorities, unlike those in Belarus or Lithuania, did not perceive the introduction of *Karta Polaka* as a threat to the security of the state. Rather, the migration of Ukrainian citizens helped to address the problem of unemployment and brought remittances to the country (Coupé & Vakhitova, 2013, p. 10, 20; Jaroszewicz, 2018, p. 11). With increased migration of Ukrainians, especially to Poland after 2014, the authorities discussed the possibility of taxing migrants or restricting their access to some social benefits. Recently, the Ukrainian government proposed a law by which the Polish Card holders or persons with double citizenship could lose the right to a pension or other social benefits (Kresy24.pl, 2020). Thus far, however, these have remained only drafts.

Karta Polaka is also criticised by the Ukrainian media, especially its more nationalistic elements. These criticise the Polish authorities for the fact that as part of the application procedure for the Card, Ukrainians have to declare their belonging to the Polish nation, which means denying their Ukrainian identity. In the same vein, they criticise the practice whereby Polish consuls ask questions on Polish and Ukrainian history as part of the application interview and require the applicant to confirm the Polish version. Some Ukrainian media regard this as interference in Ukraine's internal affairs (Vholos, 2019; WZ, 2020a).

Karta Polaka and especially the applicants for the Polish Card have also attracted criticism from among Ukrainian intellectuals. Yuriy Andrukhovych, one of the most popular modern Ukrainian poets and writers, accused Ukrainians who apply for the Card of betraying their motherland in search of material gain. He claims that, by accepting Ukrainians, Poland receives unfaithful new inhabitants.

> They are going to the Polish Consulate ... for their decisive interview for the Polish Card. Ukrainians massively want to become Poles ... Final preparations for the decisive interviews. One can hear about the renowned historic events: the Battle of Grunwald, the Lublin Union and the Constitution of 3rd of May. If they would study their

own history so attentively, then, maybe, there would be no need for *Karta Polaka*, I am thinking nastily …

People are looking for a homeland. The one which they perceived as theirs does not meet their expectations. It is worth replacing it with a neighbouring one, especially when that neighbour does not object, and even welcomes them. (Zbruch.eu, 2017)

Andrukhovych's article evoked discussions on social media. On the one hand, people agreed with his opinion and criticised Ukrainians applying for the Polish Card; on the other, Andrukhovych was criticised for elitism and for denying people the right to improve their living conditions. Andrukhovych delivered a moral evaluation of Ukrainians' desire to apply for Polish Cards, and his opinion reflects a more general tendency to frame migration either as a betrayal of Ukraine or as a threat to its demographic and economic position (Europe without Barriers, 2019; Keryk, 2004). The Ukrainian media, especially in recent years, underline that migration damages Ukraine, using terms such as 'bleeding' when analysing the situation (Europe without Barriers, 2019). The main blame for migration is attributed to the state authorities, which are criticised for not taking necessary actions to prevent it by providing stable economic growth.

Political statements and decisions as well as articles such as the one by Andrukhovych polarise public opinion, which is reflected in social media. Opinion is divided between those who view migrants as traitors and those who view them as martyrs and attribute blame to the Ukrainian authorities. The discussions about *Karta Polaka* on social media, especially in the numerous Ukrainian groups on Facebook (Ukraińcy w Polsce / Ukraintsi v Polshchi (Українці в Польщі) or groups dedicated to this topic like *Karta Poliaka. Informatsiia: Yak, koly, kudy?* (Карта Поляка. Інформація: як, коли, куди?) (e-konsulat)[5]) reflect a more practical approach. Here, applicants or Polish Card holders discuss questions related to the application procedure, mostly in Ukrainian or Russian. Moral judgements are sometimes still expressed with regard to Ukrainian citizens who obtain the card, but these relate mainly to the fact that some people apply without knowledge of Polish traditions and culture and thus 'pretend' to be a Pole. Thus, one commentator claimed that:

Your grandma was a Pole and you have a right for a Polish Card because you come from a Polish family. Many *Moskalnia*[6] come here who pretend to be Poles and have no knowledge of Polish language, history, or culture. (Quotation from a Facebook group discussion)

This post shows the complicated identity of the author, which combines Ukrainian and Polish elements but excludes Russian-speaking Ukrainian citizens. It also reflects the identity and language conflict in Ukraine, which intensified following the start of the Russian-Ukrainian war in 2014 when some accused Russian speaking citizens of being unpatriotic (Language.policy.info, 2015). This division has a long history and has been used by politicians during election campaigns since the establishment of the independence of Ukraine, deepening divisions in society.

This post offers further proof that Polish Card holders come to Poland with complicated identities, which developed under the influence of the history and politics of the countries from which they came. This also poses an integration challenge for the Polish authorities, because these Card holders require an integration package to settle in Poland (language courses, professional training, etc.), but also the possibility to cultivate the traditions and languages of their countries of origin.

Integration Challenges

Polish Card holders are a privileged group of migrants in Poland, due to the benefits conferred by *Karta Polaka*. Yet, in spite of this, the Card holders encounter integration problems similar to those faced by other migrants. They need support on the labour market, in education and in learning Polish language and culture.

The key to integration and, especially, professional advancement in Poland is proficiency in Polish. For the majority of migrants, this is the major obstacle to success in the labour market, and it applies also to Card holders. To obtain the Card they have to pass the interview and to demonstrate a knowledge of Polish on the basic level; generally, however, this level is insufficient for professional advancement (FNW and ISEE, 2015, pp. 252–255; HFHR, 2012, pp. 150–152).

For migrants, access to language courses is problematic outside the large cities, and even in the cities the prices for language courses are high. State-financed courses and those run by nongovernmental organisations are very limited in number. This is one of the reasons why Card holders apply for citizenship to the President of Poland.[7] This procedure does not require the applicant to pass a Polish-language exam, in contrast to the procedure of applying via the authorities of the province where the applicant lives.[8] Receiving citizenship via the President means that Card holders have no incentive to acquire proficiency in Polish and tend to limit their communication to the people from their country of origin, leading to problems with integration into Polish society. In by-passing the language requirement, applications for citizenship via the President also limit Card holders' possibilities for professional advancement, meaning that they tend to work in jobs not commensurate to their qualifications.

Polish Card holders are placed in the same basket as migrants in general. Research shows that it takes repatriates at least one year or more to find their first job (Opiela et al., 2014, pp. 57–58). Migrants' job applications are rejected at the CV stage, because they have foreign-sounding names (FNW and ISEE, 2015, pp. 296–301). It is important to underline that the names of Polish Card holders from Ukraine are written in the documents according to the transliteration from Cyrillic accepted in their country of origin. It is only when applying for citizenship that they can change the spelling of their name, which might help them to disguise their foreign origins.

Karta Polaka provides access to free-of-charge public education at all levels. This opportunity has brought Card holders to Poland and has even been a factor motivating people to applying for a Card in the first place. Children also face educational and integrational issues in schools. They need assistance with learning Polish and familiarising themselves with the Polish system of education in order to progress in their learning, and emotional support in order to avoid marginalisation. The problem is that schools and teachers are unprepared to teach children from a multicultural background (Januszewska, 2017, p. 140–142). University students also require special support for integration, in particular additional Polish courses in order to prepare them for study in Poland. Often these students begin their studies with a low level of Polish, meaning that they fail courses, even when they have previously attained good results in their studies (HFHR, 2012, pp. 48–52). Migrant students also face negative attitudes from Polish students, hate speech and offensive behaviour.

The lack of special integration measures at universities which recruit students from Ukraine and other neighbouring countries leads to the isolation of these students from their Polish peers and further problems in their education (HFHR, 2012, pp. 51–52).

Recognition of diplomas and qualifications is the next obstacle to labour market integration faced by Polish Card holders. Such recognition is regulated on the basis of Polish and international law and bilateral agreements, and also depends on the profession of the holders (Hołuszko, 2014; Prawo.pl, 2019). Access to professions is especially complicated, as doctors, nurses, lawyers, teachers, psychologists and others are required to undergo additional training and pass further exams in order to practise. Thus, along with many other migrants, Polish Card holders often work at levels below their competences and qualifications;[9] for instance, qualified doctors and nurses holding the Polish Card work as paramedics or physiotherapists or in other spheres related to medicine.

Polish Card holders come to Poland with the cultural codes and modes of behaviour characteristic of their countries of origin. Very often their main language of communication is also the language of their country of origin, which in the case of Ukrainian citizens are Ukrainian and Russian. They speak Polish with an accent, which means that regardless of their Polish origins, they are still perceived as foreigners and *non-Poles*. They could become victims of hate crimes on the basis of their accent, their perceived failure to abide by imagined cultural codes or simply the fact that they came from abroad. This is exemplified by the reaction in the nationalist media to the students from Przemyśl who posed with the red and black flag: despite their Polish origins they were not recognised as Poles, but rather as Ukrainians with Polish Cards.

Conclusion

The original idea behind *Karta Polaka* was to recognise Poles abroad as the part of the Polish nation. In this conception, they were imagined as a culturally and religiously monolithic group—the fact that Polish Card holders have lived in borderland regions or among other nationalities and often have multiple national and cultural identities was not taken into account. The present reality is such that many applicants for the Card feel affiliated to their country of origin and use the language of this country (as is evident from internet discussion groups), but also feel connected to Poland. Due to having lived outside of the Polish cultural context, often in a multicultural environment, they have different cultural codes. There is a need for greater understanding of this fact in Poland, so that Polish society can adjust to the 'otherness' of Polish Card holders. The cultural diversity of this group should be explained to the host society in order to counteract stereotyping and negative attitudes and provide for smoother integration.

Karta Polaka is criticised by nationalist media both Ukraine in and in Poland. In Poland, the authorities are accused of granting the Card to persons without Polish origins or to Ukrainian nationalists. Polish Card holders are presented as 'non-Poles,' especially when they do not behave in accordance with the imagined canons of Polishness. Ukrainian media and intellectuals criticise the Card holders for betrayal of their nationality and their country and blame the state authorities for not providing the necessary work places and sufficient wages to keep people in the country.

The Russian war against Ukraine and the resultant economic crisis, coupled with shortages on the Polish labour market, increased the attractiveness of *Karta Polaka* in Ukraine. Thus, instead of serving as a means of strengthening the Polish community abroad, *Karta Polaka* was transformed into a mechanism for bringing its representatives to Poland, while also motivating citizens of Ukraine with Polish ancestry to establish their Polish roots and to apply for the Polish Card in order to have access to the Polish labour market and to free education for their children.

Notes

1. Act of 7 September 2007 on the Card of Pole (Journal of Laws of 2007, No 180, item 1280, as amended); Act of 28 August 2003 amending the Act on repatriation (Journal of Laws of 2003, No 157, item 1691, as amended); Act of 13 May 2016 amending the Act on the Pole's Card and certain other acts (Journal of Laws of 2016, item 753); Act of 16 May 2019 amending the Act of Pole's Card (Journal of Laws of 2019, item 1095).
2. Ustawa z dnia 9 listopada 2000 r. o repatriacji, Dz. U. z 2000 r. Nr 106, poz. 1118; Ustawa z dnia 7 kwietnia 2017 r. o zmianie ustawy o repatriacji oraz niektórych innych ustaw, Dz. U. z 2017 r. poz. 858 tom 1.
3. There are no comprehensive statistics on migration to Poland. The data comes from different sources and cannot be easily summarised here. In the case of Ukrainians in Poland, there are several sources of data. Ukrainian citizens received 1.15 million visas in 2017 and 876,064 in 2018. Due to the establishment of the visa free regime between Ukraine and EU countries belonging to the Schengen Area in June 2017, the number of visas was reduced. Ukrainians who live more or less permanently in Poland have applied for short- or long-term residence permits, of which 214 719 had been issued by 01.01.2020 [Data from the Office for Foreigners: www.udsc.gov.pl]. The majority of Ukrainians in Poland are temporary labour migrants, who access the labour market on the basis of temporary work permits (Declaration to employ foreigner—Oświadczenia o powierzeniu pracy cudzoziemcowi) and seasonal work permits. In recent years over one million Ukrainians have received such permits and come to Poland. For instance, 971,840 Ukrainians in 2019 received 1 475 923 of such declarations. (Data from the Ministry of Family, Labour and social Policy). The company that analyses the behaviour of smartphone users has published data on Ukrainian smartphone users in Poland. According to the Company Selectivv there were 1,270,398 Ukrainians in Poland in January 2019. [Sylwia Czubkowska. Smartfony policzyły Ukraińców. Ile Ukrainek planuje mieć dzieci? Retrieved May 13, 2020 from https://wyborcza.pl/7,156282,24522397, smartfony-policzyly-ukraincow-ile-ukrainek-planuje-miec-dzieci.html.
4. On the territories of Galicia there was tradition of baptising the daughter in the religion of the mother, and the son in the religion of the father.
5. https://www.facebook.com/groups/infoKP/.
6. Moskalnia (Москальня) –an offensive term for Russians or Russian speaking Ukrainians.
7. Today, foreigners can apply for citizenship in Poland either via President or via regional authorities. Until 2012, granting citizenship was the sole prerogative of the President. The law on citizenship from 1962 underwent numerous revisions, but remained a rather restrictive document which substantially limited access to citizenship. The decision of the president was final and there was no possibility of appeal. Facilitation of the procedure was introduced through the Act on Citizenship of 2009, which came into force in 2012. The new law on citizenship broadened the categories of foreigners who can apply for citizenship, decreased the period of prior stay required for citizenship, gave regional authorities the right to grant citizenship and introduced an appeal procedure. With the adoption of this, law the number of naturalised citizens increased. For more on this topic, see: Keryk and Trochimczyk-Sawczuk (2018).
8. The latter involves an initial application for a permanent residence permit, passing the state language examination at B1 level and then, after one year, applying for citizenship.
9. The presumption is made on the basis of research done on Ukrainian migrants in Poland (Alebank.pl, 2018; Keryk & Pawlak, 2015) and the information collected during the work with migrants.

ORCID

Myroslava Keryk ⬤ http://orcid.org/0000-0002-7011-2011

References

Alebank.pl. (2018). Ukraińcy są wykształceni, ale i tak w większości pracują fizycznie. Retrieved June 19, 2020, from https://alebank.pl/ukraincy-sa-wyksztalceni-ale-i-tak-w-wiekszosci-pracuja-fizycznie/

Coupé, T., & Vakhitova, H. (2013). *Costs and benefits of labour mobility between the EU and the Eastern partnership partner countries.* Country report. Retrieved May 20, 2020, from https://www.case-research.eu/files/?id_plik=4551

Demographic Yearbook of Poland. (2019). Statistics Poland. Retrieved May 6, 2020, from https://stat.gov.pl/files/gfx/portalinformacyjny/pl/defaultaktualnosci/5515/3/13/1/rocznik_demograficzny_2019.pdf

Europe without Barriers. (2019). *Myths and facts about Ukrainian labour migration to the visegrad group.* Retrieved May 4, 2020, from https://english.europewb.org.ua/myths-and-facts-about-ukrainian-labour-migration-to-visegrad-four-countries/

FNW and ISEE. (2015). Konieczna-Sałamatin J. (Ed.), *Imigranci o wysokich kwalifkacjach na polskim rynku pracy.* Raport z badań 2014–2015. Retrieved May 10, 2020, from https://pl.naszwybir.pl/wp-content/uploads/sites/2/2015/06/raport_imigranci_nw_isee.pdf

HFHR. (2012). Mikulska A. & Patzer H. (Eds.), *Bariery po drodzę do integracji.* Retrieved May 10, 2020, from http://www.hfhr.pl/wp-content/uploads/2012/06/HFPC_Bieg_przez_plotki_bariery.pdf

Hołuszko, E. (2014). *Ekspertyza dotycząca uznawania świadectw, dyplomów zagranicznych uczelni oraz stopni tytułów naukowych w Polsce.* Retrieved May 6, 2020, from https://www.politykimigracyjne.pl/images/publikacje/Ekspertyza_uczelni.pdf

Januszewska, E. (2017). Uczniowie cudzoziemscy w polskiej szkole – między integracją a marginalizacją. In: *Studia Edukacyjne* nr 43, 2017.

Jaroszewicz, M. (2018). *Migration from Ukraine to Poland. The trend stabilises.* Retrieved May 20, 2020, from https://www.osw.waw.pl/sites/default/files/Report_Migration%20from%20Ukraine_net.pdf

Keryk, M. (2004). *Labour migrant: Our savior or betrayer? Ukrainian discussions concerning labour migration.* Retrieved May 5, 2020, from https://aa.ecn.cz/img_upload/f76c21488a048c95bc0a5f12deece153/Keryk___Labour_Migrant.pdf

Keryk, M., & Pawlak, M. (2015). Migranci o wysokich kwalifkacjach na rynku pracy. Perspektywa instytucji rynku pracy. In: FNW and ISEE (2015) Konieczna-Sałamatin J. (Ed.), *Imigranci o wysokich kwalifkacjach na polskim rynku pracy. Raport z badań 2014–2015.* Retrieved May 10, 2020, from https://pl.naszwybir.pl/wp-content/uploads/sites/2/2015/06/raport_imigranci_nw_isee.pdf

Keryk, M., & Trochimczyk-Sawczuk, I. (Керик М. Трохімчик-Савчук I.) (2018). Naturalizatsiia v Polshchi (Натуралізація в Польщі). Retrieved June 19, 2020, from https://europewb.org.ua/wp-content/uploads/2019/03/Polske-gromadyanstvo.pdf

Korrespondent. (2013). Iz ukraintsev v shlyaktichi. Ukraintsy rinulis' iskat' u sebya pol'skie korni. 8 Oktyabrya 2013 (Из украинцев в шляхтичи. Украинцы ринулись искать у себя польские корни. 8 октября 2013). Retrieved May 7, 2020, from https://korrespondent.net/ukraine/events/1611983-korrespondent-iz-ukraincev-v-shlyahtichi-ukraincy-rinulis-iskat-u-sebya-polskie-korni

Kowalski, M. (2015). Raport z badań na temat posiadaczy Karty Polaka. In: Dworczyk M. & Odkryte Karty Historii (Eds.), *Podsumowanie ustawy o Karcie Polaka.*

Kresy.pl. (2014). Banderowcy robią sobie fotki w galerii handlowej w Przemyślu. Retrieved May 11, 2020, from https://kresy.pl/wydarzenia/banderowcy-robia-sobie-fotki-w-galerii-handlowej-w-przemyslu/

Kresy.pl. (2016). Nowelizacja Ustawy o Karcie Polaka Doprowadzi do Depolonizacji Kresów. Retrieved May 5, 2020, from https://kresy.pl/publicystyka/nowelizacja-ustawy-o-karcie-polaka-doprowadzi-do-depolonizacji-kresow/

Kresy.pl. (2016). Polski MSZ: Karty Polaka Wydane Banderowcom Zostaną Unieważnione. Retrieved May 10, 2020, from https://kresy.pl/wydarzenia/polskie-msz-karty-polaka-wydane-banderowcom-zostana-uniewaznione/

Kresy.pl. (2019). Współtwórca Karty Polaka przyznaje, że obecnie może ona służyć depolonizacji Kresów, bo "repatriacja nie działa." Retrieved May 5, 2020, from https://kresy.pl/wydarzenia/wspoltworca-karty-polaka-przyznaje-ze-obecnie-moze-ona-sluzyc-depolonizacji-kresow-bo-repatriacja-nie-dziala-i-zmienila-sie-koncepcja/

Kresy24.pl. (2020a). Rząd ukraiński chce odebrać świadczenia emerytom posiadającym paszporty obcych państw i Kartę Polaka. Retrieved May 11, 2020, from https://kresy24.pl/rzad-ukrainski-chce-odebrac-swiadczenia-emerytom-posiadajacym-paszporty-obcych-panstw-i-karte-polaka/

Kresy24.pl. (2020b). SBU zatrzymała dwóch fałszerzy "Karty Polaka", którzy kierowali pogróżki wobec konsula RP we Lwowie. Retrieved May 11, 2020, from https://kresy24.pl/sbu-zatrzymala-dwoch-falszerzy-kart-polaka-ktorzy-kierowali-pogrozki-wobec-konsula-rp-we-lwowie/

Language.policy.info. (2015). Serhii Osnach. Movna skladova hibrydnoi viiny (Сергій Оснач. Мовна складова гібридної війни). Retrieved May 10, 2020, from http://language-policy.info/2015/06/serhij-osnach-movna-skladova-hibrydnoji-vijny/

Najwyższa Izba Kontroli. (2018). *Informacja o wynikach kontroli. Przyznawanie Karty Polaka Osobom Zamieszkałym Za Wschodnią Granicą RP*. Retrieved April 21, 2020, from https://www.nik.gov.pl/kontrole/wyniki-kontroli-nik/kontrole,18207.html

Niezalezna.pl. (2019). Dworczyk o aktywizowaniu Polaków za granicą do głosowania. Mówi o obecnej "mikroskali". Retrieved May 13, 2020, from https://niezalezna.pl/287113-dworczyk-o-aktywizowaniu-polakow-za-granica-do-glosowania-mowi-o-obecnej-mikroskali

Opiela, K., Skorycki, S., & Socha, Z. (2014). *Polacy na wschodzie a polityka migracyjna RP. Diagnoza i propozycje zmian*. Retrieved May 12, 2020, from https://fundacjarepublikanska.org/wp-content/uploads/2020/01/Raport-repatrianci-8-grudnia-2014-1.pdf

Polskie Radio 24. (2019). Michał Dworczyk: przez lata ograniczano prawa Polaków na Wschodzie. Retrieved May 13, 2020, from https://polskieradio24.pl/130/8303/Artykul/2365205,Michal-Dworczyk-przez-lata-ograniczano-prawa-Polakow-na-Wschodzie

Prawo.pl. (2018). Niepotrzebne obostrzenia w ustawie o Karcie Polaka. Retrieved April 12, 2018, from https://www.prawo.pl/prawnicy-sady/niepotrzebne-obostrzenia-w-ustawie-o-karcie-polaka,73818.html

Prawo.pl. (2019). Potwierdzenie kwalifikacji zagranicznego pracownika to nie lada kłopot dla pracodawcy. Retrieved May 6, 2020, from https://www.prawo.pl/kadry/potwierdzenie-kwalifikacji-pracownika-to-klopot-dla-pracodawcow,455550.html

Pudzianowska, D. (2021). Karta Polaka – New wine in old bottles. *Ethnopolitics*. doi:10.1080/17449057.2020.1808319

Sawicz, A. (2018). Karta Polaka – przepustka do lepszego świata. In: Miszewski M. (Ed.), *Imigranci z Ukrainy w Polsce. Potrzeby i oczekiwania, reakcje społeczne, wyzwania dla bezpieczeństwa*.

Snyder, T. (2003). *The reconstruction of nations: Poland, Ukraine, Lithuania, Belarus, 1569–1999*.

Szoszyn, R. (2020). Karta Polaka: Droga do Polski. Retrieved May 6, 2020, from https://www.rp.pl/Bialorus/309269893-Karta-Polaka-Droga-do-Polski.html

Vholos. (2019). Bandera ne heroi, a UPA – banditi: yak otrymaty Kartu Poliaka, yakshcho ty ne Poliak – rozsliduvannia "Vholosu." (Бандера не герой, а УПА – бандити: як отримати Карту Поляка, якщо ти не поляк? – розслідування "Вголосу."). Retrieved May 11, 2020, from https://vgolos.com.ua/articles/bandera-ne-geroj-a-upa-bandyty-yak-otrymaty-kartu-polyaka-yakshho-ty-ne-polyak-rozsliduvannya-vgolosu_1120933.html

Wyborcza.pl. (2014). Zła Flaga. Retrieved May 10, 2020, from https://wyborcza.pl/duzyformat/1,127290,16916487,Zla_flaga.html

WZ. (2020a). Eliza Dzvonkievich: "Yakshcho osoba pochuvaietsia ukraintsem, to navisshcho khoche otrymaty Kartu noliaka?" (Еліза Дзвонкєвіч: «Якщо особа почувається українцем, то навіщо хоче отримати Карту поляка?»). Retrieved May 6, 2020, from https://wz.lviv.ua/article/405808-eliza-dzvonkievich-yakshcho-osoba-pochuvaietsia-ukraintsem-to-navishcho-khoche-otrymaty-kartu-poliaka

WZ. (2020b). Yuliia Lishchenko. V Interneti I nadali proponuiut "otrymaty Kartu poliaka, navit yakshcho u vas nemaie polskykh koreniv". (Юлія Ліщенко. В Інтернеті і надалі пропонують «отримати Карту поляка, навіть якщо у вас немає польських коренів»). Retrieved May 6, 2020, from https://wz.lviv.ua/article/404498-v-interneti-i-nadali-proponuiut-otrymaty-kartu-poliaka-navit-iakshcho-u-vas-nemaie-polskykh-koreniv

Zbruch.eu. (2017). Yurii Andrukhovich, Yak liazhut karty? (Юрій Андрухович, Як ляжуть карти?). Retrieved May 7, 2020, from https://zbruc.eu/node/64189

Identities of and Policies Towards the Polish National Minority in Lithuania

DIANA JANUŠAUSKIENĖ

ABSTRACT   This paper explores the multi-layered intersecting identities of the Polish national minority in Lithuania and analyses the impact of national, local, and foreign policies on the accommodation and identities of this minority. The paper examines policies of the Government of the Republic of Lithuania at the national level, policies of the political party Electoral Action of Poles in Lithuania—Christian Families Alliance (LLRA-KŠS), (a governing political party in the south-eastern municipalities of Lithuania where ethnic Poles comprise a significant part of the population) at the municipal level, and the kin-state policies of the Government of the Republic of Poland. The paper argues that due to certain specific characteristics of the Polish national minority as well as certain policies that are applied towards it, in the short term it is not possible to predict either a strong identification with Lithuania or a strong trans-sovereign identification with Poland. One of the most important factors for the survival of this minority are schools with the Polish language of instruction. Nevertheless, the impact of this factor is twofold: on the one hand, these schools have a direct influence on the reproduction of Polish national identity; yet, on the other, they may re-create social cleavage and prevent the formation of a wider civic Lithuanian identity. Attachment to the Russian language and Russian media adds an additional important layer that shapes the identities and attitudes of the minority. However, the most solid layer within the multi-layered identity of this minority remains identification with locality (a certain village or town, or the Vilnius region in general).

Introduction

The Polish national minority in Lithuania has been studied extensively during the last three decades by national and international scholars. This national minority attracts attention due to its specificity as well as its potential for comparative research. Scholars are interested in its historical formation (Eberhardt, 2002, 2008; Stravinskienė, 2005, 2007, 2010), identity (Gordon, 1996; Kazėnas et al., 2014; Korzeniewska, 1997), models of accommodation (Kasatkina, 2002; Kasatkina & Leončikas, 2003), usage of languages (Geben, 2013; Ramonienė, 2010, 2013), schooling (Bakonis et al., 2018), as well as its political agenda (Janušauskienė, 2016; Kowalski, 2000) and the role it plays in bilateral relations between Lithuania and Poland (Kowalski, 2008; Sirutavičius, 2009). The research accomplished by Lithuanian, Polish and other scholars shares many similar findings; yet, as a rule, cross-referencing between studies published by Polish and Lithuanian researchers is almost absent. In addition, many findings published in Polish or Lithuanian remain unknown to foreign scholars.

This paper is based on a variety of empirical research undertaken by Lithuanian scholars, and one of its side objectives is to make this national research known to a wider audience. The aim of the paper is to explore the specificity of the Polish national minority in Lithuania and to analyse the impact of national, local, and foreign policies on the accommodation and identities of this minority. The paper examines policies applied by various political actors: the Government of Lithuania at the national level, the political party Electoral Action of Poles in Lithuania—Christian Families Alliance (LLRA-KŠS) at the municipal level, and the foreign policies of the Government of Poland at the international level. The goal of this analysis is to understand the preconditions for the implementation of these policies and the kind of impact these policies have (or might have) on the forms of accommodation and identities of the Polish national minority in Lithuania. The central question of the analysis is whether these policies foster or prevent development of a stronger identification with Lithuania, on the one hand, and trans-sovereign identification with Poland, on the other.

The paper argues that the identity of the Polish national minority in Lithuania is multi-layered. The inner (and most solid) layers of the identity are formed on the basis of a combination of several shared communalities: Catholic faith, Slavic origin, a long historical attachment to the Vilnius region, as well as a linguistic cleavage that separates this Slavic-speaking minority from the Lithuanian speaking majority. The outer (and weaker) layers consist of identification with Lithuania (based on citizenship and place of residence), and a trans-sovereign identification with Poland (based on culture, language and Slavic origin).

Empirically, the paper rests on the analysis of official data of Statistics Lithuania as well as other statistical data on the Polish national minority collected by Lithuanian historians; several national representative surveys; and qualitative semi-structured interviews from two empirical projects involving the author that were recently carried out at the Institute of Sociology of the Lithuanian Social Research Centre. The first project—'Subjective security in volatile geopolitical context: Traits, factors and individual strategies' (2015–2017) (hereafter 'Subjective Security')—provides substantial empirical data on attitudes of ethnic Poles, derived from two representative surveys carried out in February 2016: a national survey (N=1009) and a survey of national minorities (ethnic Poles and ethnic Russians) (N=414). In the paper, this data is used to show the complexity of the situation of the minority. The second project—'Quality of democracy and equal opportunities: Attitudes and social practice' (2017–2018) (hereafter 'Quality of Democracy')—provides data on the human rights situation of national minorities in Lithuania. In the paper, the empirical data from 30 semi-structured qualitative interviews are used for illustrating the trends. Data from other representative surveys allow the research to be placed in the context of previous studies, while official statistics show the longitudinal demographic tendencies.

The Origin and Peculiarities of the Polish National Minority in Lithuania

In Lithuania, Poles are the largest national minority, making up 5.65 per cent of the total population in 2019 (Statistics Lithuania 2019c). A key characteristic of this minority is its concentration in the south-eastern part of Lithuania around the capital Vilnius. In some administrative districts of this region, ethnic Poles constitute either the majority or a significant part of the population. According to the census of 2011, the largest proportion of the Polish population lives in Šalčininkai district (ethnic Poles make up 77.8%), Vilnius district (52.1%), Trakai district (30.1%) and Švenčionys district (26%) (Population Census, 2011a).

The Polish national minority in Lithuania formed as a result of several interrelated factors: changes of state borders over several past centuries, and processes of assimilation and migration. The Polish language played a key role in the Polish-Lithuanian Commonwealth which was established in 1569 by creating a confederation between the Kingdom of Poland and the Grand Duchy of Lithuania. The Commonwealth existed until the final partition of 1795. During this period, Polish gradually became a dominant language used by the nobility and town dwellers and was also employed as an official language in the chancellery of the Grand Duchy of Lithuania from 1697 (Barbour & Carmichael, 2000; O'Connor, 2006). The dominance of the Polish language had a significant influence on the identities of the inhabitants of Lithuania. Assimilation to the Polish language and culture was common.

Another important factor was migration during the twentieth century. During the period 1920–1939, when the capital of Lithuania Vilnius and its surroundings were ruled by Poland, around 98,000 ethnic Poles migrated from Poland to the Vilnius region. An additional 25,000 ethnic Poles had moved to Lithuania by early 1940. Historical sources suggest that by late 1944-early 1945, the number of ethnic Poles in the Vilnius region ranged from 259,325 to 264,325 people (Stravinskienė, 2007, p. 39). After the Second World War, repatriation agreements between the Soviet Union and Poland resulted in 169,000 people leaving Lithuania for Poland during 1944–1947 (Stravinskienė, 2007, p. 46). This population exchange meant that the Polish elite left for Poland, and Lithuania was left 'with a Polish population that was at the bottom of the socio-economic ladder' (Gordon, 1996, p. 221). Due to this emigration as well as deportations during the Stalin era, by 1947 the number of ethnic Poles in Lithuania diminished to 100,000 (Stravinskienė, 2005, p. 23). Later, due to natural growth of the population (on average Polish families had 3.7 children) and immigration from other republics of the Soviet Union (mainly Belarus, Latvia and Russia), the number of ethnic Poles started to grow. According to the data of the Soviet Population Census of 1959, there were 230,100 ethnic Poles resident in Lithuania (Stravinskienė, 2005, p. 24). After the collapse of the Soviet regime and restoration of Lithuania's independence, the size of the Polish minority diminished from 258,000 in 1989 (7% of the total population) to 157,871 (5.65%) in 2019 (see Table 1). This decrease corresponds to a general decrease of the population in Lithuania which has occurred due to low birth rates and emigration. Yet, in the case of the Polish minority several additional factors might have influenced change. These are mixed marriages, change of self-identification as well as assimilation. For example, in the Population Census of 2011, 0.6% of the total population of Lithuania declared that they have two native languages, and one-fifth of this proportion said that these were Lithuanian and Polish (Population Census, 2011b).

Language Usage

An important feature of the Polish national minority is its specific relation to the Polish language. According to the Population Census 2011, 77.1% of ethnic Poles considered Polish to be their native language, while 10.1% stated that their native language was Russian, 8.8%—Lithuanian, 0.2%—Belarusian, and 2.5% mentioned two native languages

Table 1. The Proportion of Polish National Minority in Lithuania in 1944–2019

Year	% of Total Population	Amount
1944–1945	-	259,325–264,325*
1947	-	100,000
1959	8.5	230,100
1979	7.3	247,000
1989	7.0	258,000
2001	6.7	235,000
2007	6.3	212,100
2008	6.2	208,300
2009	6.1	205,500
2010	6.0	201,500
2011	6.6	212,800
2012	6.6	210,600
2014	5.6	164,778
2015	5.6	163,858
2016	5.6	162,344
2017	5.6	159,486
2018	5.6	157,717
2019	5.65	157,871

Note: *Approximate data of Poles living in Eastern and South Eastern part of Lithuania based on historical sources.
Source: (Stravinskienė, 2007, p. 39); (Stravinskienė, 2005, p. 23); (Stravinskienė, 2005, p. 24); Statistics Lithuania 2019a, 2019b, 2019c.

(Population Census, 2011b). Previously, the Population Census of 1989 had shown that 85% of ethnic Poles declared their native language to be Polish (Population Census, 1989), while in the Population Census of 2001 this proportion was 80% (Population Census, 2001). An important aspect of understanding these proportions is that the Polish language spoken in Lithuania is not homogeneous and does not necessarily correspond to standard Polish as spoken in Poland. An essential linguistic characteristic of the Polish national minority in Lithuania is that in rural areas where approximately half of ethnic Poles live, people mostly use a 'Tuteishi' dialect ('Language of the Locals'), also called 'Po Prostu' ('Simple Language') (Hogan-Brun et al., 2005; Korzeniewska, 1997). This dialect is quite distinct, and might be considered close to Belarusian, meaning that a person speaking standard Polish and a person speaking 'Po Prostu' may not understand each other properly.

Notably, ethnic Poles use several languages in their everyday lives, and Polish, Russian and Lithuanian may be used interchangeably. In a representative survey taken in 2013, 95% of ethnic Polish respondents said that they use Russian on a daily basis, while at the same time 92% said that they use Polish, and 90%—Lithuanian (Geben, 2013, p. 225). Importantly, 67% stated that most often they think in Polish, 66%—in Russian, and 47%—in Lithuanian (Geben, 2013, p. 225). Yet, there remains one particular sphere where the Polish language remains dominant: namely in Roman Catholic practices. In 2013, 85% of the ethnic Poles said that they prayed in Polish only (Geben, 2013, p. 225).

Usage of the Russian language was common among ethnic Poles during Soviet times, when many families put their children into Russian schools and children were socialised into the Russian language and culture. A possible explanation for this trend could be general Soviet policies of russification as well as a heterogeneous demographic composition of the minority due to immigration from the Soviet republics of Belarus, Latvia and Russia. People coming from Belarus and Russia were already russified before World War II. Consequently, Russian remained common among ethnic Poles after Lithuania regained independence. Research by Lithuanian linguists shows that in 2013, 92% of ethnic Poles declared that they used Russian when writing short messages and personal notes. At the same time, 60% said that they used Polish for the same purpose as well. In addition, 54% of ethnic Polish respondents declared that they used Russian as a language of communication with their partner (Geben, 2013). The sociological data shows that ethnic Poles read the news, listen to the radio and search the internet more often in Russian or Lithuanian than in Polish (Geben, 2013, p. 226). Subsequent research confirms the trend of regular usage of Russian. A representative sociological survey taken in 2016 as part of the research project 'Subjective Security' found that 36% of ethnic Polish respondents read the most popular Lithuanian internet news portal 'delfi.lt' in Russian. A substantial proportion of ethnic Poles do not use Polish language media: 30% declare that they never use internet in Polish and 28%—that they never watch Polish TV. At the same time, more than half (54%) admitted that they often watched the 1st channel of Russian state television. This attachment to Russian media and Russian language corresponds to general attitudes towards the Soviet past and Russia. In a representative survey taken in 2016, 17% of ethnically Polish respondents said that they were proud of Russia, 42% supported the annexation of Crimea, and 41% agreed that life was better in the Soviet times (Janušauskienė et al., 2016).

The Lithuanian government tries to divert ethnic Poles from watching Russian TV by providing the opportunity to watch Polish TV instead. The government has bought rights to retransmit five Polish TV channels, at a cost of 349,000 Euros per year (Majauskienė, 2018, March 09). Yet, as the data show, only a small share of the ethnic Poles currently prefers Polish to Russian TV.

To conclude, a significant proportion of ethnic Poles use several languages in their private life simultaneously, and some of them prefer Russian to Polish. Yet, this linguistic heterogeneity does not damage identification with the Polish minority, since linguistic homogeneity 'is by no means a sufficient or necessary marker of a nation or nationality' (Gordon, 1996, p. 217). Polish national identity is strengthened by the existence of separate cultural and religious institutions and practices.

Patterns of Accommodation

An important peculiarity of the Polish national minority in Lithuania is a way of life that maintains a clear cleavage between the Polish community and the rest. This pattern is especially visible in rural areas, where ethnic Poles celebrate, pray, and learn at schools separately from the rest of the society. An example of separate celebrations comes from an interview with a local Lithuanian politician who lives in the Vilnius region:

> In Sudervė, last year during the festival of Mardi Gras people celebrated in the cultural centre. First, the Poles came, they celebrated and left. Then, the Lithuanians came, and celebrated. You see ... There are no common celebrations, they do not get together. < ... > The local government of Sudervė organises a Christmas event for children < ... > and this celebration always takes place in the Polish language.

A Santa Claus always comes from Poland, from Cracow. A nice celebration, everything is in Polish. < … > and each year I receive invitations for my children. But my children are Lithuanian, they do not understand Polish. < … > yet, we go. But none of my Lithuanian neighbours receive such an invitation. (Interviu No. 14, a politician of the local municipality, research project "Quality of Democracy", 2017)

The interview shows practices that, on the one hand, support and re-create Polish national identity, yet, on the other hand, create ethnic cleavages. Notably, policies of the local governments that are controlled by the political party LLRA-KŠS (as the interview shows, celebrations are organised by the local government) as well as kin-state policies of Poland (charitable organisations in Poland pay for the Santa Claus from Krakow) play a significant role in keeping the minority consolidated yet apart from the majority group.

Another important cleavage separating ethnic Poles from the majority group is separate Catholic worship in the Polish language. Usually, separate services are provided in Lithuanian and in Polish in Catholic churches that are located in multi-ethnic areas. In Vilnius, for example, 22 Catholic churches have masses in the Polish language (Archdiocese of Vilnius, 2015, August 28).

These separate religious services, in addition to education in separate Polish schools, create a basis for demarcating the minority, as well as strengthening identification with the local community. A strong identification with locality (a certain village or town, or the Vilnius region in general) is connected to the long historical presence of the minority in the Vilnius region, and is typical for 63% of ethnic Poles (Geben, 2013, p. 221). Attachment to Lithuania is weaker; yet, as data from the research project 'Subjective security' show, 35% of ethnic Polish respondents declared that they would defend Lithuania in the event of war (Research project 'Subjective Security', 2016).

In general, ethnic Poles feel an attachment to Lithuania as their birthplace and homeland, while affiliation with Poland is more cultural (Frėjutė-Rakauskienė, 2011). Other research shows that ethnicity is the second most important component of personal identity for Poles: the first being a person's profession (Petrušauskaitė & Pilinkaitė-Sotirovič, 2012, p. 30).

Policies Towards the Polish National Minority in Lithuania

Taking into consideration the peculiarities of the Polish national minority, the next part of this paper looks at education policies towards this minority that are applied by three political actors—the Government of Lithuania at the national level, the political party LLRA-KŠS at the municipal and the national level and the Government of Poland on the international level. The analysis focuses on the policies of these actors, trying to understand whether there is a substantial basis and conditions are favourable for these policies to reach their goals and what are (or might be in the future) the consequences of these policies for the accommodation and identity of the Polish national minority in Lithuania.

Policies of the Government of Lithuania

Policies towards the Polish national minority in Lithuania are twofold. On the one hand, Lithuania remains one of the few EU member states where it is possible to receive a full education (from kindergarten to university level) in a minority language. On the other hand, the Lithuanian government takes a relatively conservative standpoint and does not take into account demands by the Polish national minority to expand the areas of the official usage of the Polish language. The demands include allowing names in official documents to be written according to Polish orthography and not transliterating names according to the grammatical rules of the Lithuanian language as well as writing street signs and other signs in Polish in the areas where the Polish national minority makes up a substantial part of the population. These issues are periodically discussed, yet no major changes with regard to the acceptance of these political demands have been made.

A general problem that is faced by the state policies towards the Polish national minority is how to harmonise two contradictory demands: maintaining national Polish identity and integrating into the Lithuanian society. A collision of interests between the state and the Polish national minority arises due to different interests and different perceptions of policies: what the state considers as an improvement (e.g. more hours of studies of Lithuanian language), the Polish national minority views as a decline of the right to study in its mother tongue as a threat to its identity. On the other hand, the strict position of the government in not allowing the use of Polish in official documents and street signs prevents consensus and limits trust in the government as well as creating problems in international relations with Poland.

Education Policy

Education in Polish has a long tradition in Lithuania. Children belonging to the Polish minority are educated in separate schools with Polish as a language of instruction. Mixed schools where education is provided in Lithuanian, Polish and Russian also operate. Yet this does not mean that children learn in all these languages. Rather, separate classes with instruction in one particular language are established in one school building. In 2018, there were 49 separate schools with Polish language of instruction, and 31 schools with several languages of instruction (Bakonis et al., 2018, p. 9).

This policy provides a safeguard for the identity of the national minorities. As one of the activists of the Polish national minority put it: 'Polish schools are the basis of our existence. While schools exist, we exist < ... >. Schools are everything that we have' (Interview No. 30, an activist of the Polish national minority, research project 'Quality of democracy', 2017). The statistical data show that in the academic year 2017–2018, there were 11,209 children in schools with Polish as the language of instruction, which amounts to 3.57% of a total school population of 313,829 (Ministry of Education and Science, 2018). The proportion of students who choose to study in the Polish language started to increase after the restoration of independence. In the period 1991–2000, the number of pupils in schools with Polish language of instruction increased by 61%. Yet, from 2000, the number has been gradually diminishing (Merkys et al., 2006, p. 26).

In 2011, tensions arose between the Polish national minority and the government when the Ministry of Education and Science introduced a new law on education. The new law increased the share of lessons in the official Lithuanian language, while the number of native Polish language lessons has remained unchanged. In addition, subjects such as Lithuanian history, geography and citizenship should be studied in the Lithuanian language (Ministry of Education and Science, 2011). Previously, in the schools with Polish language of instruction, these subjects were studied in Polish. The government claims that the new law is intended to improve the standard of Lithuanian-language teaching and ensure equal opportunities for ethnic Poles to study at university and compete in the labour market. According to data from 2008, only 68% of people belonging to national minorities knew the Lithuanian language, up from 65% in 2006 (Report of the Department of National Minorities and Émigrés, 2008). Nevertheless, the LLRA-KŠS as well as non-governmental organisations representing the interests of the minority do not agree with these changes and think that they would damage Polish national identity. In response to the policies of the Ministry, protest meetings and pickets, strikes, petitions, appeals to courts, and Catholic masses took place (LLRA-KŠS, 2015; LLRA-KŠS, 2015; LLRA-KŠS, 2015).

To conclude, state education policies guarantee the survival of Polish national identity and the Polish language. Nevertheless, the latter outcome is not always considered as a positive thing. For example, when analysing this situation, American scholar Ellen Gordon mentioned the 'state's failure to achieve linguistic hegemony' (Gordon, 1996, p. 222). Nonetheless, state education policies deepen social exclusion and re-create a separate 'imagined community' which is not fully integrated into wider society, receives a worse education and has lower chances of upward social mobility. According to data of the Programme for International Student Assessment (PISA), the results of pupils from schools with Polish as the language of instruction are lower than those of their peers studying in schools with Lithuanian as the language of instruction. In 2015, the results for 15 year-olds showed that pupils from Polish schools reached 87% of the average level in reading. A similar situation occurs with Science and Maths scores: pupils from the Polish schools had 88% and 92% of the total average correspondingly (PISA report 2015 as quoted in Bakonis et al., 2018, p. 32).

The Policies of 'Electoral Action of Poles in Lithuania—Christian Families Alliance'

The LLRA-KŠS plays a specific role within the Lithuanian political party system. It is a 'niche' political party enjoying a long lasting popularity among the ethnic Poles in Lithuania. Due to the weak competitive position of other political actors that represent the interests of the Polish minority, this political party tends to retain a monopoly and remains a ruling political party in the municipalities of the Vilnius region where ethnic Poles make a significant part the population, occasionally also becoming an important partner in governing coalitions at the national level (Janušauskienė, 2016). The LLRA-KŠS was established in 1994. Since then, the party has constantly participated in politics forming the governing coalitions in the municipalities of the Vilnius region as well as overcoming the threshold and forming a fraction in the Parliament after the national elections of 2012 and 2018. In summer 2019, LLRA-KŠS became part of a governing coalition and obtained two ministerial posts in the Government.

The roots of the political mobilisation of the Polish national minority can be found in the initial phases of democratisation in Lithuania in the early 1990s, when Polish autonomy within the re-established Lithuanian state was proclaimed in the Vilnius region. This political move was perceived by the pro-independence Lithuanian elites as showing a lack of loyalty to the re-established independent state of Lithuania. Until recently, this shadow of the political past has played an important role in national politics and to a large extent rules out any consensus between the demands of the Polish national minority and the position of the government.

Ideologically, the LLRA-KŠS is a traditional right-wing political party with ideas that could be described as radical in a rather secular Lithuanian society. The prohibition of abortion and introduction of compulsory religious education in schools are permanent demands of the LLRA-KŠS, while the major political demands that represent the interests of the minority include the full restitution of land in the Vilnius region, allowing the writing of names in official documents such as passports using the letters of the Polish alphabet that do not exist in their Lithuanian counterpart (e.g. 'W', 'Ł') and not transliterating names according to the grammatical rules of the Lithuanian language. In the same vein, LLRA-KŠS demands that street signs and other official signs should be written in Polish in the areas where the ethnic Polish population lives (Janušauskienė, 2016). Until recently, almost no decisions that would satisfy these political demands were made, partly due to the strict regulations of the 1995 Law on the State Language and the generally cautious and reserved attitudes of Lithuanian political elites towards the possibility of adopting a law on the official use of the Polish language.

One characteristic of the policies applied by the governing LLRA-KŠS in the municipalities of south-eastern Lithuania is sustaining the status quo of the education system in the Polish language and preventing lithuanisation. As the data from the research project 'Quality of Democracy' show, the LLRA-KŠS applies preferential treatment policies to the population of Polish ethnic origin and some ethnic Lithuanians feel discriminated against, since they have restricted access to education in Lithuanian. The data show that there is a lack of schools with Lithuanian language of instruction (especially pre-primary schools) as well as after-school activities in the Lithuanian language. As one local politician puts it:

A Polish school was closed due to a lack of pupils. And we asked to open a Lithuanian pre-primary school in that building. The municipality did not agree, they said they would have a Polish cultural centre in that building instead. < ... > It is a property of the municipality. Each school, each kindergarten is a centre of Polish culture. The policy [of the municipality] is like this. (Interview No. 14, a politician of the local municipality, research project "Quality of Democracy", 2017)

In order to ensure access to education in the Lithuanian language, the Ministry of Education, Science and Sport administers the network of Lithuanian schools. In 2018, there were 31 schools administered by the Ministry (Lietuvos švietimas skaičiais, 2018, p. 69). In addition to the schools administered by the local municipalities (except those 31 mentioned), the Ministry is building new ones because of growing demand due to the urbanisation of the suburban territories of Vilnius and the increasing proportion of ethnic Lithuanians living in that area. In such a way, for example, a new Lithuanian school was opened in Ažuaukė village in September 2019 just a few hundred metres away from an empty former Polish school building.

To conclude, the policies of the LLRA-KŠS strengthen the cleavage between the Polish national minority and the Lithuanian majority group, prevent deeper integration of the minority into Lithuanian society as well as preventing the integration of Lithuanians into municipalities where ethnic Poles constitute a majority or a plurality of the population. Yet most importantly, the policies of the LLRA-KŠS strengthen the Polish identity of the minority.

Foreign Policies

The problems of the Polish national minority are an issue not simply for national and local politics, but also for international politics between Lithuania and Poland. Due to the unrealised demands of the Polish national minority, Lithuania was criticised by Poland for violating the rights of ethnic Poles. Thus, on the one hand, Lithuanian-Polish relations suffered due to Poland's dissatisfaction with the policies of Lithuania towards the Polish minority, yet, on the other hand, they worsened because of the kin-state policies of the Government of Poland, mainly the decision by Poland to distribute the *Karta Polaka* to the Lithuanian citizens of Polish ethnic origin that was considered as an interference in the internal affairs of Lithuania. In 2019, developments in inter-state relations showed some tendencies towards warming: the LLRA-KŠS entered the coalition government, and Lithuania's new President Gitanas Nausėda described the Lithuanian-Polish relations as a 'strategic partnership' (lrpt.lt, 2019).

Returning to the issue of the *Karta Polaka*, it is important to note that it is perceived very negatively among the Lithuanian political elites, since it is regarded as interference in the internal affairs of a sovereign state (Debates in the Committee on Human Rights of the Seimas, 2011; Delfi.lt, 2008; Kazėnas, 2012; Seimo nario G. Songailos pranešimas, 2011). Each year the Polish Embassy in Lithuania issues about 1,000 cards to Lithuanian nationals of Polish ethnic origin (15min.lt, 2012). The *Karta Polaka* confirms that a person belongs to the Polish nation. In Lithuania, this circumstance provoked political debates about the possibility of a collision of loyalties towards the Lithuanian and Polish states (Debates in the Seimas, 2013). This dilemma is especially important in the case of members of the Parliament and the European Parliament possessing the *Karta Polaka*. Right-wing politicians have regularly raised this issue in Parliament (tv3.lt, 2014), yet no formal decisions in the Parliament have been reached. In 2013, the Parliament rejected for the third time a proposal to apply to the Constitutional Court for an interpretation of the status conferred by the *Karta Polaka* (15 min.lt, 2013). A leader of the LLRA-KŠS and member of the European Parliament Valdemar Tomaševski (Waldemar Tomaszewski), who holds such a card, claims that the *Karta Polaka* does not create any conflict of loyalties, since in 2008 the Ministry of Foreign Affairs of the Republic of Lithuania acknowledged that the *Karta Polaka* is a certificate of national identity and nothing more (tv3.lt, 2014).

Financial support coming from Poland is very important for the Polish national minority. Poland helps Polish-language schools financially and supports non-governmental organisations and their co-operation with Polish counterparts. Since the financial reports are not made public on the official sites of the Polish foundations, the only source of information about the proportion of this aid is the media. For example, the Lithuanian online news portal 15 min reported that in 2018 the Polish foundation Aid to Poles in the East (Pomoc polakom na wschodzie) donated 10,000,000 Polish zloty to the organisations of the Polish national minority in Lithuania (15 min.lt, 2018-06-07). A significant part of the financial support goes to schools with Polish language of instruction in the Vilnius region. In 2011, the Senate of the Republic Poland declared that it had dedicated 24,000,000 Polish zloty for reconstruction and other needs of schools with Polish language of instruction in Lithuania (15 min.lt, 2011). In addition, this money is used to attract families and to encourage them to choose schools with Polish language of instruction. A family receives 1,000 Polish zloty if it chooses to put its first-grade child into a school with Polish language of instruction. The latter is perceived by the Lithuanian side as bribery, while the Government of the Republic of Poland and the LLRA-KŠS portrays it as support for families (Baltic News Service, 2011). On a yearly basis, theAid to Poles in the East foundation provides school appliances for schoolchildren and 'scholarships for parents'. In 2018, for the third time, this foundation organised a charity event in

Vilnius and distributed school backpacks and scholarships for 980 ethnic Polish schoolchildren (Baltic News Service, 2018). As an interview of the research project 'Quality of democracy' shows, parents look for better options and could change their decision in favour of Polish schools and kindergartens even if initially they had decided to put their child in a Lithuanian kindergarten:

> My hairdresser ... her child went to the same group [in the kindergarten with the Lithuanian language of instruction]. Then, a Polish kindergarten was opened, and she left to this Polish kindergarten. And now she goes to a Polish school. This is, as you see, a competition. (Interview No. 14, a politician of the local municipality, research project "Quality of Democracy", 2017)

In addition to the financial support for schools, charitable organisations from Poland support the activities of non-governmental organisations and the Polish-language press, organise courses for teachers, and support events that promote Polish culture Due to this important financial support from Poland, the Polish national identity of the minority is strengthened. In rural areas where the population is poor, the financial support provided by charitable organisations from Poland is perceived as a benefit of being Polish (research project "Quality of Democracy", 2017). Thus, Poland's kin-state policies include financial mechanisms that evidently enhance a Polish identity and reinforce the group's detachment from the rest of the society.

Conclusion

This paper has sought to analyse the determinants and possible impact of national and international policies towards the Polish national minority in Lithuania. It argues that due to specific characteristics of the Polish national minority, as well as certain policies applied towards it, it is not possible to speak either about a strong civic Lithuanian or a strong trans-sovereign Polish identity, while an important factor remains an attachment to the Russian language and Russian media. This paper advocates the idea that the identity of the Polish national minority in Lithuania is multi-layered. The inner (and most solid) layers involve strong identification with the locality (the village or town, or the Vilnius region in general), strong Catholic identity, as well as an awareness of Slavic uniqueness (based on ethnic origin as well languages used on the everyday basis). The outer (and much weaker) layers consist of identification with Lithuania as a citizen, trans-sovereign identification with Poland as a member of a kin-minority group, and, as empirical data from the surveys show, a certain identification with 'the Russian speaking world'.

Analysis of the implementation of national and international policies shows that all these policies have one common feature—they tend to foster the detached development of the minority. The paper shows that national education policies have a direct influence on the survival of the Polish national identity, while local municipality policies foster the cleavage between the minority and the majority and at the same time foster the development of local Polish identity. National policies that do not acknowledge the demands of the minority concerning usage of Polish language in the public sphere prevent the formation of a wider civic Lithuanian identity. Poland's kin-state policies foster a Polish identity within the Lithuanian state, yet they have not created a significant basis for the development of a trans-sovereign

Polish identity due to the specificity of the minority (mainly its linguistic heterogeneity and strong identification with locality).

References

Archdiocese of Vilnius. (2015, August 28). *Parishes and Mass times*. https://www.vilnensis.lt/holy-mass-times-parish-search/?lang=enawpl.lt

Bakonis, E., Balevičienė, S., Gražytė-Skominienė, A., Jevsejevienė, J., Kalvaitis, A., Mikėnė, S., Paurienė, L., & Zablackė, R. (2018). *Lietuvos tautinių mažumų būklės analizė*. [*Analysis of the situation of national minorities in Lithuania*]. Nacionalinė mokyklų vertinimo agentūra. http://www.nmva.smm.lt/wp-content/uploads/2019/02/Lietuvos-tautini%C5%B3-ma%C5%BEum%C5%B3-%C5%A1vietimo-b%C5%ABkl%C4%97s-analiz%C4%97-2018-m.1.pdf

Baltic News Servise. (2011, October 7). *Lenkiškų mokyklų pirmokų tėvams - 1000 zlotų parama iš Varšuvos*. [*For parents of first-graders in Polish schools – Support of 1000 zlotys from Warsaw*] Delfi.lt. https://www.delfi.lt/news/daily/lithuania/lenkisku-mokyklu-pirmoku-tevams-1000-zlotu-parama-is-varsuvos.d?id=50292134

Baltic News Service. (2018, September 1). *Lenkų pirmokams – mokinio krepšeliai su finansine parama*. [*For Polish first-graders - student baskets with financial support*]. Delfi.lt. https://www.delfi.lt/news/daily/lithuania/lenku-pirmokams-mokinio-krepseliai-su-finansine-parama.d?id=78958595

Barbour, S., & Carmichael, C. (Ed.) (2000). *Language and nationalism in Europe*. Oxford University Press.

Debates in the Committee on Human Rights of the Seimas. (2011, November 16). https://www.lrs.lt/sip/portal.show?p_r=15424&p_k=1&p_t=116839

Debates in the Seimas. (2013, May 3). https://www.lrs.lt/sip/portal.show?p_r=35727&p_k=1&p_a=sale_klaus_stad&p_moment=20130523&p_kl_stad_id=-34551

Delfi.lt. (2008, May 23). *Seimo teisininkai įžvelgia požymių, jog Lenko korta susijusi su pažizadėjimu kitai valstybei*. [*Seimas lawyers see signs that the Karta Polaka is linked to a promise to another state*]. Delfi.lt. https://www.delfi.lt/news/daily/lithuania/seimo-teisininkai-izvelgia-pozymiu-jog-lenko-korta-susijusi-su-pasizade jimu-kitai-valstybei.d?id=19581380

Eberhardt, P. (2002). Ethnic problems in Poland and in her eastern neighbours. *Geografický ČAsopis, 54*(3), 191–201.

Eberhardt, P. (2008). *Problematyka geopolityczna ziem polskich*. [*Geopolitical issues of Polish lands*]. PAN IGiPZ.

Frėjutė-Rakauskienė, M. (2011). The impact of the EU Membership on ethnic minority Participation. Parties of Lithuanian ethnic minorities in the European Parliament elections. *Politikos Mokslų Almanachas, 10*, 7–30.

Geben, K. (2013). Lietuvos lenkai ir lenkų kalba Lietuvoje. [Lithuanian Poles and Polish language in Lithuania]. In M. Ramonienė (Ed.), *Miestai ir kalbos II. Sociolingvistinis Lietuvos žemėlapis*. [*Cities and Languges II. Sociolinguistic Map of Lithuania*] (pp. 217–233). Vilniaus universiteto leidykla.

Gordon, E. J. (1996). The revival of Polish national consciousness: A comparative study of Lithuania, Belarus, and Ukraine. *Nationalities Papers, 24*(2), 217–236. https://doi.org/10.1080/00905999608408439

Hogan-Brun, G., Ramonienė, M., & Grumadienė, L. (2005). The language situation in Lithuania. *Journal of Baltic Studies, 36*(3), 345–370. https://doi.org/10.1080/01629770500000131

Janušauskienė, D. (2016a). Ethnicity as political cleavage: The political agenda of the Polish national minority in Lithuania. *Nationalities Papers, 44*(issue 4), 578–590. https://doi.org/10.1080/00905992.2016.1156073

Janušauskienė, D., Vileikienė, E., Nevinskaitė, L., & Gečienė, I. (2016b). *The research project "subjective security in volatile geopolitical context: Traits, factors and individual strategies" (2015-2017)*. [data set]. *Vilnius: Lithuanian Social Research Centre*.

Kasatkina, N. (2002). Lietuvos etninių grupių adaptacijos ypatumai. [Peculiarities of Adaptation of ethnic Groups in Lithuania]. *Filosofija. Sociologija, 4*, 15–22.

Kasatkina, N., & Leončikas, T. (2003). *Lietuvos etninių grupių adaptacija*. [*Adaptation of ethnic Groups in Lithuania*]. Eugrimas.

Kazėnas, G. (2012, April 18). *Lenko korta – tai ne išimtinai politinė, bet ir teisinė problema* [*Karta Polaka – it is not a purely politial but also a legal issue*]. Delfi.lt https://www.delfi.lt/news/daily/law/gkazenas-lenko-korta-tai-ne-isimtinai-politine-bet-ir-teisine-problema.d?id=58166754

Kazėnas, G., Jakubauskas, A., Gaižauskaitė, I., Kacevičius, R., & Visockaitė, A. (2014). *Lenkų tautinės mažumos Lietuvoje identiteto tyrimas*. [*Research of the Polish national minority in Lithuania*]. Mykolo Romerio universitetas.

Korzeniewska, K. (1997). Tutejszy, polak, katolik. Tożsamość religijno-etniczna mieszkańców południowo-wschodniej Litwy. Badanie empiryczne w Dziewieniszkach, Kierniowie i Turgielach. [Tuteish, Pole, Catholic. Religious and ethnic identity of the inhabitants of south-eastern part of Lithuania. Research in Dieveniškės, Kernavė, and Turgeliai]. *Przegląd Polonijny, XXIII-1997-1*(83), 59–86.

Kowalski, M. (2000). Spatial Differentiation of Electoral Behaviour in Poland and Lithuania. In J. Kitowski (Ed.), *Eastern borders of European integration processes* (pp. 717–733). Filia UMCS.

Kowalski, M. (2008). Wileńszczyzna jako problem geopolityczny w XX wieku. [Vilnius region as a geopolitical problem of the 20th century]. In P. Eberhardt (Ed.), *Problematyka geopolityczna ziem polskich. [Geopolitical issues of Polish lands]* (pp. 267–296). PAN IGiPZ.

Law on the State Language. https://e-seimas.lrs.lt/portal/legalAct/en/

LLRA-KŠS. (2015, June 1). *National minorities in Lithuania will stand for their schools.* http://www.awpl.lt/?p=522&lang=en

LLRA-KŠS. (2015, June 3). *Prayers in the intention of the protection and development of the Polish education in Lithuania.* http://www.awpl.lt/?p=524&lang=en

LLRA-KŠS. (2015, August 28). *Statement rearding the strike.* http://www.awpl.lt/?p=1044&lang=en

LRA-KŠS. http://llra.lt/

lrpt.lt. (2019, November 21). *Media center of the President of the Republic of Lithuania.* https://www.lrp.lt/lt/ziniasklaidos-centras/naujienos/prezidentas-lenkijos-ir-lietuvos-santykiai-pasieke-strategini-lygmeni/33432

Majauskienė, D. (2018, March 9). *Nuo gegužės Pietryčių Lietuvoje bus transliuojami bent penki Lenkijos TV kanalai. [From May, at least five Polish TV channels will be broadcast in Southeast Lithuania].* Delfi.lt. https://www.delfi.lt/news/daily/lithuania/nuo-geguzes pietryciu-lietuvoje-bus-transliuojami-bent-penki-lenkijos-tv-kanalai.d?id=77379931

Merkys, G., Telešienė, A., Balžekienė, A., Lapienienė, A., & Pauliukaitė, Ž. (2006). *Mokymosi prieinamumas Vilniaus rajono gyventojams. [Accessibility of learning to Vilnius district residents].* Ministry of Education and Science. https://www.smm.lt/uploads/documents/kiti/Mokymosi_prieinamumas.pdf

Ministry of Education and Science. (2011). Lietuvos Respublikos Švietimo ir mokslo ministro įsakymas „Dėl ugdymo lietuvių kalba bendrojo ugdymo ir neformaliojo švietimo mokykloje tvarkos aprašo patvirtinimo" [Order of the Minister of Education and Science of the Republic of Lithuania "On Approval of the Description of the Procedure of Teaching in the Lithuanian Language at the General and Non-formal Education School]. https://e-seimas.lrs.lt/portal/legalAct/lt/TAD/TAIS.409318?jfwid=-9dzqnu8os

Ministry of Education and Science. (2018). *Lietuvos švietimas skaičiais. [Education in Lithuania in numbers].* ŠČA. https://www.smm.lt/uploads/documents/teisine_informacija/statistika/Lietuvos%20%C5%A1vietimas%20skai%C4%8Diais%202018_%20Bendrasis%20ugdymas.pdf

O'Connor, K. (2006). *Culture and Customs of the Baltic states.* Greenwood Press.

Petrušauskaitė, V., & Pilinkaitė-Sotirovič, V. (2012). Rusai Lietuvoje: Etninės grupės raida ir socialinės integracijos iššūkiai 2001–2011m. [Russians in Lithuania: Evolution of the ethnic group and Challenges of social integration]. *Etniškumo Studijos*, 1–2. 14-50.

Population Census. (1989). https://osp.stat.gov.lt/statistikos-leidiniu-katalogas?publication=7453

Population Census. (2001). https://osp.stat.gov.lt/statistikos-leidiniu-katalogas?publication=6613

Population Census. (2011a). https://osp.stat.gov.lt/statistikos-leidiniu-katalogas?publication=14625

Population Census. (2011b). https://osp.stat.gov.lt/documents/10180/217110/Gyv_kalba_tikyba.pdf/1d9dac9a-3d45-4798-93f5-941fed00503f

Ramonienė, M. (2010). *Miestai ir kalbos. [Cities and Langugages].* Vilniaus universiteto leidykla.

Ramonienė, M. (2013). *Miestai ir kalbos II. Sociolingvistinis Lietuvos žemėlapis. [Cities and languages II. The Sociolinguistic Map of Lithuania].* Vilniaus universiteto leidykla.

Report of the Department of national minorities and émigrés. (2008). http://tmid.lt/

Seimo nario G. Songailos pranešimas. (2011, May 15). [*The notification of the MP G. Songaila*]. https://www.lrs.lt/sip/portal.show?p_r=15371&p_k=1&p_t=108884

Sirutavičius, V. (2009). Lietuvių ir lenkų santykiai 1988–1990m. (lenkų autonomijos genezės klausimu) [Lithuanian – Polish relations in 1988-1990. On the Genesis of the question of Polish autonomy]. In J. Volkonovski & R. Gaidis (Eds.), *Lietuvių–lenkų santykiai amžių tėkmėje. Istorinė atmintis* (pp. 290–320). Vilniaus universiteto leidykla.

Statistics Lithuania (2019a). https://osp.stat.gov.lt/statistiniu-rodikliu-analize?indicator=S3R162#/

Statistics Lithuania (2019b). db1.stat.gov.lt/M3010215.

Statistics Lithuania (2019c). https://osp.stat.gov.lt/statistiniu-rodikliu-analize#/.

Stravinskienė, V. (2005). Lietuvos lenkų teritorinis pasiskirstymas ir skaičiaus kaita (1944m. Antrasis pusmetis – 1947 metai). [Territorial distribution and change in the number of Poles in Lithuania (second half of 1944–1947]. *Lituanistica, 64*(4), 13–27.

Stravinskienė, V. (2007). Rytų ir pietryčių Lietuvos gyventojų repatriacija į Lenkiją (1944m. Pabaiga–1947m.). [repatriation of the inhabitants of eastern and south-eastern Lithuania to Poland (end of 1944 - 1947)]. *Lituanistica, 69*(1), 6–50.

Stravinskienė, V. (2010). *Tarpetniniai lenkų ir lietuvių santykiai Rytų ir Pietryčių Lietuvoje 1953-1959m. [Interethnic Relations between Poles and Lithuanians in Eastern and South-Eastern Lithuania in 1953-1959*], Istorija. Mokslo darbai. 77 tomas.

tv3.lt. (2014, April 10). https://www.tv3.lt/naujiena/lietuva/784764/v-tomasevskis-atsake-j-bernatoniui-apie-lenku-kortas

Žvinklienė, A., Kublickienė, L., Šėporaitytė-Vismantė, D., & Janušauskienė, D. (2017). *The research project "Quality of democracy and equal opportunities: Attitudes and social practice" (2017-2018)*. [Data set]. Vilnius: Lithuanian Social Research Centre.

15 min.lt. (2011, September 13). https://www.15 min.lt/naujiena/aktualu/pasaulis/lenkijos-senato-vadovas-zada-toliau-remti-lenkiskas-mokyklas-lietuvoje-57-169518

15 min.lt. (2012, October 17). https://www.15 min.lt/naujiena/aktualu/lietuva/lenko-korta-kasmet-gauna-per-tukstanti-lietuvos-pilieciu-56-190482#ixzz2Og1FywEp

15 min.lt. (2013, May 23). https://www.15 min.lt/naujiena/aktualu/lietuva/seimas-atmete-siulyma-kreiptis-i-konstitucini-teisma-del-lenko-kortos-56-338303

15 min.lt. (2018, June 07). https://www.15 min.lt/naujiena/aktualu/lietuva/itarimai-michalui-mackeviciui-lenkijos-mokesciu-moketoju-pinigus-leido-kaip-savus-56-983302

National Bonds, Foreign Policy and the Future of Europe

JAN ZIELONKA

The topic of this collection of essays sounds narrow, but it deals with the basic story of politics since time immemorial, namely the relationship between territory, authority, and rights (Sassen, 2008). Borders are central to this volume, which again brings us to the core of political analysis. Max Weber and different generations of his disciples always argued that the whole history of human organisations could largely be read as a series of continuing efforts to bring territorial borders to correspond to, and coincide with, systemic functional boundaries, and to be in line with the consolidated socio-political hierarchies of corresponding populations (Bartolini, 2005; Rokkan et al., 1987, pp. 17–18; Tilly, 1975). Cultural and political identity also features prominently in this volume, a topic only recently rediscovered by political scientists, but central to social sciences for many decades (Fukuyama, 2018; Gilbert, 2010). While the volume offers an in-depth analysis of only a few empirical cases, its theoretical significance goes well beyond the limited geographical context.

Foreign policy analysis sounds narrow, if not trivial in comparison, even if kin-state policies are usually handled by diplomats and belong to this particular academic discipline. The problem is that foreign policy analysis often displays a narrow understanding of states and their borders. It is ill-suited to talk about cultural and political identities. And it neglected the topic of national minorities and kin-state policies towards them for many decades.

Central and Eastern Europe (CEE) is an ideal case for analysing the relationship between territory, authority, and rights (Smith & Hiden, 2012). The region is also ideal to test the utility of the foreign policies applied to sort out this relationship. Romantic nationalism was largely born in CEE, and the region has shed a lot of blood to create nation-states and to defend or enlarge their borders. Territories changed their 'owners' on a regular basis, leaving millions of people on the wrong side of the new 'ethnic' border. I was born in Silesia, the region tackled by three chapters in this volume (Cordell, Łodziński and Nowosielski). The region has changed affiliations several times throughout its history. Silesia was part of Greater Moravia, Bohemia, the Piast duchy, the Holy Roman

Empire, the Habsburg Monarchy, and Prussia. At the Potsdam Conference in 1945 Silesia was given to Poland by Atlee, Truman and Stalin as a 'compensation' for the Eastern part of pre-1939 Poland that was incorporated into the Soviet Union. The Cold War border between the Eastern and the Western camp was artificial, but it was firm and guarded by the Soviet tanks. With the fall of the Berlin Wall, the unification of Germany and the EU's successive waves of enlargement, the East–West divide has lost its meaning.

This constant geopolitical reordering was not in sync with cultural realities on the ground. During the Cold War, in my school in the city of Opole/Oppeln, Polish was the official language and you could learn Russian, English and French, but not German, although a significant number of my schoolmates spoke German at home. In the 1970s Poland's government received Germany's economic help in exchange for 'family re-unification.' One third of my schoolmates went to Germany, and I was not even aware that all of them were German. Although I grew up in Silesia, I speak Polish with an Eastern accent, like people who grew up in Lwów (present-day Lviv) which is now part of Ukraine. I never visited Lwów in my life and my family does not originate from there. I acquired this accent during my study in Wroclaw/Breslau, a German city which was 'given' by Stalin to Poland and which became a 'safe haven' for the Poles who had to leave Lwów after it became part of the Soviet Union. The local Germans from Wroclaw either fled the city or were expelled. There are other similar cases from Central and Eastern Europe tackled in this volume. They show why we are dealing with a perfect case to understand the roots and nature of kin-state policies. In hardly any other part of the world have borders been so 'fuzzy' and the relationship between territory, authority and rights so complicated.

This concluding chapter will shed some light on the difficulty of grasping kin-state policy solely through a diplomatic lens. It will then deal with 'indirect' ways of handling ethnic groups living on the 'wrong' side of Europe's borders. The third section will try to assess the apparent return of nation-states to the centre of European politics, especially following the outbreak of the Covid-19 pandemic.

Foreign Policy's Blind Spots

Until the fall of the Berlin Wall, foreign policy in Europe was chiefly about ideological confrontation. West German policies towards the native Germans living around my native city of Opole/Oppeln was perceived in terms of East–West confrontation. Nationalism within the 'Socialist camp' was conceived as a relic of the past by the local authorities, and thus there was no official foreign policy debate about the Poles in Ukraine, Russia, Belarus and Lithuania or Hungarians living outside Hungary.

The fall of the Soviet Union and the re-unification of Germany have sparked discussions about the national question, but foreign policy analysts have focused on other issues such as European integration, trade promotion and Europe's security architecture. Supporting co-nationals in neighbouring countries was usually identified with atavistic Russian imperialism and not with liberal countries promoting universal values. Although the ethnic question was politically salient from Berlin to Warsaw, Bratislava, Budapest, Bucharest and Vilnius, foreign policy handled the issue chiefly through legal instruments. A concerted effort was made to depoliticise the ethnic question, with modest results, however.

The war in Yugoslavia was a stark reminder that the ethnic question had not disappeared, but the liberal foreign policy discourse has focussed on efforts to secure peace and protect human rights (Caplan, 2005). Foreign policy went hand in hand with military 'humanitarian' interventions, with mixed results as manifested most sadly in Srebrenica. After the war in Yugoslavia a more ambitious foreign policy project was launched in Europe, namely democracy promotion. This concept aspired to address the national minority issue through institutional engineering rather than foreign policy proper.

The reasons for the neglect of the ethnic question in inter-state relations was not just political. Foreign policy was poorly equipped analytically to deal with this topic. This is because states are the key if not only actors taken seriously by foreign policy analysts. These states are seen as sovereign and demarcated from other states by firm and clearly identified borders. As Christopher Hill put it:

> Borders and foreign policy are inextricably bound up with each other (...) foreign policy depends on the existence of borders. The word 'foreign' originally referred to that which is 'outside,' and where there is an outside there must not only be an inside but also a line of demarcation between the two. (Hill, 2002, p. 95)

The sovereignty concept assumes that matters within states' borders are not for other states to question or meddle in. Of course, diplomats can request a different treatment of certain minorities, but it is for the sovereign to decide how to respond to such requests. A different reasoning would represent an 'illegal interference' in domestic affairs; a rule recognised not just by the United Nations, but also by the Organization for Security Cooperation in Europe (OSCE). Both the UN and the OSCE have provisions for defending human rights, but these provisions do not necessarily extend to national minority rights, at least not explicitly (Gerner, 1991, pp. 159–176).

Foreign policy specialists feel equally uncomfortable with the notion of identity, despite the growing popularity of such terms as soft power or cultural diplomacy (Melissen, 2005; Nye, 2004). The way foreign policy specialists handle identity issues is chiefly through the demarcation and enforcement of legal, administrative and military boundaries. Such boundary construction helps to identify those on behalf of whom foreign policy is being conducted, and those who are on its receiving end, friends and enemies alike.

The above approaches have been criticised by representatives of other academic disciplines. They pointed out that borders are not just lines on the map where one jurisdictions ends and another begins. Borders are complex set of institutions determining market transactions, powers of coercion, politico-administrative entitlements, identity clusters and communication flows. These arrangements can be formal or informal to various degrees, but they are neither given nor stable; they are subject to historical change driven by technological, economic, social, cultural, political, and military developments (Rosenau, 1997). Control of borders is never absolute even in well-functioning states; nor is the fit between various types of borders. In our context, for instance, it is important to stress that some states are multi-cultural and some nations live in more than one state or have no state. Moreover, some specialists argue that personal and cultural borders determine our daily practices to a greater extent than legal or institutional ones (Barbour & Carmichael, 2000; Carsten, 2000). As states are unequal and eager to export their rules to other states, sovereignty is a relative rather than absolute concept. Some scholars have gone as far as to label sovereignty an 'organized hypocrisy' (Krasner, 1999). Besides, transnational jurisdictions and plural trans-border allegiances have proliferated in recent decades.

Unbounding and Rebounding

The above intellectual critique of the approach to foreign policy has not made much impact on either diplomatic analysis or practice. However, two political processes have re-defined the discussion on ethnic minorities and kin-state policies towards them. One was the process of European integration and the other was an upsurge of Euro-scepticism in response to this integration. The former was chiefly about unbounding and the latter about rebounding. Unbounding signifies efforts to open borders between states or to make them less relevant. Rebounding implies the opposite, namely policies aimed at reinforcing borders or sealing them altogether.

The process of European integration was chiefly about economics and regulatory realignment facilitating the movement of goods, money, services, and labour within Europe's 'single market.' As pointed out by different contributions to this volume, there is no European body of laws trying to regulate the inter-state relations regarding national minorities. States which wanted to join the EU were expected to respect human rights and refrain from questioning existing borders, but ethnic issues were not the EU's major preoccupation (Liebich, 2002, pp. 124–125). The Council of Europe and the OSCE contained provisions protecting minority rights, but these provisions were not part of EU law. However, the progress of European integration had an indirect impact on cross border contacts and movement. With borders open for economic flows it made less difference on which side of the border certain ethnic groups resided. Members of the EU had fewer incentives to argue with each other. Cross border economic zones have emerged with the help of European institutions and have generated considerable local wealth.

However, European integration went hand in hand with neo-liberal economics, which stimulated inequalities within and among states (Bohle & Greskovits, 2012). Borders were relatively open not only within the EU, but also globally, which helped to shift production to countries with cheap labour. Migration within the EU has also increased. According to Eurostat data published in May 2018, one sixth of Romania's workforce has left the country and this could not but create numerous problems, especially in Romania itself. It is estimated that over two million Poles have emigrated since accession to the EU. At the same time, it is estimated that over a million Ukrainians live and work in Poland.

With the passage of time, European integration came under fire from a group of Right-wing politicians in Central and Eastern Europe in particular (Krastev & Holmes, 2019). When hundreds of thousands of desperate refugees from the Middle East and North Africa began to cross Europe's borders in 2015, Viktor Orbán, Jarosław Kaczyński and other leading politicians from CEE decided to close their countries' borders and refused to host any significant number of these refugees as stipulated by the EU redistribution scheme. From then on, the politics of rebounding was ever more pronounced in the political discourse, with direct implications for cross-border relations and for the respective ethnic minorities.

The open borders policy has been accused of inviting migrants who take local jobs and introduce 'alien' cultural habits. Brain-drain from CEE was also on the agenda and linked to the issue of open borders. European integration was criticised for siding with transnational markets against ordinary citizens. EU institutions were seen as interfering too much in sovereign decisions of member states. All this is described in more depth in this volume by Cordell.

While the anti-European discourse has not specifically focused on national Diasporas, Right-wing politicians started a campaign to re-interpret the history of their relations with their neighbours. Combatants seen as traitors and murderers by one side of the conflict were celebrated as heroes by the other side. This could not but sour diplomatic relations between states in Central and Eastern Europe, some of which were already members of the EU and others—most notably Ukraine—candidates for membership.

Similar political developments could be observed in Western European member states of the EU (Zielonka, 2018). Brexit was partly about Polish migrants in the UK. Migrants from Central and Eastern Europe were also under fire from nativist politicians in other states. Calls for reinforcing borders in Europe intensified. No wonder therefore that with the outbreak of Covid-19 EU governments decided to seal their national borders with no convincing medical argument justifying such a drastic step, and with no consultations with the EU headquarters.

With borders restored in one form or another, and with the EU's pacifying effect waning, one can envisage a proliferation of conflicts regarding national groups residing on the 'wrong' side of a border. This means that international law and traditional forms of diplomacy are likely to be in vogue again. This is why normative proposals such as those made in this volume by Udrea and Smith are timely and important. However, this does not mean that the proposed instruments will be sufficient to address the problems; indeed, it is not even certain that these legal and diplomatic instruments will be utilised, even if created.

Peering into the Future

With the outbreak of pandemic, the nation-state seems to be experiencing a striking renaissance. Borders are back, and with them national selfishness. Each national government is focusing on its own people, and each claims to be better prepared to fight the crisis than its neighbours. Virtually overnight, national capitals have effectively reclaimed sovereignty from the EU. The Italian term *sovranismo* (soverenism) has become the most commonly used buzzword. Not only globalisation, but also European integration has been declared in danger if not already dead (Gray, 2020; Maak, 2020). All this seems to suggest that ethnic minorities across Europe, in Central and Eastern Europe in particular, can no longer expect to enjoy their rights freely. Once again they are likely to be at the receiving end of diplomatic bargaining between states interested in national pride and glory. Symbolic politics seldom produces pragmatic outcomes and mutually satisfying compromises. Should we therefore expect policies of curbing what Waterbury called in her essay 'multiple membership' of national minorities? Will the return of the nation state stop what Sendhardt termed 'reconfiguration of citizenship, territory and national belonging?'

The answer to these questions may well be positive, but we are not condemned to this black scenario. This is because the pandemic has demonstrated the weaknesses of nation-states more graphically than it has validated their strengths. None of Europe's states was prepared for this pandemic regardless of numerous warnings, and most of them handled the emergency poorly. States have indeed closed national borders, but this was a rather symbolic step as the most vital borders were around cities or regions where we observed concentrated outbreaks. States may be tempted to retain hard borders after the end of the pandemic scare, but it is hard to see any good in such a move. Effective migration policy requires multinational trans-border engagement with countries of the Middle East and North Africa. Cyber-attacks can hardly be stopped by state borders.

Internet-based communication and financial flows do not respect state borders either. And it is difficult to imagine how nation-states on their own can cope with climate change.

Some national politicians have promised to liberate their states from dependence on imports and promised to reduce international supply-chains. Yet economic autarchy is not conducive to innovation and crisis prevention. Besides, the EU's single market is vital for recovery from this pandemic and it would require trans-border flows of not only goods and money, but also of people.

Moreover, cultural identities are no longer as simple and dominant as nationalist politicians claim. Urban identities are gaining in importance, but cities are not interested in passports, sovereignty and borders. Even in such a traditional nation-state as Poland, liberal Poles are at odds with illiberal ones, urban Poles are at odds with peripheral ones, and Catholic Poles are at odds with secular ones (the secularisation of young Poles is striking). If there is anything that unites the Poles at present, it is their enthusiasm about the European Union, which is supported by nearly 90% of the population. In the twenty-first century the sovereigntist idea that people across the continent will unite under national flags is wishful thinking, and hence the difficulty in recreating a Europe of nation-states alone.

All this is bad news not only for nativists and sovereigntists. Nation-states are here to stay in Europe, but they will have to work in tandem with other states and European institutions. Reinstating if not sealing Europe's internal borders will not be possible without harming respective economies. Intra-European disputes will again be handled by 'soft diplomacy.' The crisis caused by Covid-19 may lead to long awaited reforms of the EU rather than to its demise. It is only to be hoped that these reforms will give greater rights and protection to national minorities and make the topic of this book less important.

In sum, the national minority question can hardly be tackled satisfactorily by traditional foreign policy, which operates with the traditional or, if you wish, old-fashioned concept of sovereign nation states with fairly hard borders. National minorities can only enjoy their rights in Europe where borders are open and states are sharing sovereignty. The current effort to restore Europe's borders will negatively affect national minorities, but we are not condemned to such a scenario. In an integrated Europe, resembling a complex web of cooperation between a variety of territorial actors—states, cities, region and the EU— there is no particular need for a kin-state policy protecting fellow nationals across a border. This scenario looks unlikely in the coming years, but in the long-term perspective borders are not just a function of political decisions, but also, if not chiefly, a function of technological and societal trends which seem to spur unbounding.

References

Barbour, S., & Carmichael, C. (2000). *Language and nationalism in Europe*. Oxford University Press.

Bartolini, S. (2005). *Restructuring Europe: Centre formation, system building, and political structuring between the nation state and the European Union*. Oxford University Press.

Bohle, D., & Greskovits, B. (2012). *Capitalist diversity on Europe's periphery*. Cornell University Press.

Caplan, R. (2005). *Europe and the recognition of new states in Yugoslavia*. Cambridge University Press.

Carsten, J. (2000). *Cultures of relatedness: New approaches to the study of kinship*. Cambridge University Press.

Fukuyama, F. (2018). *Identity: Contemporary identity politics and the struggle for recognition*. Profile Books.

Gerner, K. (1991). Ethnic rights as human rights: The case of the Baltic States and Hungary. In V. Mastny & J. Zielonka (Eds.), *Human rights and security. Europe on the eve of a new era* (pp. 159–176). Westview Press.

Gilbert, P. (2010). *Cultural identity and political ethics*. Edinburgh University Press.

Gray, J. (2020). Why this crisis is a turning point in history. *New Statesman.* https://www.newstatesman.com/america/2020/04/why-crisis-turning-point-history

Hill, C. (2002). The geopolitical implications of enlargement. In J. Zielonka (Ed.), *Europe unbound* (p. 95). Routledge.

Krasner, S. (1999). *Sovereignty, organized hypocrisy.* Princeton University Press.

Krastev, I., & Holmes, S. (2019). *The light that failed. A reckoning.* Allen Lane.

Liebich, A. (2002). Ethnic minorities and long-term implications of EU enlargement. In J. Zielonka (Ed.), *Europe unbound* (pp. 124–125). Routledge.

Maak, G. (2020). Na de ramp heeft Europa wonderen nodig. *NRC Handelsblad.* https://www.nrc.nl/nieuws/2020/03/27/na-de-ramp-heeft-europa-wonderen-nodig-a3995163

Melissen, J. (Ed.). (2005). *The new public diplomacy: Soft power in international relations.* Palgrave.

Nye, J. (2004). *Soft power: The means to success in world politics.* Public Affairs.

Rokkan, S., Urwin, D., Aarebrot, F. H., Sande, T., Malaba, P. (1987). *Centre-periphery structures in Europe.* Campus.

Rosenau, J. (1997). *Along the domestic-foreign frontier: Exploring governance in a turbulent world.* Cambridge University Press.

Sassen, S. (2008). *Territory, authority, rights: From medieval to global assemblages.* Princeton University Press.

Smith, D. J., & Hiden, J. (2012). *Ethnic diversity and the nation state: National cultural autonomy revisited.* Routledge.

Tilly, C. (Ed.). (1975). *The formation of nation states in Western Europe.* Princeton University Press.

Zielonka, J. (2018). *Counter-revolution. Liberal Europe in retreat.* Oxford University Press.

Index

accommodation 16, 49, 71–73, 77–78, 113, 136–137, 140–141; patterns of 140
Act on Citizenship 18, 20
actual political practices 34
adaptation 31, 33–35
agreements 97, 99, 102
amendments 15, 20–21, 58, 60, 124
ancestors 19, 60, 83, 88, 125–126, 128

Bellamy, R. 70
Boxenbaum, E. 34
Boyle, E. H. 33
Brand, L. A. 29
Brubaker, R. 2, 5, 30–31

card holders 15, 123–126, 130–131
children 45, 83–84, 87, 131, 133, 138–142
citizenship 13–15, 18–20, 26–27, 29–35, 41–42, 45, 67–68, 70, 72–73, 75–76, 125, 128–129, 131
contemporary situation 86
co-operation 114–119, 145
country of origin 54, 57–58, 109–111, 113, 118, 131–132
country of residence 110–112, 118, 125

democracy, quality 137, 141–142, 144, 146
diaspora engagement policies (DEP) 25–32, 34–35
diasporas 12, 15, 20–21, 25–30, 33–34, 83, 88, 98, 106, 110, 112–113
divided nationhood 39–41, 44, 47, 49

economic migrants 83–84, 90
education policies 141–142
ethnic Germans 85, 87, 98, 102
ethnic Poles 42, 53, 55, 73, 83, 88, 137–145
ethnic question 151–152
ethnocultural minority groups 70–71, 74–75, 77
European integration 16, 71, 75, 151, 153–154

Federal Republic of Germany (FRG) 97–98, 105, 109
financial support 21, 42, 100–101, 125, 145–146
flexibility 44, 46, 49
foreign policy 53–54, 56, 137, 144, 150–153; blind spots 151
Fowler, B. 30
Framework Convention for the Protection of National Minorities (FCNM) 105

Gamlen, A. 32, 98
German citizenship 97, 105
German minority 1, 86, 91, 97–98, 101–103; in Poland 86, 88, 96–97, 100–101, 103–104, 106
German public administration 111, 116, 118–119
Germany 1, 5, 83–88, 90–93, 96–106, 109–110, 112–118, 151
globalisation 29, 32, 35, 89, 91–92, 154
global models 26, 32–33

Hill, Christopher 152
Hooghe, M. 112
Hungarian citizenship 45, 48, 58, 60, 74–75
Hungarian language 45, 60
Hungarian minority communities 41, 45, 47
Hungarian nationality 41, 58, 71
Hungarians 13, 40, 45, 47–48, 55–58, 60, 73, 75, 151

immigrants 35, 110, 112
integration challenges 123–124, 131
integration policies 58, 110, 112–113, 116
international organisations 2, 70, 72, 74–76, 98
international relations 26, 72, 142
inter-state relations 46, 69, 72, 77, 99, 145, 152–153

Jonsson, S. 34

INDEX

Karolewski, Pawel 7
kin-minorities 3, 5, 12–13, 53–58, 60–62, 67–68, 71, 73, 106
kin-state: actors 47, 73; citizenship 41, 48, 77; community 40, 42–43, 46, 48; engagement 5–6, 54, 67–69, 71–73, 76–78, 98; laws 28, 35, 58; legislation 27, 30; policies 6–7, 27–28, 35, 39–40, 42, 44, 46, 49, 53, 72–73, 150–151, 153, 155; politics 5–7, 49
Krasner, S. D. 29
Kröger, S. 70

language usage 138
Lithuania—Christian families alliance 143

Meyer, J. W. 33
migration crisis 58
Mikołajczyk, Barbara 3
minority: communities 40, 42–45, 47–49, 124; ethnocultural groups 2, 68–72, 77–78, 99; groups 70–72, 77, 96–98, 100–103, 106; language 43–45, 99–102, 141; protection 3, 6, 67–73, 75–78, 99, 102
moral obligation 13–14, 17, 57, 104
multiple membership 39–40, 42, 44, 46, 48–49, 154

national bonds 150
national community 46, 53–54, 56–58, 61–62
national minorities 39–40, 42–44, 46, 49, 69–70, 72, 98–100, 102, 104–106, 129, 136–146, 150, 154–155; communities 40, 42–43, 46, 49; groups 46, 72
national sovereignty 26–29, 32–35
nation-state model 26, 28–31, 33, 35
native languages 110, 116, 138–139
NATO 56, 88, 90, 99, 104
Nausėda, Gitanas 145
non-governmental organisations 113, 124, 143, 145–146
Nowak, W. 111
Nowosielski, M. 97, 111

O'Neill, S. 68

Palermo, F. 72
Pickering, P. M. 46
Poland's diaspora policy 113–114, 119
Poles in Germany 85, 96–97, 99–106, 117
Polish: citizens 14, 18–19, 21, 34, 84, 97, 109; citizenship 14–15, 17, 19–21, 31, 33–35, 57, 62, 87, 97, 124; communities 49, 57, 84, 104, 110, 113–116, 118–119, 126, 132, 140; diaspora 15–16, 20–21, 27, 83–84, 106, 118–119, 124; diplomacy 117; government 48, 54, 62, 88, 98–100, 103, 124–125; identity 43, 45,

113–114, 117, 119, 128, 144, 146; language 18, 43, 97, 100, 102, 115, 130, 138–144, 146; origins 13–17, 20, 55, 61, 93, 100–101, 105, 116, 123, 125–129, 132; population 13, 98, 138, 144; zloty 145
Polish card 4, 5, 15, 17–21, 123–133; holders 123; 'industry' 126
Polish-German relations 91, 102, 110
Polish-German Round Table meetings 98–99, 101, 105
Polish–German Treaty 110
Polish immigrant organisations (PIOs) 109–119
Polish minorities 42–43, 48, 55, 84, 87, 99, 101–102, 123–124, 126, 138, 140, 142–143, 145; in Germany 83, 86, 91, 93
Polish national minority, in Lithuania 18, 136–146
Polish organisations 98, 100–103, 116, 127; in Germany 100–101, 103–105, 114
political communities 26, 28–30, 32, 40, 43, 75
political mobilisation 2, 77, 143
populism 89–92

Romania 13, 40, 43, 47, 55–56, 71, 74, 77, 153
Russian language 139–140, 146

Shain, Y. 28
Sherman, M. 28
Silesia 150–151
Smith, R. C. 29
sovereignty concept 152
state borders 54–55, 62, 138, 154–155
state-diaspora relations 25–30, 32; paradoxical nature of 28–30, 32
strategic partnership 145

trans-border nationalism 53–54, 56
triadic nexus 2, 68, 70

Ukraine 12–13, 16–17, 40, 42, 45, 48, 55–56, 73, 77, 123–124, 126–133, 151, 154
Ukrainian citizens 12, 90, 123–124, 126–127, 129–130, 132, 153
Universal Declaration of Human Rights 69
Upper Silesia 85–87

Vilnius region 137–138, 140–141, 143–146

Waterbury, Myra 54
Weber, Max 150
Western Europe 58, 92, 117
world-cultural models 27, 33–35
world polity theory (WPT) 27, 32–35

Zolberg, A. 98